D0322840

ONE WEEK LOAN

FEMINIST PERSPECTIVES SERIES

Series Editors:

Professor Pamela Abbott, Glasgow Caledonian University
Professor Claire Wallace, Institute for Advanced Studies, Austria
and Glasgow Caledonian University

Published Titles:

Feminist perspectives on the body
Barbara Brook

Feminist perspectives on politics
Chris Corrin

Feminist perspectives on disability
Barbara Fawcett

Feminist perspectives on language
Margaret Gibbon

Feminist perspectives on environment and society
Beate Littig

Feminist perspectives on ethics
Elizabeth Porter

FEMINIST PERSPECTIVES SERIES

Feminist Perspectives on Sociology

Barbara Littlewood

PEARSON

Prentice
Hall

Harlow, England • London • New York • Boston • San Francisco • Toronto
Sydney • Tokyo • Singapore • Hong Kong • Seoul • Taipei • New Delhi
Cape Town • Madrid • Mexico City • Amsterdam • Munich • Paris • Milan

Pearson Education Limited
Edinburgh Gate
Harlow
Essex CM20 2JE
England

and Associated Companies throughout the world

Visit us on the World Wide Web at:
www.pearsoned.co.uk

First published 2004

ISBN 0 13 040461 6

British Library Cataloguing-in-Publication Data
A catalogue record for this book is available from the British Library

10 9 8 7 6 5 4 3 2 1
08 07 06 05 04

Typeset in 10/12pt New Baskerville by 35
Printed and bound in Malaysia

The publisher's policy is to use paper manufactured from sustainable forests.

Contents

Preface and acknowledgements

This book began its life alongside an undergraduate course I teach at Glasgow University, on feminist issues in sociology. Although there are many feminist sociologists who write in various specialised areas, and sociology is arguably the social science that has been most affected by the feminist revolutions in thought and politics, I was surprised to find how few texts there were that provided a broad review of the field. The completed book is not an exhaustive review however, either of feminist analysis, of sociology, or their interconnections. It does not take the form of a long march through the orthodox sociological areas of institutions, family, school, employment, and so on (largely because this has already been excellently accomplished by the one of the few general reviews there were when I began: Abbott and Wallace 1997). The type of book that I decided to write relates to the two reasons I wanted to teach the course in the first place.

Transforming sociology

The first reason was my perception that feminism has been the single most transformative influence on the shape of postwar sociology, at least in Britain. The book is, then, a review of the issues that I saw as central to this transformation, of places where feminism rewrote the script of sociological knowledge (and joined with other critics who were attacking fundamental concepts such as 'knowledge' as well). Perspectives on familiar areas (the family, school, and so on) would never be the same. But even more radically, feminism opened up new areas that had never been seen as interesting to sociologists. These areas included much of what had passed as 'private' life, but not only the complementary family relations that functionalists were analysing.

Questions of sexuality, motherhood, violence and housework were all pioneered by feminist sociologists and, at least in the case of the first area, gay and lesbian theorists too (there were no queer theorists in the 1960s and 1970s). Comparing introductory textbooks from the 1960/1970s and the 1990/2000s brings home just how far sociology has travelled. At the very least, it is now pretty much obligatory to introduce students to the concept of 'gender' and its difference from 'sex' very early in their courses. Most sub-areas contain some reference to 'feminist approaches to . . .', or 'women and . . .'.

I would argue, though, that the single most significant change has been in our conception of 'work'. Once it simply meant a paid job, normally done outside the home and was contrasted with 'leisure' (especially for men), or being a mother (as in the phrase 'working mother'). Studies of housework *as* work changed that. It is not simply a matter of recognising that housework is labour, or is sometimes tiring and demanding, and arguably necessary. It is not recognising that housework can be studied like any other job, although this was a first step. It is recognising that there is a deep connection between these two kinds of work, paid and unpaid. These divisions of labour, in the house and in the workplace, emerged together and one cannot be fully understood without looking at the other.

Feminist perspectives, feminist politics

The second reason I wanted to teach the course and write this book is to explore the connections between feminism as a politics and feminism as a perspective on the world. Generally, academics shy away from making explicit connections between their teaching and research activities and their political interests and activities. Political commitments are generally seen as incompatible with objectivity, and would undermine the status of sociological work.

It is, however, impossible to appreciate the impact of feminism in sociology unless we see it as a politics as well as a perspective. Like Marxism, feminism began as a movement and analysis outwith academic life and continues to retain much of its vigour through its commitment to achieving change and social justice. Its campaigns have often inspired feminist sociologists to research particular issues. Research, in turn, informs further campaigning.

The feminist slogan that 'the personal is political' captures the perception that broader social forces structure our personal lives. It implies a radical reconception of 'politics' too, not as something disconnected from our lives, to do with voting and government, but as something that relates to our most personal and intimate experiences and relationships. This was the cue for feminist sociologists to break open the unspoken conventions that governed what was a proper area of research.

This connection between researchers and campaigners (who could also be the same person of course) does not imply that the research is therefore biased. Critics, though, may often wish that uncomfortable results, documenting the prevalence of male violence, or the few hours men spend on housework compared to their female partners, *could* be dismissed that easily.

Who's for feminism and who is feminism for?

This book aims to demonstrate that feminism has had and will continue to have a powerfully transformative presence in the world, including on sociology. Like sociology itself, it offers a new angle of vision on the world. That alone makes it a fundamental aspect of students' education. It also means that you do not have to be a feminist to study feminism anymore than you have to be a Marxist or a neo-fascist to study these philosophies and movements.

Feminism also raises important questions for students and teachers when it is studied in the context of a highly socially selective institution such as a British university or college. We have to be conscious of our relative privileges, which include the privilege of dissent, of exercising a critical imagination. The ideas we explore can, when expressed in different social contexts, lead to intimidation and persecution. Educational institutions can, though not without struggles, be tools to make changes. Having a feminist perspective, moreover, implies that we learn to question established categories and practices, of forms of knowledge, ways of theorising, and of what constitutes the proper subject of 'sociology'.

Acknowledgements

No preface to a book is complete without some acknowledgement of the people who helped. Several friends read draft chapters and/ or provided generous amounts of feminist inspiration, including Paul Littlewood, Chris Corrin, Michele Burman, Ruth Madigan, Angela McRobbie, Liz Bird, Elinor Kelly, Eleanor Gordon, Catherine Eschle, Linda Mahood and Eileen Yeo. The students I have taught over the years also deserve some thanks, including those whose eyes glazed over when I failed to express my arguments clearly. Many, though, were generous in their responses, sharp in the questions they asked, and pushed me to cover issues that they told me mattered. I would specially like to acknowledge one ex-student, 'Madam Mischka', who saw this book when she read my tea leaves one Chinese New Year. Unfortunately it was too small (and concave) for us to scan directly onto a Word document. Getting my jumbled bibliography onto a presentable Word document was the accomplishment of Andy Smith.

I would also like to acknowledge the musicians who kept me company in my office when everyone else had sensibly gone home. Indeed I sometimes felt I would like to compile a soundtrack for the book – 'Play tracks 3–5 while you read Chapter 3'. In lieu, I will just thank Salif Keita for *Moffou* and Gramma Funk for *Universal Unfolding*. And many thanks to Lisa and Matt who have been largely responsible for my musical education in recent years.

They and Paul are also part of the family that loved and fed me, materially and spiritually. Thanks.

Further reading

Abbott, P. and Wallace, C. (1997) *An Introduction to Sociology: Feminist Perspectives.* London: Routledge.

Series editors' preface

The aim of the Feminist Perspectives series is to provide a concise introduction to different topics from a feminist perspective. The topics were chosen as being of interest for students on a range of different degree courses and in a range of different disciplines. They reflect the current interest in feminist issues and in women's studies in a wide range of fields. The series aims to provide a guide through the burgeoning and sometimes rather arcane literatures which have grown around various feminist topics. The texts are written by experienced teachers and academics providing lively and interesting accounts of topics of current interest. They include examples and case studies or statistical information where relevant in order to make the material more accessible and stimulating. The texts contain chapter outlines and summaries for convenient, quick access. There are also suggestions for further reading.

We are pleased to be able to present our readers with this volume by Barbara Littlewood on *Feminist Perspectives on Sociology*. In this volume Barbara Littlewood presents a lively and engaging account of the transformative impact that feminism had on Sociology in the late twentieth century. Her account demonstrates that in a discipline where women were systematically erased from the cannon, feminism has come to stay – it is not possible to conceive of a sociology in the twenty-first century where feminist perspectives are not core to the discipline. Feminism has not only contributed to our theorised understanding of social phenomena but has also opened up new areas of sociological concern and raised new questions and ways of looking at areas of traditional concern. She also considers the dialectical relationship between feminism as a theory and feminism as political action and argues that this tension between theory and action is central to sociology as a discipline. In the book Barbara challenges not only the patriarchal assumptions of much sociology but also the Eurocentrism of much contemporary sociology and feminism as taught in the UK. She does this by discussing both postcolonialist feminist theory and feminist accounts of feminism and contributions to debates on globalisation.

This book will be essential reading for all undergraduate students of sociology and women's studies as well as those studying related disciplines.

Claire Wallace and Pamela Abbott

Chapter 1

Feminist perspectives on sociology

Chapter outline

This book is primarily intended for students of sociology and related disciplines, although others may also find it of interest. It is
based on a university course I teach, designed for third and final
year students, and so assumes that readers will already have some
familiarity with sociology and with feminist approaches.

The chapter aims to introduce several fundamental points about
both sociology and feminism that will recur in other chapters:

- There are several ways of doing sociology, it has various
  approaches and contending perspectives.
- Similarly, feminism is not a single perspective, or politics.
  Its different forms have sometimes been described as
  'waves', or prefixed by terms such as '**Marxist**', or 'lesbian'
  or '**postcolonial**'.
- A number of factors have shaped the relations between
  feminism and sociology, including dominant models in
  sociological analysis, and developments in the wider
  feminist movement.
- Feminism has made a significant contribution to
  contemporary sociology, in criticising the adequacy of
  previous explanations and in changing what is considered
  as relevant and interesting.

Many sociologies, many feminisms

What counts as 'sociology' nowadays is different from the time when I – and probably most of your teachers – began doing sociology. In Britain, there have been attempts at a national level, in the quality assurance and benchmarking exercises, to specify what is part of a core with which all students should be familiar, but different college and university departments approach it in a wide variety of ways. There is even less consensus about where boundaries might be drawn, with history or philosophy for example. Particular historical and cultural influences have also produced different sociological traditions in different countries, where there may be more or less emphasis on, for example, gender studies. Students and other readers should therefore be aware that topics they encounter in the following chapters are just one view of what constitutes 'sociology'. Although I have tried to make it a reasonably typical overview, there will undoubtedly be readers who will identify (in their view) crucial omissions and/or eccentric inclusions.

If it is hard to speak of sociology in the singular, feminism has always been multiple (though it is often more convenient to write of it in the singular). At different moments, one strand, one approach, one issue has been or seemed to be dominant, but there have always been alternatives and challenges. I have tried to represent what have been sociologically and politically significant ways of thinking and acting at different moments over the past thirty years or so while not losing sight of other approaches. Sometimes the changes have been called 'waves', where the First signifies the nineteenth- to early-twentieth-century movements, for the vote, for rights to education and for reforms to property, marriage and divorce laws among many. Typically, Second Wave feminism refers to the reappearance of a widespread movement in the late 1960s and early 1970s, which is associated (in the UK) with various demands, for equal pay, for 24-hour nursery care, for access to contraception and abortion, and to the end of discrimination against lesbians. More controversially, some commentators (Arneil 1999) have identified a Third Wave, consisting of the 'daughters' of Second Wave feminism and who have moved on (as they may see it) from older demands. Many Third Wavers are careful, however, to distance themselves from conservative 'post-feminists' who claim that Second Wavers have achieved these demands, and even gone too far.

This model of waves signifies different generations of feminists with different priorities *and* between whom there was a certain tension. Sheila Rowbotham remembers growing up in the 1950s and 1960s when:

> From dim childhood memories I had a stereotype of emancipated women: frightening people in tweed suits and horn-rimmed glasses with stern buns at the back of their heads. Feminism was completely asexual. It didn't occur to me that it was anything to do with the double standard of sexual morality that hurt and humiliated me. Feminism seemed the very antithesis of the freedom I connected with getting away from home and school. My recognition of women as a group was as creatures sunk into the deadening circumstances from which I was determined to escape.
>
> (Rowbotham 1973: 12)

Part of the tension is caused by a misunderstanding, or even ignorance of what earlier generations had written and done. Rowbotham imagined that hers was the first generation to rebel against that double standard and to seek sexual freedom. At the time, she knew nothing of the campaigns around what we would now call sexual politics that date back to the early nineteenth century (Taylor 1983), and nothing about the men and women, sometimes called 'sex reformers' at the time, who attempted to live out their ideas about free love, including Karl Marx's daughter Eleanor (Hall 2000). We cannot suppose, either, that once a history of feminism has been written, the task is complete; memories have to be kept alive, actively, and different generations will find different parts of that history more and less relevant.

Kimberley Springer, however, argues that this model of waves is one that effectively obliterates the contribution of Black feminists in America who came to consciousness at different times and through different routes. In particular, the model neglects the role of race-based activism through which many Black women became politically active and which served as a model for gender activism (Springer 2002).

The varieties of feminism have often also been described by a prefix such as 'liberal', 'anarcho', 'eco' or 'Marxist/socialist' that obviously refer to wider political allegiances or affinities. 'Radical' or 'revolutionary' feminism marked itself off from the others as placing its feminism first and unqualified. Later, feminism multiplied again into forms that emphasised the identity of its formulators, as lesbian, as Black or Generation X. In the 1990s, theoretical qualifiers became more common: postmodern, post-structuralist, postcolonial and even postfeminist. The latest, that seems to have gained widespread currency, is 'transnational'. In certain respects, it is this varied nature of feminism that contributes to its vitality and relevance: it is not a single thing, either as a movement or an ideology. It adapts and responds to local conditions and changing times, it is the creation of generations of (largely) women and (occasionally) men, and sometimes it contributes to changing those conditions and times.

Feminism in sociology: influences

While reviewing the contribution that feminism has made to sociology is the central purpose of this book, it is also necessary to acknowledge four factors that have, in turn, shaped the development of feminism in sociology. First, when feminism is considered in relation to an academic discipline such as sociology, one aspect of the local conditions mentioned above is the (changing) dominant sociological paradigm. Feminism has, I will be arguing, considerably altered the sociological landscape but sociology has also affected the form of feminist inquiry and research. In Britain from the late 1970s, for example, sociology was profoundly affected by the revival of interest in Marxism and much feminist work could, in turn, be loosely categorised as 'socialist feminist', if not Marxist feminist.

Second, feminist studies have been interdisciplinary studies. This has partly been a matter of historical accident. The 1960s were a time both of higher education expansion and experimentation. Non-standard ways of teaching were on the agenda, and a range of interdisciplinary courses began to appear, although Women's Studies were a relatively late beneficiary in Britain and Europe compared with North America. Nevertheless, collaboration across disciplines was encouraged and this was especially important for feminists, relatively few in number across colleges and universities. Exposure to the work that historians, anthropologists and political scientists, for example, were doing was often very influential for sociologists' research. In addition, in the early 1970s, there were so few feminist books that they were read eagerly and widely. Although thirty years on, feminists may have similar attitudes of open-minded curiosity, the explosion of publishing makes it barely possible to keep up with developments in one's own, let alone other, disciplines. Feminists, then, were often the means by which the concerns of and approaches from other subjects leaked into sociology. The current fuzziness of sociological borders may partly, then, be a consequence of this feminist inventiveness.

The third factor relates to profound changes in gender relations over the past thirty or so years. In a feedback loop, one of the contributory factors was the women's movement of the 1970s. It provided a new vocabulary to think about roles and relations as gendered, to identify certain forms of behaviour as sexist and/or discriminatory, and to formulate visions of alternative, less oppressive ways of living. On a practical level, it contributed to changes in the law, changes in policies in schools and workplaces, and changes to practices in the media and healthcare. There was not one area of public life that was untouched by feminist campaigns, though not all were by any means successful. By the 1980s, although feminism was pronounced 'dead' in the media and unpopular with 'ordinary' women, it was beginning to form a taken-for-granted background consciousness. The popular disclaimer 'I'm not a feminist but . . .' often prefaced sentiments, both against discrimination, and for equal treatment. Such opinions, although disavowing their feminist origins, indicated how far what one might call the basics of feminism had transformed consciousness.

Finally, sociological feminism has been profoundly affected by developments in the wider feminist movements that have, in turn, drawn inspiration from other social justice movements. Feminism – like Marxism – is also a collection of political movements that occupy a ground outside the academy where not only campaigns go on, but thinking and research do too. This face of feminism refreshes and invigorates the academic side of feminism, it provides an inspiration for students, teachers and researchers who can come to see that these are all activities that can go on in many places, and in which many people can engage. It also tends to make feminism a democratic movement – although it has had distinctly authoritarian and elitist tendencies – since there is no vanguard and no centre who elaborate the 'correct' line.

Probably more than any other sociological perspective including Marxism, feminist sociology is open to influences from beyond the traditional academic community of scholars. The studies academic feminists produce, especially if they have focused on a topic, such as domestic violence, inspired by community movements and campaigns, are likely to be read by people in those movements.

Not only does feminist work have a wider readership, it also has a highly critical readership, and most feminist writers and researchers will feel at least as concerned about the way this readership responds to it as the way non-feminist sociologist colleagues do. In certain areas, the critical mass of this collectivity lies outside the academy. Black feminists, for example, have had to spend time in justifying their research and political commitments to Black communities who may see this as a *lack* of commitment to antiracist struggles (Springer 2002). This critical non-academic readership has, however, made recurrent accusations of elitism, of inaccessible language and a detachment of 'academic' from 'activist' feminists. This, I would argue, generally provides a healthy deflation of intellectual pride, a reminder that writing clearly and concisely is often harder than not writing in that way – especially after many years of academic training and of reading typical academic prose.

Sociology too has regularly been attacked on similar grounds, that it is little more than common sense dressed up in impenetrable jargon in order to pose as a difficult, and therefore 'real' subject. Criticisms by feminists, however, have an extra edge; if only a highly educated elite minority can understand and engage with the debates going on in colleges and universities, feminism is the loser. This is not to say that certain topics, or forms of language, or references to, say, dead German philosophers should be avoided, but it is to recognise that there is a politics to communication. Different styles are more and less appropriate to and effective for different contexts, media and audiences. I would further suggest that this means there is a particular affinity between feminism and sociology since this is a social science discipline that takes the stuff of everyday life as its subject matter, that directs students' attention to the world around, and that presents itself as a way of cultivating a critical gaze on that world. Learning about sociology, like learning about feminism, often means students never see the world in the same way again.

Feminism and sociology: developments and directions

Although most sociology students study feminist perspectives at some point in their courses, it is most commonly in association with a particular area, such as education, stratification, the media, or crime. There is, though, a case to be made for making feminist approaches the central focus and using these to consider their impact on sociology more generally. Feminism has had an enormous impact on sociology, possibly more than on any other social science discipline, and this book aims to review the contributions of feminism not simply to the various sociologies of the sub areas, but to the discipline itself.

The survey that follows concentrates on developments since the late 1960s and early 1970s, largely in Britain and America since that is the field I know best. Readers should not assume that nothing much of interest happened elsewhere but should look to feminist sociologists in their countries and continents to provide better commentaries than I could attempt. They should not assume either that the chronologies, trajectories and interweavings of sociology and feminism will match those I outline here. Indeed, the term 'feminism' in any of its forms might not make sense in certain places, though 'women's movement' might.

Finally, I intend to show that feminism's perspectives on and contributions to sociology have been twofold. First, feminists have provided alternative and illuminating criticisms of existing areas and, perhaps more significantly, have opened up new areas within sociology, transforming the area it occupies.

The first thing that struck feminists looking at sociological research, in the late 1960s and early 1970s, was the absence of women in accounts of the social world. Although in certain areas such as crime or employment, for example, there were significantly fewer women than men to be found and studied, this could not explain the lack of attention to women in areas such as schooling. Furthermore, feminists began to see that the relative *absence* of women could be an interesting question in itself. Why were there so few women in prison, or in boardrooms? And, on the other hand, why so few men working as secretaries, or at home looking after children? These questions were both sociological and political; they were about the adequacy of sociology's claims to document and explain the social world, and about the structures that might discriminate against women.

Related to this awareness of the invisibility of women was another move, to enlarge sociology to include areas where women *were* present, and to pose questions that were relevant to women's lives and experiences.

Women carried out much of the initial work, but in the 1970s there were growing numbers of men who were learning lessons

from feminism. Two well-established British sociologists who engaged in seriously rethinking work in their respective areas were
Ronald Frankenberg (community studies) and Richard Brown
(industrial sociology). Frankenberg also criticised his own earlier
work as incomplete because of its blindness to gender relations
(Frankenberg 1976).

Richard Brown pointed out that where women had not been
ignored altogether, industrial sociologists had treated them in one
of two ways: either as indistinguishable from men in their attitudes
and behaviour, or as a special problem, for their employers or their
families (Brown 1976). He identified a very common approach,
which was by no means confined to industrial sociology alone,
and that was 'an assumption that one can safely generalise and
"theorise" about organisations without giving any significance to
the sex of their members' (Brown 1976: 22).

Examining progress five years later, Helen Roberts (1981) con-
cluded that although there were some changes in sociology, the
core high-status areas of study, of power, class conflict and order,
had been relatively untouched, although there was a very good
case for regarding gender differentiation as crucial to their full
analysis. Roberts did point out though that in assessing progress,
it was important also to look at the organisation of social relations
in the sociology profession, and here there were more positive
changes. Not only were more women studying the subject, and
university and colleges including issues of gender in their courses,
but were organising in their professional associations and places
of employment to ensure that gender issues were taken seriously
in very practical ways too, such as implementing equal opportunities
policies (Roberts 1981).

But as well as criticising and revising already established fields
of sociology, feminists were also opening up new ones, most notably
in areas of 'private' life, in sexuality, the domestic division of labour
– motherhood and housework – and crimes of violence against
women. These will be examined further in later chapters.

Summary

- Sociology has changed significantly over the past forty
  years, partly under the impact of feminists working both
  inside and outside universities and colleges.

- Feminist approaches to sociology have developed alongside feminist political movements.
- They have contributed to shifting sociology away from a preoccupation with men's experiences and lives to a more inclusive picture of the social world.

Further reading

Delamont, S. (2001) *Changing Women, Unchanged Men?: Sociological Perspectives on Gender in a Post-industrial Society.* Buckingham: Open University Press.

Evans, M. (1997) *Introducing Contemporary Feminist Thought.* Cambridge: Polity Press.

Oakley, A. (1981a) *Subject Women.* Oxford: Martin Robertson.

Oakley, A. (2002) *Gender on Planet Earth.* Oxford: Polity Press.

Chapter 2

The epistemological challenge

Chapter outline

Feminists have, inevitably, had to challenge existing views in society regarding women's (and men's) proper place. They have had to question dominant views and practices and to elaborate an alternative knowledge. These views are not only found in the wider society but in academic subjects of all kinds. These can be particularly influential, and can present themselves as objective fact backed up by impartial research. In the process of criticising the flaws and omissions in sociological knowledge, feminists began to develop more extensive critiques of knowledge **construction** more generally, and formulate alternative ways of validating knowledge. In this, they have often been inspired by currents and campaigns in the women's and other emancipatory movements, and have felt accountable to these as much as to an academic audience.

The chapter will examine:

- The nature of dominant sociological models and their approaches to knowledge.
- Stages in the development of feminist critiques, explaining the significance of 'feminist empiricism', 'feminist standpoint' and postmodern epistemologies.
- The relations between activist and academic feminists: how campaigns originating outside the academy came to inspire feminist researchers.
- Issues surrounding the politics of research: how researchers should behave towards each other, their subjects and their audiences.

• Questions of 'useful knowledge'. What should feminist research be about? How should it be communicated? Should it have links with 'useful' projects and campaigns?

Introduction

There have been a number of stages in the development of the feminist critique, beginning with the 'feminist archaeology' stage (finding the hidden women). The limitations of this in turn led to a critique of conventional sociological methodologies and the development of alternative 'feminist standpoint' epistemologies. This was also a moment of intense feminist political activism and debate, both in the sense of establishing what were the 'demands of the women's movement' and initiating and campaigning for appropriate policies and provisions (such as women's aid refuges). The significance of feminist standpoint(s) can be understood in this political context, as an 'academic' response to the centrality that was being given to women's experiences in the wider movement.

The relations, however, between 'academic' and 'activist' feminists were not always easy, and a gap also appeared to be opening up between 'feminists' and 'ordinary' women. These divisions led to a new interest in the 'politics of research', a concern not only with the ethics of research practices and the academic division of labour, but also profound questions about the purpose of research, what 'useful knowledge' might be, and who are the producers and consumers of knowledge. These issues are still under debate, but feminists have been at the forefront of opening them up for sociology.

In the 1960s, the 'classic' sociological perspectives of functionalist and conflict theories largely shaped sociological debate and research, and can be examined for what they offered (and failed to offer) to feminism.

The theoretical background: functionalism and conflict theory

When any sociologist begins to investigate any area of social life, they approach it from a particular theoretical perspective. This not only guides the questions and issues that sociologists research, what topics they find interesting, but also contains an epistemology. This is a theory of knowledge that establishes conventions by which valid knowledge is produced. In sociology, epistemological questions can be divided into debates about fairly abstract issues, and about more practical issues, the methods and methodology sociologists should adopt. Sociology has been subject to epistemological debates for a long time, especially arguments between those who favour an approach based on a model of the natural sciences and those who argue for a different, an interpretativist, approach.

In 1970s sociology, two main perspectives dominated debate and argument. In both Britain and North America, the dominant perspective, which had been the basis for most postwar sociology, was structural functionalism, but was increasingly being challenged by an alternative. The alternative was different in Britain and North America; in the former it was conflict theory, especially in its New Left Marxist version, while in America it was interactionism. All were able to point to ideas drawn from the various founding fathers of the discipline, though some such as Karl Marx had not called themselves sociologists.

Structural functionalism largely drew on the ideas of the French sociologist Emile Durkheim who emphasised the system-like nature of society. In this case, 'system' signifies both the ways society is organised, as a unity, rather like an organic system, and it also signifies the systematic nature of this organisation. Society, like an organism in the natural world, is more than the sum of its parts. The structure of this system consists of sets of norms, values and expectations some of which cohere into institutions such as the family, religious and educational institutions. The functionalism consists of the manner in which the structure works to meet certain needs of society, as the heart functions to pump blood around. This view has largely been associated with a positivist epistemology, an investigation of social facts using specific research techniques that are based, as far as possible, on scientific methods. This, it is claimed, is the way sociological knowledge is produced. Such knowledge is true because it is value-free and objective: the values and beliefs of the researcher do not enter into it.

Although feminist sociologists had been quick to challenge or at least modify the functionalist versions of the sociology of the family and sex roles, conflict theory offered more. Originally devised to account for **class** formation and relations, conflict theory appeared to offer a model for the analysis of gender as well. It draws largely on the perspectives of Marx and Weber, though 'Weberian feminism' has never become a label for a strand of analysis, in the way in which 'Marxist feminism' has. Weberian conflict theory is a major example of interpretative sociology. In distinction from positivism, the epistemology often associated with this argues that sociologists should be producing knowledge about the meaning of human action and interaction whether on a large or small scale.

Conflict theory emphasises divisions, power and inequalities, rather than consensus and cohesion. The concept of 'class' is fundamental, although defined in different ways by different schools of sociology. Conflict theorists hold certain basic ideas in common, however: we can usefully note three main ones.

- First, groups (such as classes) are formed through differential access to scarce and desired resources, and through the unevenly distributed possession of these resources. They struggle for access to them, they struggle to gain a greater share of them, and they struggle to maintain their hold over them.

- Second, those groups which have the greatest access to the important resources in society, also have more power over those who have the least resources, although this power is often contested: hence, conflict.

- Finally, there is an emphasis on 'interests' rather than 'needs'. 'Interests' stem from the social location of a group, whereas 'needs' implies an almost biological reductionism. 'Needs' must be met if any society is to survive, whereas 'interests' may only have to be met in a particular type of society. They exist only in relation to one group and, typically, are in conflict with the interests of another, subordinate, group. The bourgeoisie in a capitalist society, for example, have an interest in maintaining current property and inheritance laws. Many of the institutions in society reflect the ideas and interests of the dominant group; they do not, after all, reflect 'society's' needs, but the interests of the dominant group. The law, for example, which punishes crimes against property, embodies and maintains the interests of the group that owns most property.

These basic ideas, therefore, could be adapted to analyse men's dominance over women. The social groups of men and women could be conceived of as competing over scarce resources, such as

well-paid careers. The 'needs' of a society (which structural functionalists listed) for a division and specialisation of gender roles
and labour turned out to embody *men's* interests, and their power
was manifest in many of society's institutions, which continued
to reproduce that dominance. For example, in the past, trade
unions have attempted to maintain control over jobs, to the detriment not only of women but also **ethnic** minority groups, and those
others whose labour might be seen as less skilled, and therefore
cheaper.

Conflict theory, knowledge and ideology

Conflict theories of all kinds, including feminist ones, also have a
distinctive view on issues about knowledge and therefore implications for the way we do sociology. Sociology, in common with many
other academic disciplines, aims for a better view of and account
of the world than that provided by unreflective common sense. It
aims to tease out the things below the surface, to identify patterns
and regularities that are not apparent at first. But although many
of the classical theorists supposed they could come up with objective claims about society, identified and investigated *facts*, and
provided true explanations, the conflict theorists were far less sure
that there was only one kind of true, disinterested knowledge. Many
held what we can call a theory of **ideology**, that much of what passes
as knowledge actually reflects not only the social location of the
knower, but his/her interests. Ideology literally means the science
of ideas, the study of beliefs, but is more particularly understood
to refer to false or mistaken ideas that get a grip on people,
including those who promote them. Those who do not believe in
them often call both religious and political beliefs 'ideological'.

The contemporary sociological analysis of ideology owes much
to Marx's writings on ideology, and here it is closely tied to bourgeois interests. He attacked not only religion for being an ideological system which served to pacify the proletariat by promising them
rewards in the afterlife, but also political economy which mystified
people about the real workings of economics and politics. Part of
this mystification derives from the claim that ideology is simply
objective knowledge, and a critique of ideology suggests we should
therefore be particularly wary of any knowledge that claims to be
objective and true. Ideologies often present their claims in terms

of human nature, timeless truths about the human condition, that we are naturally competitive and acquisitive, for example. Such appeals imply that a social system that encourages competition is just allowing our natures to flourish and that attempts to alter the system will be doomed to failure. This example demonstrates how these claims serve the interests of the bourgeoisie, who are the ones benefiting from competition, how their ideas are the dominant ones and even often accepted by those who suffer from competition. There are, however, divisions between the theorists over whether there ever can be objective knowledge (as opposed to ideology).

One significant feature of analyses of ideology is that they reverse normal assumptions about many forms of knowledge and expertise. As well as appearing in many common-sense views, ideology is also to be found in expert knowledge, as Marx's analysis of 'bourgeois' political economy illustrates. So, rather than the professionals and experts producing valid and objective knowledge about the world and our place within it, they are actually producing politically interested ideology that serves the dominant class. The real experts and knowledge producers are actually located in the exploited class: they not only have a clearer view of the workings of society, but have an objective interest in producing real knowledge that will emancipate them. This is a crucial aspect of theories of ideology, one that appealed to feminists who added that the dominant group was also male. Ideologies they identified were patriarchal (as well as capitalist and racist). Women, many feminists wanted to argue, were in a position analogous to that of Marx's proletariat: they were in a position to see through **patriarchal** ideologies (though many women did not), and they had an interest in producing an alternative, better and emancipatory knowledge.

Feminist critiques of sociological knowledge

The feminist critique of knowledge began by making two basic points: first, that sociology does not offer an analysis of women's lives. Existing sociological knowledge was excluding half the population – women – and was concentrating on men and men's lives (often under the guise of analysing the experiences of 'people' in general). The answer to this was a simple injunction to include women. But this turned out to be not so simple after all, and part of the difficulty relates to the second critique, that sociology as it stands *cannot* provide an adequate analysis of women's lives. Both of these contained a claim that current sociological knowledge has been written from a male perspective, is riddled with unexamined bias, and marginalises women's lives and experiences.

Feminists also pointed out that the work of many of the classic theories of sociology were masculinist theories, written from a male perspective. Not only did both Durkheim and Weber concentrate on men's lives, they also assumed the sexual division of labour to be natural and inevitable, so not worthy of analysis (Sydie 1987). Although Marx (and Engels) did acknowledge inequalities between men and women, the emphasis was on exploitative class and not **gender** relations, which has the effect of relegating women's **oppression** to a by-product of class inequalities (Delmar 1976).

However, the first 'include women' approach did do much to remedy some of the existing gaps in sociological knowledge. As well as studies of (male) factory workers (Beynon 1973), we began to get studies of female factory workers (Pollert 1981; Cavendish 1982) and secretaries (McNally 1979), and the first studies directed to the broader division of labour in employment were also starting to emerge (Hakim 1979). This last was a very important break-through enabling sociologists to chart men's and women's places in the occupational structure, a necessary first step for assessing changes and identifying key factors which explained that division.

The first problem with the 'include women' approach was that there were not necessarily 'women' *there* to be researched. Although, up to a point, it was possible to 'include' women in studies of schools, offices and factories, it became harder in socio-logical areas such as crime. Women were *not* in courts and prisons to nearly the same extent as men, were not causing the same prob-lems as boys in gangs, had not been there all the time though somehow overlooked by sociologists. Feminist researchers therefore had to approach such an area from a different perspective, to ask about their *absence*, to examine their status as victims rather than as perpetrators, and perhaps as Frances Heidensohn (1985) argued to explain their *conformity* rather than their deviance. Indeed, this early interest on women's experiences as victims of crime was to lead into one of the most significant new areas of sociological research, of violence (though feminists often now prefer to use the term 'survivor' rather than 'victim').

The second, more radical point was that both the content of and the nature of conventional sociological inquiry made it im-possible to ask meaningful questions or get proper answers about women's lives. A good example of this critique was Helen Roberts' article 'Do Her Answers Fit His Questions?' (Roberts 1983). Roberts argues that the standard, survey based, sociological method was particularly inappropriate for researching women's lives. The researcher using surveys and questionnaires begins with a set of assumptions or a hypothesis, devises questions into which people must fit their answers, and which will enable him/her to draw conclusions and make statistically reliable generalisations. But Roberts argues that not only might women's experiences not fit with the researcher's assumptions and categories, but that the whole interviewing process is based on a 'masculine' approach, of distance and neutrality which is unlikely to elicit knowledge about women's lives. An even stronger criticism was that the whole nature of scientific inquiry (of which much of sociology was a part) was highly **gendered**.

There is, in the West, a long-standing opposition between reason and emotion (often called irrationality), and these categories are also associated with masculinity and femininity respectively. Insofar as the ideal stance for the researcher is taken to be one of separation, objectivity and the application of disinterested reason, then science can be described as a masculine activity. Emotion is also normally relatively devalued as a means of producing knowledge. But it has not always been so. In Chapter 3 we look at the argument of some of the early women social scientists, accepted also by many men at the time, that both reason and emotion were necessary to the advancement of science.

There is, though, some confusion about whether this claim about the opposition and association relates to differences between 'real' men and women's ways of knowing, or to the labelling of ways of thinking as 'masculine' and 'feminine' (see the discussion in Hekman 1990). However, all agree that the consequence is that women, unless they adopt 'masculine' ways of knowing, have typically been excluded from the category of knower. For liberal feminists, the answer is straightforward: dispel the associations between women and irrationality, admit that women can be as 'rational as men and include women as full members of the category of knower. For other feminists, the answer is not so simple. Harding (1984), for example, insists that our conception of 'reason' is a distorted one and is not a standard that feminists should emulate. Other radical feminists argue that feminine ways of knowing *are* different but better, and the categories of reason and emotion should be revalued in order to privilege the latter (Daly 1978; Griffin

1978). For their critics, this comes dangerously close to antifeminist arguments about women's essential natures, and leaves the dichotomy intact: 'Only a move that dissolves the dichotomy can successfully remove the prescribed inferiority' (Hekman 1990: 42). It still remains the case, though, that women's *experiences* of the world are different from men's.

Related to this was an observation that sociology, though it typically claims to investigate social life, relations and institutions, actually investigates only some of these, typically the public world. It is no accident that women are largely excluded but is related to the development of sociology as discipline, as a mode of understanding and analysing the social changes precipitated by **capitalism**. These were numerous, but as the early founders of sociology were by and large men, they focused on the changes that seemed, most dramatically and profoundly, to have affected the lives of men, such as changes in employment and **production** relations. The legacy of that focus is that 'sociology is oriented not simply to men, but the social arenas to which men have privileged access' (Roberts 1983: 135). Although many women (and children) had been employed in the mines, fields and textile factories of the early nineteenth century, by the time the early sociologists were writing employment had come to be seen as the proper preserve of men. In contrast, women's place was, equally properly, the home (which, until recently, we could imagine was without a history).

We now know that women's lives have been as dramatically changed as men's have, but in different ways. They may not have become the main wage earners of families, but neither – ever – have their lives been confined to the private realm of families and households. The ideas about men and women's proper places, however, were so strong that sociologists could imagine that women had no 'public' life and men had no 'private' one. The sociology of employment for example, has usually treated male workers as if they had no 'private' life, or no private life that has consequences for their lives as workers. Furthermore, as the Canadian sociologist Dorothy Smith (1974) explained, some very basic sociological categories such as 'work' and 'leisure' rest on men's experiences where such divisions make sense to them. They do not make sense to many women where the work they do in the house and caring for children is not counted *as* work, and where 'leisure' is meaningless when being a housewife and mother is a '24/7' kind of job.

Through the 1970s and 1980s, there were a number of campaigns around issues of housework and childcare. They included campaigns for nurseries, for maternity and paternity leave, and a Wages for Housework campaign. Many of the actions, however, took place in 'private', between couples and partners, as women attempted to renegotiate the domestic division of labour to share tasks more equitably (Coote and Campbell 1987). These campaigns and actions had a number of motivations: not only did women object to assumptions that these tasks 'naturally' fell to them to perform, this division of labour had consequences for men's wage bargaining. The idea that men had to earn a 'family wage', enough to 'keep' his wife and children, has a long history within trade unions (Lewis 1984). Feminists argued that this was actually a means of justifying women's lower pay that kept them dependent on a male earner. In addition, some feminists were arguing that women's maternal role has profound effects on women's lives:

> Women's mothering determines women's primary location in the domestic sphere and creates a basis for the structural differentiation of domestic and public spheres. . . . Culturally and politically, the public sphere dominates the domestic, and hence men dominate women.
>
> (Chodorow 1978: 10)

With so much attention focused on family life, feminist sociologists felt it was time to investigate just what was going on there, to ask just what women (and men) were and were not doing in and around the home. Indeed, it was a couple of early studies of housewives that were to break open the confines of 1970s functionalist sociology of the family.

Case study 2.1 Feminist studies of housework

At this time, the women's movement in Europe and North America was much concerned to put the question of housework on the political agenda. Some feminist researchers such as Ann Oakley in England and Meg Luxton in Canada took up the challenge to put it also on the sociological agenda. As Oakley explained:

> The conventional sociological approach to housework could be termed 'sexist': it has treated housework merely as an aspect of the feminine role in the family – as part of women's role in marriage, or as a dimension of child-rearing – not as a work role. The study of housework as *work* is a topic entirely missing from sociology.
>
> (Oakley 1974: 2)

One of the implications of this is that to examine housework as work puts it in the context of the sociology of occupations and employment, and takes it out of the sociology of the family. It means you ask different questions, about job satisfaction and dissatisfaction, for example. Industrial sociologists have typically found that certain patterns of job satisfaction and dissatisfaction are associated with particular kinds of jobs and conditions of employment.

Treating housework *as* work means both a reconceptualisation of the term 'work' in sociology, and a different method of investigating it. Indeed, a more common formulation now is 'paid' and 'unpaid' work to deal with employment and housework/childcare respectively. On the issue of methods, Oakley insists that one consequence of the mystification of housework as non-work is 'a failure to represent the meaning of housework to the actors (actresses) themselves' (1974: 27).

To correct this 'involves going back to the women themselves and looking through their eyes at the occupation of housewife' (Oakley 1974: 28). This observation introduces what was to become a central preoccupation of feminist sociology, documenting and drawing on women's experiences.

Another major study of housewives also began in the 1970s, though the author, Meg Luxton (1980), adopted a rather different approach. Basing her study in a small mining town, Luxton interviewed three different generations of housewives not only about their attitudes to housework, but she put this in the wider context of the occupational division of labour. (Flin Flon was largely a single industry town where very few mothers of small children were employed.) She returned to the town five years later to see whether any changes had occurred to what was a very traditional set of attitudes and division of labour. The decline in the mining industry where most men were employed had precipitated a significant increase in the employment of women, including those with young children. But if women were entering or returning to jobs, what was happening to the domestic division of labour? Luxton found three basic patterns in the households. The smallest group of her respondents tried valiantly to maintain a traditional division of labour, insisting they were only taking jobs because of a crisis in mining. They held onto their beliefs that a married woman's place was in the home, and that housework and childcare were entirely their responsibility. As Luxton comments:

> As a result, these women set themselves up in a never-ending vicious circle and ran themselves ragged. Their fatigue and resulting irritability and occasional illnesses only served to

> convince them that their original prognosis was correct: paid
> employment is bad for women and harmful to their families.
> (Luxton 1990: 43)

About a third of Luxton's sample *had* changed both in their
attitudes and actions. While arguing that a traditional division of
labour was desirable, they recognised that they could not do it all
by themselves. They could not be superwomen. In the same way
that they were 'helping out' with wage earning, their husbands
and children should 'help out' with domestic labour.

Just over half, however, had changed dramatically. They now
regarded wives and husbands as partners who should share the
responsibilities of both domestic labour and wage earning. They
were putting increasing pressure on their husbands and children
to share the burdens of domestic labour. However, Luxton makes
quite clear that their husbands often fiercely resist these
demands:

> At some point a man's increasing involvement in domestic
> labour starts eroding his ability to engage in other activities
> he values highly. There is a substantial difference between
> washing dishes and watching TV, and in coming home early
> to cook dinner or staying with one's mates in the pub.
> (Luxton 1990: 50)

Luxton's study also illustrates that not all women are happy to
give up their responsibilities in the home. Housework is not
uniformly regarded as a burden: 'For most women, the kitchen
is the closest they ever have to having a "room of one's own"'
(Luxton 1990: 47). The jobs they took on and the wages they
earned did not necessarily compensate for this loss.

In conclusion, Luxton notes that her study suggests that
changing patterns of paid employment are provoking a crisis
in the way labour, both in and outside the home, is divided by
gender. Each household feels it is facing and negotiating these
changes in isolation. When women (and men) try to change
the divisions of labour in employment, they have collective
organisations, such as trade unions and sometimes the law, to
back them up, but no such practical support for changing the
domestic division of labour. Ideas about men's and women's
proper places are undoubtedly changing, but no single dominant
idea has emerged. As a result, 'The current situation is thereby
generating a great deal of confusion and often pain and
interpersonal conflict, especially between women and men'
(Luxton 1990: 54).

Both of these studies relate to a significant claim made by
feminists around this time: that the family, and especially

women's major responsibility for domestic work, is at the heart of women's oppression. As long as women retain overall responsibility for domestic work, they are not 'free' to compete with men on equal terms when it comes to paid work. They are the ones expected to take time out to have and raise children, and to take time off when children are ill. These expectations contribute to a perception of women as less career oriented than men, which in turn makes them poorer promotion prospects. We will be looking at these claims in more detail in Chapter 3.

Metaphors of silencing or, alternatively, giving women a voice run through both studies discussed in Case Study 2.1 and combine to indicate that women have a different set of experiences, a different form of knowledge about the world from men. Typically, qualitative research methods are better at exploratory research, when the researcher is either less sure of just what it is she/he wants to investigate, or is committed to tapping into the subject's own understanding of her/himself and her/his life.

These methods, face-to-face in-depth interviews with a small sample, observation, and the recording of life histories were those favoured by feminist researchers in the 1970s. But there were two other reasons why they were adopted. First, they are (relatively) cheap, at least compared with large-scale surveys, and questionnaires that need teams of assistants to administer and code them. In the first stages of feminist research, when the women often only had the limited budgets of postgraduate grants and scholarships, this was an important factor. Second, other sociologists in Britain and America, especially in the areas of crime and deviance were also adopting these more ethnographic and naturalistic methods in their research (Becker 1963; Young 1971). In the 1960s and 1970s, these fields of sociology appeared to be at the cutting edge of radical sociology, and the use of their methods seemed to guarantee radical answers. This methodological preference also characterised the emerging field of (sub)cultural studies (Hall and Jefferson 1976). Subsequently, feminists have drawn on a wider range of methods and now no single type can be seen as particularly 'feminist'.

The emphasis on beginning with women's experiences rather than researchers' categories led to the development of a distinctive feminist epistemology, an approach to acquiring adequate knowledge of women's lives and/or viewing the world from the point of view of a woman. Sandra Harding (1986) has identified two major variants, feminist empiricism and feminist standpoint epistemologies.

Feminist empiricism

Feminist empiricism underpins some of those earlier 'include women' studies, and may proceed from the assumption that there is nothing inherently wrong about sociology, that it only needs correction, to include women, document their experiences, and to study them in an open-minded manner. The sexism that Oakley, for example, identified is, from this perspective, just a bias that can be eliminated. But also as we saw in the case of the sociology of crime and deviance, bias lies not just in how things are studied, but in what is studied (and not studied) too. Sociology identifies key aspects of society for investigation, such as its structures of ownership and wealth and the unequal distribution of life chances. But feminist critics of sociology have argued that things are not just problems in isolation, they are problems *for* someone, and in this they are following one of the basic precepts of sociological analysis. As C. Wright Mills (1959) pointed out many years before, people have many problems and troubles that they may see as personal – unemployment, divorce, being a victim of crime – but which are also public issues rooted in the structures of society. Making connections between personal problems and public issues is what sociology is about and requires the exercise of what he called the sociological imagination.

Even on the same issue, different things might be problematic. To take examples from various areas of sociology, the 'problem' of 'race relations' appears very differently depending on whether we examine it from the perspective of many politicians, police and immigration officers or from the perspective of those experiencing racist attacks or harassment. The problem of strikes is different for employers and for workers (and their wives might have a different view again). What feminists add to this is that because of the socially and historically constructed differences between men and women, different things matter, different things are problematic for them (though there are overlapping interests and problems too). As Harding notes, feminist research takes its cue from the issues that women regard as problematic (Harding 1987). Another study by Ann Oakley illustrates well this approach, her study of childbirth from the point of view of first time mothers that is discussed in Chapter 4, Body Politics.

This term 'experience', however, is not a simple one. Many feminists concerned to eradicate sexist bias, wanted to begin with documenting women's experiences, to set these against their neglect and/or their dismissal in **mainstream** sociology. But experiences are not infallible guides to how things 'really' are. They are not immediately given to us, but are shaped by our understandings of social reality. Many women as they learn the language of **feminism**, for example, come to see certain interactions and relationships in different ways. When a man makes a remark about their bodies, whether they see this as 'sexual harassment' or not will depend on the context and the language they have available to make sense of the situation. This is not only a point about feminism however.

All kinds of political **discourses** enable us to see things differently, and hence to *experience* the world differently. Sociology itself enables us to reinterpret the world and our places within it, to break down common sense assumptions about why people do things. Sociologists also learn to identify certain explanations as instances of dominant ideologies that basically serve as justifications of the status quo. Another problem with feminist empiricism is that there was no single category of 'women' with the same set of experiences. By the 1970s, this point was being forcefully made by Black, working-class women and by lesbians. *Their* experiences are often different from those of the predominantly **White** middle-class women who were carrying out most of the academic research in sociology and other disciplines. Black women, for example, were criticising the emerging feminist research and theories, arguing forcefully that both were profoundly **ethnocentric** (produced from an unexamined perspective of White women), and limited. While still situating their analyses within feminism, they argued that neglect of the structures of **racism** seriously compromised 'White' feminist theory's claims to analyse *all* women's situation. Valerie Amos and Pratibha Parmar (1984), for example, focused their critique on a number of central issues in White feminism (or as they called it 'Imperial feminism'), including sexuality and the family. The problem, they pointed out, was not simply one of **Black** women's absence (which could be remedied by another filling in of the gaps). Rather, the way analyses had been constructed, to examine the intertwined development of capitalist and patriarchal relationships, neglected how they were also intertwined with racism and imperialism. Both capitalist and patriarchal relations have positioned women (and men) differently, depending on their 'racial' categorisation. If we remember this, then we can see that Black women do not always share experiences with White women, and that they share others with Black men (which are different from those of White men). The same year, in America, bell hooks (1984) also attacked the implicit racism of much American feminism, or that which had official recognition as 'feminism'. She pointed out that White women, even when victimised by sexism, were always in a position of dominance over Blacks, and that their lack of consciousness of this power undermined their attempts to understand class and gender relationships.

Feminists, though, were reluctant to leave the matter here, simply recognising the existence of a multitude of different experiences, different knowledges. In common with other sociologists, feminists wanted to argue that some knowledge *is* better than others are – feminist knowledge *is* better than malestream knowledge. Many sociology students learn in the first year to deconstruct 'common sense' explanations about the world, such as 'it's only natural for women to want babies', or 'poor race relations are caused by too many immigrants'. But the common sense that sociologists learn to unpack is usually other people's. But they (we) too, privileged intellectuals, future professionals, and members of the dominant class in the world order, also operate with common sense assumptions, ways of *not* seeing which are intimately bound up in power relations. We tend to assume that our superior education gives us an edge over other, less privileged, people's vision of the world who have only a partial understanding of those links between personal troubles and public issues which Wright Mills talks of. But privilege as well as domination also produces partial ways of knowing. If feminism has shown many people how far the ways of knowing of the dominant male group are limited by position in gender relations, other critiques, especially from Black women, can show how White women's ways of seeing are not necessarily impartial either. Comprehending our (relative) privilege requires wrenching ourselves out of our own common sense.

In addition, not all (or even most) women are feminists and so not all accounts of the world from women's perspectives will look like the accounts feminists want to offer. In the early stages of feminist research, there was a tendency to select topics that lent themselves to an excavation of a kind of submerged or muted feminist worldview which feminist researchers would articulate. This tended to elide a feminist and a woman's perspective, avoiding the problem of multiple perspectives and their relative validity.

Case study 2.2 Right-wing women and feminism

A study, by the American feminist researcher, Andrea Dworkin (1983), even managed to uncover this submerged feminist perspective from apparently very unpromising material, right-wing women. Dworkin's basic argument is that the right-wing women she interviewed had, like radical feminists, seen the truth about gender relations, about male dominance and female submission. These women, unlike liberals who, to the extent they even recognised gender discrimination, saw it as a problem of individual bias or prejudice, recognised it as a deep-seated problem which structured the whole world. This is what made them, in effect, sisters under the skin to radical feminists. The right-wing women felt that, for women, the world was a dangerous place, violent, unpredictable, and unforgiving of women who fail or refuse to conform. The Right, Dworkin claims, manipulates these fears, promising to reveal the rules of the game on which women's lives depend, and promising to make men too abide by their side of the bargain:

> A woman is loved for fulfilling her female functions: obedience is an expression of love and so are sexual submission and childbearing. In return, the man is supposed to be responsible for the material and emotional well-being of the woman.

> As long as the sex-class system is intact, huge numbers of women will believe that the Right offers them the best deal.
> (Dworkin 1983: 22, 234)

The difference between right-wing and feminist women is that the former believes the world is unchangeable, and the latter see that the bargain right-wing women make will not keep them from harm:

> The home is the most dangerous place for a woman to be, the place where she is most likely to be murdered, raped, beaten, certainly the place where she is robbed of the value of her labor.
> (Dworkin 1983: 232)

The problems with simply grounding feminist sociology in 'women's experiences' lead us on to the second version: feminist standpoint epistemology.

Feminist standpoint

Standpoint feminists generally want to distinguish between 'experience' and 'standpoint'. Nancy Hartsock's account clarifies what is meant by 'standpoint', which here she calls 'vision', and its relation to experience (Hartsock 1998). Drawing on a Marxist influenced epistemology she argues that:

- Material life structures and sets limits to our understandings.
- If material life is structured in opposing ways, the visions of each party will be different and/or opposed.
- The vision of the ruling group structures material relations which are shared by all, so they are not false.
- The vision of the oppressed must be struggled for.
- This engaged vision exposes real relations, and is emancipatory.

Hartsock draws a parallel with Marx's view that it is through the labour we perform that our visions emerge. But in societies such as ours where there is a sexual division of labour, there are epistemological consequences of the different labour that, typically, men and women perform. The reproductive labour (housework and childcare) which women in capitalist societies perform (though not to the exclusion of productive labour) produces a distinctive vision, which enables them to formulate a distinctive standpoint. By this, Hartsock means a knowledge that is achieved through engagement, through the struggles women wage with their oppressors. A standpoint, therefore, is a second stage of knowledge, based on a distinctive set of experiences.

Another important point to recognise about feminist standpoint epistemologies, also parallel with a Marxist view of the proletarian standpoint, is that this standpoint is not simply another way of looking at the world, it is a better means of generating knowledge. As Hartsock explains, in a later reflection on her original formulation of standpoint epistemology:

> I argued . . . that for [White] women in Western industrial society, the experience of life under patriarchy allows for the possibility of developing an understanding both of the falseness and partiality of the dominant view and a vision of reality that is deeper and more complex than that view.
>
> (Hartsock 1998: 243)

In the case of women, it is their experiences of performing reproductive labour that allows for a new understanding of the world. Their labour is dismissed as non-work, something they perform for love, or because of instincts. But this invisible, de-valued labour is essential. The vision does not come automatically, however:

> The difficulty of the problem faced by feminist theory can be illustrated by the fact that it required a struggle even to define household labor, if not done for wages, as work, to argue that what are held to be acts of love instead must be recognised as work whether or not wages are paid.
>
> (Hartsock 1998: 124)

Feminist theory, therefore, is based on women's experiences, but is mediated through a feminist standpoint. Hartsock, however, assumes here that women have enough experiences in common to generate a single standpoint, distinct from that of men.

Although Hartsock was aware that there were certain perils in generalising about women, that 'it contains the danger of making invisible the experience of lesbians or women of color' (1998: 112), she believed that women in Western class societies do have enough in common to justify a general claim. She implies that we can somehow abstract their shared 'womanness' from any other aspect of their identities, presumably based on the reproductive labour they all perform. This is still problematic. **Reproduction** is a social, not a biological fact (and Hartsock recognises this with her qualification that she is analysing women's position under capitalism), and so Black and White women, heterosexual women and lesbians are positioned very differently in relation to reproduction. Heterosexual women, for example, are expected to have a 'natural' desire to become mothers, and if they find they are infertile will have a sympathetic hearing if they want to consider adoption, or use one of the various means of assisted conception. They may have some problems but these are very different from the problems infertile lesbians who want to have a child routinely face. Again, Black women not only perform reproductive labour within their own households but also often within the households of others, 'freeing'

White women from these chores. The assumption that Hartsock makes, therefore, is highly suspect. Does this plunge us into relativism? Does this mean we can never use the term 'women' or without following it with a long list of specifications about **sexuality**, (dis)ability, age, religion, ethnicity and so on? Allesandra Tanesini (1999) warns of the opposite error, of putting too much emphasis on **differences** between women and neglecting what they have in common. It may also imply people can only talk about *their* experiences which consequently means everybody else can ignore what they have to say.

The African American writer Patricia Hill Collins (2000) offers a clear and helpful way through this problem by a focus on Black women and the production of what she calls Black feminist thought. Hill Collins distinguishes three levels of consciousness:

- First, there is a distinctive Afrocentric worldview, though it may not be fully articulated. It is produced not by 'race', but by the experience of living in a **racist** world.
- Second, there is a conscious and collective articulated worldview or standpoint, which is arrived at through struggle. More women than men develop a feminist standpoint since women have more negative experiences of gender **oppression**, and more Blacks than Whites develop an Afrocentric standpoint.
- Third, there is Black feminist thought that reflects on and articulates these standpoints: 'One key role for Black women intellectuals is to . . . investigate all dimensions of a Black woman's standpoint with and for African American women . . . the consciousness of Black women may be transformed by such thought (Collins 2000: 30).

She acknowledges that there are different forms of experience, and different standpoints generated by oppressed groups. Black feminist thought draws on a number of such standpoints including what she calls Afrocentric, Black women's and feminist standpoints, though it is not a simple addition of them. By Black women's standpoint she refers to those ideas and experiences shared by African American women, while Black feminist thought refers to the theoretical interpretations of Black women's reality by those who live it. Collins recognises that not all African American women generate such thought, manage to articulate this alternative standpoint, and that other groups may contribute to Black feminist thought.

Collins also notes that Black feminist epistemology has a different set of criteria for producing valid knowledge, different from the normal sociological criteria. The criteria include.

*   Lived experience. This is a claim that those who have lived through particular experiences are more credible than those who have simply read or thought about them.
*   Use of dialogue. New knowledge claims are developed through dialogues with other community members. Connectedness rather than separation is an essential part of the validation process.
*   Ethics of caring. Value is placed on individual expressiveness, on emotional connectedness, and a capacity for empathy.
*   Ethic of personal responsibility.

There are also, often, different ways of coming to and expressing knowledge:

> Traditionally, the suppression of Black women's ideas within White-male-controlled social institutions led African-American women to use music, literature, daily conversations and everyday behaviour as important locations for constructing a Black feminist consciousness.

> (Collins 2000: 251)

Black church services have been one paradigmatic location for this epistemology where all four elements interact:

> Neither emotion nor ethics is subordinated to reason. Instead, emotion, ethics and caring are used as interconnected, essential elements in assessing knowledge claims. . . . Moreover, when these four dimensions become politicised and attached to a social justice project, they can form the framework for Black feminist thought and practice.

> (Collins 2000: 266)

A further important element in Collins' account is that each group with a distinctive standpoint should recognise that its knowledge, though true for them, is also partial. They should be open to recognising the validity of other standpoints. Although Collins concentrates on Black women and Black feminist thought, this does not imply that their experiences, their thought, have a particularly privileged or central position. Instead, as she says, 'Black women's experiences serve as one specific location for examining points of connection among multiple epistemologies' (Collins 2000: 270). It is open to members of other oppressed groups to formulate their equivalents to Black feminist thought, learning from and in turn enriching what Collins calls a transversal knowledge in which no single standpoint, no single version of the truth is recognised. From this point of view, knowledge is not a fixed body of truth, but is forever in process, always emerging.

This position has certain similarities with what Harding (1986) calls a **postmodern** epistemology. This is an epistemology sceptical of any claims about a universal and singular truth, or about any one group's special claim to produce *the* truth. In so far as all kinds of feminism have been sceptical about the superiority of malestream knowledge, there may appear to be an affinity between feminism and **postmodernism**, but many feminists feel postmodernism is too close to relativism to be politically useful. We will be examining the affinities and tensions between postmodernism and feminism in more detail in a later chapter.

So far, much of the discussion about feminist epistemology, what constitutes good and reliable feminist knowledge, has been carried out at an abstract level. We have seen how some feminists have tried to put this into practice, but there are many problems in translating these arguments into the everyday practicalities of carrying out research. One area where these problems surfaced was in the arguments between 'activists' and academic feminists.

Academics and activists: the politics of research

The 1970s, when many of these questions were first being aired, were a time of intense feminist political activism. We have seen how one issue, housework, was translated into an effective and novel programme of feminist sociological research, and there were several others, including issues around violence. Conferences and discussions in local and national groups were often devoted to establishing what were the demands of the women's movement, and initiating and campaigning for appropriate policies and provisions. Women's refuges and rape crisis centres were just two of the achievements of these years, services initiated by women for women. Although many local authorities have since provided some funding for them, the services have never been able to meet the needs of all the women who apply to them.

In a very straightforward way, campaigns and services like these began with women's experiences, experiences that had previously been neglected or explained away, and proceeded to build an alternative. This alternative was both material – a place to live when escaping from a violent man – and political, in the sense that women's aid workers campaigned for changes in the law, and in attitudes that saw domestic violence as a private matter between a man and his wife. If starting with women's experiences could lead to such improvements in women's lives, it was obviously a powerful tool and provided the rationale for feminist research in the academy which also began with these experiences. The significance of feminist standpoint(s) can be understood in this political context, as an 'academic' response to the centrality that was being given to women's experiences in the wider movement.

Although feminist sociologists often saw their work as a contribution to feminist politics, documenting hitherto neglected experiences, their work was not always received as such by all feminists. Mary Evans (1981), for example, recounts the problems in establishing what was the first Women's Studies course as part of an academic degree in Britain. Prepared to face considerable hostility from academic colleagues, she was less prepared for the criticisms from 'sisters', some of whom could not see its relevance to 'real' women and their 'real' problems. A gap seemed to be opening up between activists and academics, with the former accusing the latter of only analysing the world instead of changing it. Academics, of course, replied that doing theory was necessary to effective political action, and was not divorced from the real world at all.

But what the arguments did do was open up another angle on research, a new interest in the 'politics of research'. This meant a concern not only with the ethics of research practices and the academic division of labour, but also profound questions about the purpose of research, what 'useful knowledge' might be, and who are the producers and consumers of knowledge. These issues are still under debate, but feminists have been at the forefront of opening them up for sociology.

Another feature of feminist research was reflexivity. This means a critical reflection on the process of research, and/or locating the 'knower' in the production of knowledge. To an extent, it is a part of standpoint and constructivist epistemologies that insists on the relevance of the social production of knowledge. As Mary Maynard (1994) points out, there are two ways in which this reflexivity has been incorporated in feminist research. It may refer to critically examining the research process to reveal assumptions about gender that are built into the process. It may also refer to reflecting on the 'intellectual' autobiography of the researcher. Stanley and Wise (1993), for example, discussing their research on obscene telephone calls argue that their personal histories and experiences of receiving them informed their analyses. In both cases 'gender is seen, not just as something to be studied, but as an integral dimension of the research process and therefore also to be studied' (Maynard 1994: 16). This is obviously at odds with the standard injunction that the best, most scientific, knowledge is produced by a detachment of the researcher from the subject being studied.

As Glucksmann explains, reflexivity is part of a constructivist epistemology. It is a 'principled response to the belief that researchers together with their research subjects construct a negotiated reality, on the premise that there is no one reality . . . The researcher's own responses and understandings, and the meanings it has for her, thus become integral components of the final product' (Glucksmann 1994: 159).

Originally, feminist research was defined as research by, on and for women, but this soon proved too simple a formulation (Kelly et al., 1994). Each of these three terms was questioned. In what sense could historical research be called 'for' women when the women were dead? Could and should not men's lives and experiences also be a topic for feminist research? And if men could not, perhaps, carry out *feminist* research, could they at least carry out non-sexist research? Might they not, also, have an advantage when it came to researching men's lives? The varying answers to these questions relate to the theoretical perspective adopted. To answer 'feminist' is not enough, as there are several varieties of feminism.

Without necessarily reaching agreement on these questions, researchers began to scrutinise various stages of the research process and their roles within it. They tried to break down hierarchical relations within research teams, and between the researchers and their subjects, attempting to treat all as active participants in the production of knowledge. Not all feminists believe this is possible, however. Miriam Glucksmann, for example, reflecting both on writings on feminist research and on her own experiences of conducting empirical research, says 'I want to suggest that it is impossible to overcome within the research context the inequalities of knowledge between researcher and researched' (Glucksmann 1994: 159). What Glucksmann highlights is that there are:

> real social divisions of knowledge that are created between people in contemporary society [that] represent a central contradiction that inevitably characterizes academic feminist research. No amount of sensitivity or reciprocality can alter the fact that while the task of the researcher is to produce knowledge, those being researched have a quite different interest in and relation to their situation.
>
> (Glucksmann 1994: 150)

Glucksmann goes on to illustrate what she means by these social divisions of knowledge, in the context of her research on women factory workers and the dynamics of gender subordination (Cavendish 1982; note that Cavendish is former name of Glucksmann). She could not rely entirely on the women's testimonies, she explains:

> precisely because a central aspect of their subordination was that they acquired only a fragmented and partial knowledge of the assembly line process as a whole. . . . Thus one clear instance of gender inequality on the shop floor was knowledge: men controlled the machinery, which included knowing more about the production process, while women operated it.
>
> (Glucksmann 1994: 157)

Glucksmann's work also returns us to the question of a feminist standpoint discussed above. The 'standpoint' nature of different knowledges is clearly evident, and not only women's standpoints. Not only do different groups, of men and women, of workers and managers, have different standpoints, these are related to their objectively different interests deriving from their places in the division of labour. 'For example, the supervisors had an interest in assemblers working as fast as possible since the size of their wage was linked to output' (Glucksmann 1994: 157). Glucksmann also reflects on her own position, her standpoint and *her* interests. Her education, her status as a researcher put her in a relatively privileged position. She was able to add data deriving from interviews with managers and supervisors, company archive material, official statistics and so on to the women assemblers' accounts. The final account not only recounts the different views, but explains why they experienced things differently.

Glucksmann's work is also a good example of the way that the concerns of the women's movement fed into academic feminist sociology. She took a job working on an assembly line in a factory in order to try and understand why feminism seemed to be irrelevant for many working-class women. This was not just a matter of interviewing such women, but trying to gain direct experience into what it was like to be an unskilled manual worker. Although this and other projects she later undertook depended on the co-operation of working-class women, these were not collective productions of knowledge. She and the women had quite different interests and she recognised that the study she produced would be of little interest to the women it was about. She also recognised that it would be of greater benefit to her, in the short term, in spite of her political commitment to feminism.

The politics and ethics of feminist research contain a commitment to non-exploitative relations between the researcher and her/his subjects. In her research on first-time mothers, Ann Oakley argued that she had to abandon the textbook recommendation to remain neutral and detached, not to offer comment or reveal personal details and opinions when conducting interviews. She also found that this also meant she got better information from the women she interviewed (Oakley 1981b). Subsequently, however, other feminists have pointed out that establishing friendly relations with women subjects may lead to them revealing more about their lives than they might, on reflection, have wished (McRobbie 1982; Finch 1984; Glucksmann 1994). Other feminists pointed out that, in addition, the ease with which some researchers established good relationships was a matter of shared class or ethnicity. Simply being a woman was not in itself enough (Phoenix 1994).

Ann Phoenix uses her experiences of research, and the impact of 'racial' **identity**, to clarify the difference between realist and constructionist epistemologies. Realist or reflectionist epistemology asserts or assumes there is one truth to be uncovered and that interviews aim at uncovering it. Matching Black interviewers with Black subjects when studying '**race**' for example is more likely to produce this 'truth', and it has been established that Black people are more likely to express more radical opinions than when White people interview them. By contrast, constructivist epistemology treats accounts as constructions of knowledge, not as repositories of a single 'truth': 'This necessitates analysis of the interview situation as the site where specific accounts are produced, rather than the taking for granted of interviews as productive of "truths"' (Phoenix 1994: 66). For the constructionist, the very fact that matching or not matching by 'race' produces different results is not an indication that one strategy is inferior to the other as a truth producing formula. The difference is in itself important data. Phoenix also notes that the matching strategy can contribute to the marginalisation of Black interviewers who, it is assumed, can research only 'Black' topics and subjects. Remember Tanesini's warning above.

Useful knowledge

One important aspect of feminist research that, as yet, has not been explored, is the question of useful knowledge. Many feminists such as Hartsock and Collins have insisted that feminist knowledge is or should be emancipatory, although others such as Glucksmann have worried that is hard in practice to achieve.

The material base of research matters, and different countries have different practices. In Britain, sociological research has largely been carried out in higher education institutions and this can lead to resentments and hostilities between feminists inside and outside these institutions. Our society has a division of labour in which some skills, especially academically validated ones, are more highly regarded and rewarded than others. Feminists in colleges and universities seem to have privileged access to the means of funding, conducting research and communicating their findings, although many inside would also point out that feminist research in universities has its own problems of recognition (McRobbie 1982).

Many feminists are concerned to see their ideas communicated beyond a closed circle of other academics, not least to introduce younger generations to feminism. Alternative publishing companies, film co-operatives and resource centres provide some of the means of doing so. Such enterprises also begin to challenge male domination of the conventional media and forms of education and can offer women the chance to acquire new skills.

The positive side of the location of feminist research in academia stems from the growth in numbers of women there since the 1960s, and more recently the growth of young women registering for a higher degree. This has allowed for the beginnings of a feminist 'intellectual' culture around the research projects such higher degrees entail. Feminist research networks have been established, both academically based ones and also ones open to a wider community of feminist activists. The resources of universities and colleges   hough not without a struggle, be put to instrumental ends.   hink, since the early 1980s when both McRobbie and   ?, that matters have progressed. But women's, fe   dies, both as independent modules and   have a chequered history, at least in   n that was largely the inspiration   in a year to get approval at Glasgow

w, it is in the context of academic courses   serious consideration of feminism for the   have made some gains in shifting the academic   , paradoxically, it sometimes seems the world   cided that feminism is old hat:

> y's cultural climate feminism is at one and the same time   ed with furthering women's independence and dismissed as irrelevant to a new generation of women who no longer need to be liberated from the shackles of patriarchy because they have already 'arrived'.
>
> (Whelehan 2000: 3)

Although the academic context may be one important way that feminism now gets circulated and 'consumed' (even reluctantly, simply because it's 'on' the curriculum), it does not necessarily remain there. Students who learn about feminism as part of degree courses may well take it out of universities and colleges and into the jobs they take. Jobs in local government and authorities, in private companies and in the commercial media can all provide ways in which feminist ideas circulate more widely (McRobbie 1999).

There is, then, no single way of doing or communicating feminist research, no guaranteed way of validating or defining it, and feminists have to be flexible in making judgements on the most appropriate and effective strategy in different contexts. It must be emphasised that research is collaborative and feminist research has benefited enormously from the links made between feminists inside and outside academic locations. Academic feminist researchers answer to at least two audiences and this is not always easy, but it is a socially responsible and democratic view of the research process. The forms of knowledge it produces aim to contribute to (rather than cause) the transformation of sociology and also to empowering lives.

Since both McRobbie and Evans were writing, another gap has been opening up between academic feminists and others, related to the development of 'high' feminist theory in the academy. Many of the arguments now assume a familiarity with philosophy, psychoanalysis and relatively abstract literary and linguistic theory. The literature may be rich and stimulating for readers versed in these areas, but is often inaccessible for readers without this background. The American literary critic, Barbara Christian (1989), deplored what she called 'the race for theory' especially in studies of Black and 'minority' literature. This 'race' consists not in critical, close readings of Black literature, but in the elaboration of a theory: 'Critics are no longer concerned with literature, but with other critics' texts, for the critic yearning for attention has displaced the writer' (Christian 1989: 225). Christian deplores the language that is not only ugly, but mystifies all but a select few readers. She finds it significant that it dates from a time when the literature of minorities began to gain attention, and thus high theory also serves to control the critical scene, limiting access to those who can reproduce it.

Christian concludes her essay with a reflection on the usefulness of literary criticism. She acknowledges that expertise in Theory can be useful – to a small number of people. It has become a major factor in getting published, finding a job or getting promotion in a university, but this is not what she understands by 'useful':

> But what I write and how I write is done in order to save my own life. And I mean that literally. For me literature is a way of knowing that I am not hallucinating, that whatever I feel/know *is*. . . . My readings do suppose a need, a desire among folk like me also want to save their own lives. My concern, then, is a passionate one, for the literature of people who are not in power has always been in danger of extinction or of cooptation, not because we do not theorize, but because what we can imagine, far less who we can reach, is constantly limited by societal structures. For me, literary criticism is promotion as well as understanding, a response to a writer to whom there is often no response . . . I know, from literary history, that writing disappears unless there is a response to it.
>
> (Christian 1989: 235)

One final issue relating to the question of useful knowledge is that of the relations between feminist and policy-related research. Obviously, all sorts of people as well as feminists, not least funding bodies, government departments and charities, want sociologists to do useful research. And funding often brings with it constraints.

Feminists have often preferred to use more qualitative research methods, but the 'hard' statistical evidence of surveys may be what impresses others. It can therefore be an important device of persuasion when, for example, it documents the extent of pay gaps between men and women. Many feminists now co-operate with all the above bodies and more, in the interests of bringing a feminist perspective to research, in recording the prevalence of a phenomenon (such as domestic violence) and also in order to influence policy-making decisions. It is another way of communicating findings, as well, to an audience perhaps in need of convincing of feminism's relevance. We will be looking at one instance of the effectiveness of feminist research and campaigns in relation to violence in a later chapter, on Patriarchy.

Summary

- All sociologists begin from the claim that knowledge is a social **construction**. Feminists further argue that sociological knowledge is inadequate unless it properly reflects the lives of women as well as men.
- The two major approaches, feminist empiricism and feminist standpoint, insist that we will see the world differently if we look at it from women's perspective. The knowledge women have about the world is a different knowledge, though there are also differences between women that will affect this.
- Feminist standpoint epistemology shares some features with Marxist epistemology. What passes for expert knowledge is not neutral, objective truth but a form of a dominant ideology that legitimates the status quo. For feminists, this dominant ideology actually reflects a masculine standpoint. Both Marxists and feminists agree that the subordinate group (the proletariat, women) is in a position to produce knowledge that challenges the existing order.
- Feminist sociologists are also committed to producing knowledge that is, in some sense, empowering for women. Their work stems from a base not only in feminist theories but has often taken its inspiration from the wider feminist movement and its campaigns.

- In the process of criticising and revising sociological theories and practices, feminists have been at the forefront of opening up a whole host of important questions, particularly about the politics and ethics of research.

Further reading

Harding, S. (ed.) (1987) *Feminism and Methodology: Social Science Issues.* Bloomington: Indiana University Press and Milton Keynes: Open University Press.

Maynard, M. and Purvis, J. (eds) (1994) *Researching Women's Lives From a Feminist Perspective.* London: Taylor and Francis.

Tanesini, A. (1999) *An Introduction to Feminist Epistemologies.* Oxford: Blackwell Publishers.

Chapter 3

Divisions of labour

Chapter outline

This chapter and the following one will be concerned to contextualise feminist sociology by examining trends and tendencies from the 1970s on. Feminist sociology advanced on a number of fronts, and this advance will be addressed through a more detailed analysis of the key concepts of production and reproduction. These concepts were both reworked within established areas of sociological analysis, such as education and employment, and also led to the development of new areas of analysis, such as motherhood and housework.

Both chapters will point out some of the links between 'private' and 'public' worlds; this one will concentrate on paid and unpaid work, in the home and outside, and the next will focus on education and the family, including motherhood.

The major contributions of this stage of feminist sociology have been:

- To establish that the conventional analysis of the social division of labour (in the sense of paid employment) cannot be understood without an analysis of the sexual and domestic division of labour (particularly in the sense of unpaid work).
- To establish that 'the housewife' is a socially and historically constructed role.
- To assess the relative importance of capitalist and/or patriarchal structures and practices in explaining both divisions of labour.

In the 1980s this rather narrow Eurocentric focus was expanded:

- To consider women's diverse locations within a global division of labour and the feminisation of the labour force.
- To identify the factors that have drawn women into employment.
- To examine the features and implications of this feminisation.

Feminist sociology in the 1970s

As we saw in the previous chapter, feminist sociology in the 1970s had been concerned both to revise old areas (such as employment), and also add some new ones (such as housework and motherhood). These normally occupied parts of our lives that could be called the public and the private realms respectively. Both were, and are, important areas of sociology in their own right, but a major break-through came from examining both of them together. In turn, this led to a reconceptualisation of the term 'work', to analyse the assignment of certain tasks to the public and others to the private area. This is also a gendered division of labour: Certain tasks such as housework and childcare, which women typically perform, take place in the private sphere of the home, while much paid work is seen as falling into the public sphere. Women, of course, also undertake paid work too, but the originality of the feminist approach was to argue that women's place in the public sphere had to be understood in relation to their place in the domestic division of labour. It was therefore necessary to analyse both, to examine how women's primary responsibility for the unpaid work of housework and childcare affected the paid work they did.

There was a precedent for analysing both types of labour, in Marxism, where they were called production and reproduction. Engels, in *The Origin of the Family, Private Property and the State* in 1884, had argued that:

> the determining factor in history is, in the final instance, the production and reproduction of immediate life. . . . The social organisation under which the people . . . live is determined by both kinds of production: by the stage of development of labor on the one hand and of the family on the other.
>
> (n.d.: 71)

Marx and Engels had been most concerned to outline the successive stages of human social evolution whereby classes and forms of private property ownership had developed, culminating in the capitalist mode of production. But passages where Engels discusses the emergence of the nuclear family and monogamy laid the ground for an analysis of women's oppression. This form of marriage and the family:

> comes on the scene as the subjugation of the one sex by the
> other. . . . The first class opposition that appears in history
> coincides with the development of the antagonism between man
> and woman in monogamous marriage, and the first class
> oppression coincides with that of the female sex by the male.
>
> (Engels n.d.: 129)

Engels explains this family form in terms of the emergence of male-owned private property, and the desire of men to pass it on to their sons. Monogamous marriage and women's subjugation to their husbands is the way a man can be assured that his wife's children are really his own. When discussing contemporary family relations and women's position, Engels wrote in language that would have been extremely shocking at the time:

> This marriage of convenience turns often enough into the crassest
> prostitution – sometimes of both partners, but far more commonly
> of the woman, who only differs from the ordinary courtesan in
> that she does not let out her body on piece-work as a wage worker,
> but sells it once and for all into slavery.
>
> (Engels n.d.: 134)

However, since this oppression is tied directly to private property ownership, Engels' analysis only holds for the bourgeoisie. In the non-property owning class, there is no basis for monogamy and male supremacy 'except, perhaps, for something of the brutality towards women that has spread since the introduction of monogamy' (Engels n.d.: 135).

For feminists looking at Engels' work a hundred years later, this was inadequate as a picture of women's oppression from which all men benefited, although it pointed to some of the areas to which a later generation of feminists would return: class, the state and the family. In terms of contemporary analysis, the main area that was missing in Engels' analysis was that of ethnic relations and racial stratification, but this was also to be an omission in some later feminist accounts.

'Production' and 'reproduction' in sociology

For the next eighty or so years, however, Engels' insight about the links between production and reproduction were all but ignored, partly because of an emerging division between areas of sociological analysis. 'Reproduction' was largely placed within the sociology of the family where a functionalist model was dominant in the years after the Second World War. The family, from this perspective, had two main features: first, the emergence of the nuclear family was seen as functional for modern industrial society, insofar as its small size made geographical mobility easier, as the breadwinner moved around in search of jobs and promotion. Although the modern family had shed many of the functions of the pre-industrial family, it retained two that it alone could meet. These were the primary socialisation of small children, and personality stabilisation, which means meeting individuals' needs for emotional support.

Second, the modern family is characterised by a sexual division of labour, a role specialisation between men and women, with husbands filling 'instrumental' and wives 'expressive' roles. For Talcott Parsons, an influential American functionalist of the times, the well functioning family had to have someone who earned the money to maintain the family, and also someone who did the caring and support work for its members (Parsons and Bales 1956). It was better if these roles were kept separate, assigned to the different sexes, thus reducing competition between husbands and wives, and minimising conflict between them. So, although functionalists *had* made links between production and reproduction, the picture was one of harmony and 'fit'. Any tensions and contradictions were ignored, either between families and the economy, or between husbands and wives within the family. Ideas about women's oppression by men *within* the family had disappeared.

The area of production, in turn, was allocated to the sociology of work and employment and was, even more than the sociology of the family, severed from any connections with the other sphere, in this case the family, with reproduction. The general social division of labour, what happened at work, and workers' attitudes and militancy, were all to be explained by reference to the sphere of production alone.

The social and domestic division of labour: the historical background

Feminist work in the 1970s prepared the way for all this to be seriously questioned. No longer could the domestic division of labour be seen as in some way a 'natural' division of labour, based on women's biological functions of childbearing. As we saw in relation to functionalist analysis, housework and childcare had previously been seen as simple extensions of women's role; they had been 'naturalised'. Ann Oakley's study, however, clearly demonstrated that this division of labour between men and women, and the assignment of certain tasks to men and others to women, was actually the product of historical and social developments. There was no inevitable connection between being a woman and doing housework, and raising children (Oakley 1974).

In many pre-industrial households, many of the tasks we now would call 'housework' were shared by all its members, men, women and children. This is not to say that the labour was interchangeable. Typically, there was a division of labour, both on the basis of sex and of age. But the labour of all was essential to the maintenance of the household.

The Industrial Revolution is commonly thought to mark the break with this pre-industrial system of household and family manufacture. The place of production shifted from the household to the factory and wage labour became the characteristic form of labour, as the mass of propertyless producers had nothing to sell *but* their labour. It is also often thought that this process involved the migration of men to factories in search of work and wages, marooning their wives and daughters in the household. Not all women, however, became housewives in the modern sense of the term. In many of the early textile factories and mills, women and children were the preferred labour, since they were believed to be both more docile than men, and also cheaper. Men were employed too of course, but often acted as overseers or took up the jobs labelled as skilled. Frederick Engels, Marx's collaborator, wrote about the consequences of women's employment in a number of English towns in the 1840s in *The Condition of the Working Class in England*:

> In many cases, the family is not wholly dissolved by the
> employment of the wife but turned upside down. The wife
> supports the family, the husband sits at home, tends the children,

sweeps the room and cooks . . . this condition, which unsexes the
man and takes from the woman all womanliness . . . is the last
result of our much praised civilisation.

(Engels 1972: 173–4)

**Case study 3.1 The division of labour in pre-industrial
households**

Ruth Schwartz Cowan describes various household routines in
pre-industrial America (Schwartz Cowan 1989), common to all
but the very rich who employed servants to carry out the tasks,
and to the very poor, who had no home to maintain. Although
certain material goods had to be bought or traded, households
were to a considerable degree, self-provisioning. They produced
and manufactured many of the things they ate, wore and used,
such as bread, butter, bacon, beer, candles, soap and fabrics,
even when they had to buy or trade for other necessary goods,
such as tools, salt and pots and kettles. She points out that even
if we look at a particular task that was commonly regarded as a
woman's work, such as cooking, or caring for a baby, a closer
examination reveals that a woman alone could not have
managed. Breadmaking, for example, depended on the wheat or
barley that men grew; brewing (women's work) also produced the
yeast that caused the bread to rise.

Although, in times of crisis, men and women could and did
exchange tasks, women could cut down the wheat, men could salt
the beef, the preferred solution was to hire someone of the right
sex to perform the task. So even if there was a sexual division of
labour, there was also a mutual dependency between men and
women.

Discussing the impact of changes in household equipment and
store bought goods on households and the division of labour,
Schwartz Cowan argues that far from decreasing women's labour,
they often actually increased it. It was the men's jobs in the
household that were eliminated; manufactured cloth meant
women no longer had to spin, or men to weave and children to
card, but still left women with the job of sewing clothes. Indeed,
people often expected to own more clothes and so there was
even more sewing for women.

Those housewives who could afford it may have employed
seamstresses to come and help from time to time, but the advent
of another item of domestic technology, the sewing machine, if it
eliminated the need to hire labour, put the burden back onto
the housewife.

But a further comment by Engels reveals this is not simply regret for the reversal of the wife's proper submission to her husband:

> We must admit that so total a reversal of the position of the sexes can only have come to pass because the sexes have been placed in a false position from the beginning. If the reign of the wife over the husband, as inevitably brought about by the factory system, is inhuman, the pristine rule of the husband over the wife must have been inhuman too.
>
> (Engels 1972: 174)

However, this division of labour was not the typical one of the nineteenth century. The majority of women who were employed in factories and mills were unmarried, and overall more men were employed in them than were women. The majority of women in textile production were not working in factories but in small workshops or in their homes. Domestic service was actually the biggest employer of women and, again, most of these women were also unmarried (Pahl 1984). As Ray Pahl says, 'Perhaps the best way to view women's employment in the nineteenth century is as the employment of *daughters* but not mothers' (1984: 64). He goes on to point out that these families were following pre-industrial patterns of household work strategies: there was nothing new in sending daughters out to find employment. The wages that daughters earned might either have been used to bolster their family's total income or as savings, to help establish another household when they married.

By the start of the twentieth century in Europe only about 10 per cent of married women were employed (Scott and Tilly 1975). This might be taken as evidence for the wholesale adoption of a separate spheres ideology, that married women's proper place was at home, caring for small children who should be dependent on their parents. But even if working-class families aspired to an ideal of dependent wives and children, few working-class men earned wages that were adequate to support them. The ideology of separate spheres did not mean that married women did not work, did not find other ways of earning money. The work they found, though, was less likely to be officially registered. They may have taken seasonal and casual work, done outwork in their homes, taken in lodgers and washing, minded children for neighbours, or cleaned for wealthier families. When examining official counts of women's employment in the nineteenth century, we have to bear in mind that they probably seriously underestimated women's income generating activities. More and more, throughout the century, 'work' came to mean full-time waged employment outside the home.

For much of the nineteenth century, then, what could be described as pre-industrial work strategies survived: new income earning activities were incorporated into older patterns of household collaboration. But more and more, women's employment *outside* the home became a temporary strategy, one suitable only for unmarried daughters and for families hard pressed by a man's unemployment, death or desertion.

Further, the skills that housewives and mothers were learning to exercise were ways both of stretching a man's wages and ensuring that the children they raised would be fit workers and soldiers for capital and the state. There was no assumption that these skills came 'naturally' to women, especially if they were women of the working class. They had to be taught, and women were invited to enter into alliances with experts in basic hygiene, plain cooking, laundering and nutrition, whose lessons were leavened by a strong dose of Christian sobriety.

By the early years of the twentieth century, there are two features of patterns of women's employment that we can note. The first seems to indicate an intensification of the pattern of the nineteenth century, and the second points to a break with it. First, proportionately more young women and fewer married women were employed, possibly as opportunities for casual and home based work declined (Gittins 1982). But second, the types of jobs young women were now taking up were increasingly in the service sector and light industry. Domestic service was beginning to decline. For those young women going out to work, it was less and less likely to be in someone else's home. Although there were clear class differences to this pattern, since for middle-class families it was often a mark of respectability to be able to 'maintain' daughters as well as wives, there were also certain commonalties between women across the classes. It was marriage, and especially motherhood, which largely determined whether a woman was employed or not.

Women and employment: contemporary issues

It was the Second World War that marked the decisive break with this pattern: by 1945 more than five times the number of married women were in employment compared with the numbers before the war. There was some reduction in the 1950s, but by the 1960s, the numbers were increasing again (Pahl 1984). By the second part of the century, it was the presence of small children rather than marriage that was becoming a decisive factor and the bi-modal pattern of employment was becoming the norm (that is, when mothers took a break from employment while children were young). Contributing to this new growth in married women's employment was the increasing availability of part-time jobs enabling married women, it was said, to combine their 'dual roles', of mother and worker.

Whatever the reasons for this dramatic turnaround, this feminisation of the labour force (though the majority of women are part-time employees), one important feature stands out, distinguishing women's and men's work patterns. For women, 'work' always and still combines unpaid work for their families and households with income earning activities, whether undertaken for an employer or not. Arguably, it is *men's* work patterns that have changed more over the past two centuries, as they have shed the labour they once performed within the household, for a concentration on full-time, waged employment outside their homes.

There is now a huge literature identifying and analysing current patterns of men and women's employment. For a full discussion see Walby (1990) and Bradley (1989). We can divide this into sociology that concentrates on identifying the key features (the types and character of jobs men and women do), a mid-range type of theory that identifies the contributing factors, and a more 'grand' theoretical sociology that asks about the underlying reasons for the patterns.

Features of women's employment

Some of the key features of women's employment patterns that have been identified are:

- Horizontal and vertical job segregation. Horizontal segregation means that men and women work in different sectors of the economy; women are concentrated in clerical work, in professional and related jobs in education, health and welfare, and in personal service work. There are far more male dominated jobs than there are female dominated jobs. Vertical segregation means that within a sector, men are more likely to be in the top jobs; within the health service, the majority of consultants are men while the majority of nurses are women.

- Full-time versus part-time jobs. In Britain, there has been a huge expansion of part-time jobs and these are overwhelmingly filled by women, often married women.
- Pay. Some 25 years after Equal Pay legislation in Britain, there is still a significant gap between men's and women's take-home-pay. Part of this may relate to the two factors mentioned above, but female full-time workers on average still earn 82 per cent of a male full-timer's wage, although better than the 69 per cent it was in 1971. We might expect female part-time workers to earn less than the hourly wage of a full-time employee, but at 61 per cent it still compares badly with a European average of 73 per cent (Equal Opportunities Commission 2001).

Factors contributing to women's employment patterns

Sociologists and others, including employers, unions and pressure groups have argued about the reasons for these patterns, especially low pay. In particular, they have considered how far (covert) discrimination is at work, or whether women's low pay can be explained by their concentration in certain lower paid jobs and/or taking time off to have children. Certain changes in employment law have affected the pay gap, such as the introduction of a minimum wage in 1999, and of maternity leave, but here again British women lag behind others in the EU. The average woman in Britain has eight weeks' maternity leave on full pay compared with a European average of thirty-two weeks (Ryle 2001).

Behind these arguments, however, lies a more important issue: why women are in the types of jobs they are – basically, the poorer-paid jobs. The main alternative to feminist explanations is advanced by neo-classical economists who argue that women (on average) possess less 'human capital' – skills, qualifications and job experience – than men. It is linked with a functionalist view, that men and women rationally choose to specialise both in terms of the domestic and social division of labour. Because of their domestic responsibilities, women have less commitment to forging careers for themselves. They want to be able to take time out and this means they will choose less skilled jobs (because they don't put time in to gaining skills and qualifications), and jobs where they can move in and out without interrupting career paths. A by-product of this choice is lower pay. However, other economists have found that this explanation does not account for the entire pay gap. Neither does it account for why women who do not start at a lower level of qualification, or who do not take time out, remain stuck at lower levels, in jobs with poorer pay (Beller 1982; England 1982). In addition, even if human capital theory accounts for vertical segregation, it cannot explain horizontal segregation, why women are clustered in such a narrow range of 'women's jobs'.

In contrast, feminist sociologists have identified a number of other factors that shape these employment patterns. They include:

- the 'gendering' of jobs;
- employer strategies;
- employee strategies;
- the construction of women's labour as cheap and less skilled.

Gendering jobs

There has been some debate among feminist sociologists and others about the link between women and poor work. Does the low status and poor conditions of certain jobs mean that they are reserved for workers of low status (that is, women, ethnic minorities, migrants), partly because other workers have been in a better position to refuse them? Or does the already inferior status of women and others spill over into the way these jobs are regarded? The first view is associated with a claim by Marxist feminists such as Heidi Hartmann, that capital creates 'empty' places in the division of labour, while patriarchy (and racism) decides who will fill them. The second view results from work by writers such as Phillips and Taylor about how the label of 'skill' is socially constructed in ways that naturalise women's skills therefore making them invisible (Phillips and Taylor 1980). This view captures the connections between 'traditional' or pre-existing modes of gender and racial control with the 'modern' experience of employment.

The association of certain types of jobs as suitable for certain types of workers (men or women) is a long-standing one, and there is a close correlation between what it is thought *fitting* for people to do, and what people are thought *capable* of doing (Burman

1979). Typically, this has meant that jobs demanding heavy physical labour and technical expertise have been seen as suitable for men, and that men, with greater muscular strength and mechanical know-how are better suited for these jobs. Conversely, jobs demanding nimble fingers, a tolerance for routine, repetitive labour, or that demand personal, caring, servicing skills and an attractive demeanour have been seen as suitable for women who, 'naturally' possess these qualities. Of course, this is ideology, and has often been disregarded in the case of working-class and Black women who, miraculously, *can* work in fields and mines, and disregarded for all women who *can* work in munitions factories and shipyards during wartime.

However, the gendering of jobs has powerful consequences, both for employers and employees. Employers recruit people who will 'fit' the unwritten job specifications, unless pressed by labour shortages or high wages bills to widen their intake. Men's reluctance to move into 'women's jobs' can be related to two factors: material and ideological. Women's jobs *do* on average pay less, and in addition the gender typing means that they may be seen as unsuitable for 'real' men.

Sometimes, one occupation may contain within it two competing forms of gendering. This is the case with teaching and although many women enter this profession, relatively few attain the ranks of head teachers or professors (Bradley 1989). This is a prime example of vertical segregation. Harriet Bradley relates this internal segregation to two views of the nature of teaching that are in turn linked to ideas about gender. The first emphasises the childcare aspects of teaching going back to a time when children's basic education was part of a mother's duty. Teaching is akin to socialisation. The second view emphasises the passing on of specialised academic knowledge and the links between many universities and the church, which was overwhelmingly a male preserve, strengthened the association with masculine traits. Teaching here is akin to instruction.

For much of the nineteenth century, mass education was available only to younger pupils and it was women who predominated in these schools. In Britain in 1851, there were more than twice as many women as men teachers (Bradley 1989). When teaching is seen as an extension of or substitute for a mother's role then it's a proper job for a woman. When teaching is seen as instruction, especially the instruction of boys, and when it goes along with the direction of a large school, then it's a job for a man. Not surprisingly, men have come to dominate the higher ranks of the occupation. Men have also been more successful in monopolising bodies of knowledge and ensuring limited access to the higher ranks by insisting on lengthy and expensive training:

> Thus, while professional work provides women with the best career chances and puts them on a closer footing with men . . . [they] are nonetheless subjected to ideologies of sex-typing which confine the majority to subordinate positions within the hierarchy.
>
> (Bradley 1989: 219)

However, the gendering of jobs changes. Women have made their way into occupations that once were male preserves, not just the occasional female 'captain' of industry, but whole occupations have changed in character. The job of clerk is the archetypal example. If once this was regarded as a good and suitable job for a man that had the possibility of promotion into managerial grades, the huge expansion of this type of post necessitated the recruitment of women at the end of the nineteenth century. By the 1950s, most clerks were women (Lockwood 1958). The men were, however, like the printers, worried about the consequences for their pay, promotion prospects and for their prestige. Most women did not, however, compete directly with men. They entered the lower routine levels, occupying a set of new jobs that were created by office mechanisation, notably by the advent of the typewriter. Ann Witz examines a range of jobs within medicine that are more and less marked by gender segregation (and changes to this) in order to identify the factors (including technology, employer and employee strategies) that explain current patterns (Witz 1992).

However, more recently, women have been moving out of the poor work ghetto. A factor that accounts for the move of some women into certain professional and administrative 'male' jobs is the use of the 'qualifications lever'. Sex Discrimination legislation now makes it impossible for employers openly to discriminate against women when recruiting or promoting people, but often the qualifications required for a job or a promoted post served to disqualify many women. With rising numbers of women now attaining formal qualifications, at school and after, this informal, covert barrier is falling.

Employer strategies

There is considerable evidence that employers have used women strategically, to fill certain types of jobs that are seen as more suitable for women than men. These include jobs where a woman's attractiveness or sexuality is a key component (if unwritten) of the job description (Adkins 1995). Such jobs include work in the travel, tourist and leisure industries. Many girls also see these jobs as quite glamorous, attractive alternatives to basic office and shop work (Sharrat 1983).

Other jobs for which women appear to be particularly suited include teaching and nursing. To some extent, these jobs can be seen as extensions of women's 'natural' domestic roles and qualities, and Victorian women pioneers often drew on this idea to argue for their entry to these professions. Cooking, sewing and cleaning are also aspects of 'the housewife' role that can be turned into paid work, though few women are able to turn these into well-paid careers.

The rise in the numbers of part-time jobs, and the use of women to fill them, has also been related to employers' strategies. From the 1950s when there was a labour shortage, employers saw married women as an untapped reserve that could meet their needs. The expansion of part-time jobs was a way they could recruit women who had other domestic responsibilities. Such jobs were also heralded by some women sociologists at the time as enabling married women to enter the world of paid work (Myrdal and Klein 1956). A later study examining part-time jobs in both the public and private sectors argued strongly that part-time work is an important device by which employers can achieve a flexible labour force, one that can cover peaks and troughs in the working day and week, *but* it was only women's jobs that were constructed on this part-time basis (Beechey and Perkins 1987). Employers found other ways of making men's jobs flexible, through overtime working in factories, or by instituting three eight-hour shifts to provide 24-hour cover (in the case of hospital portering). In other words, the question of gender cannot be separated from employer strategies; they operate with a set of assumptions about their employees and what kinds of work they can do, what kinds of wages they need. In the case of married women, employers are working with the assumption that they do not need a full-time wage, that their husbands also support them, and they have other calls on their time. These assumptions do not operate in the case of male employees, though the demand for a 'family wage', enough for a married man to support his wife and children, has often been used by unions to claim higher wages for men.

Because of the assumption that working women only need a secondary wage, women have also been used by employers to drive down labour costs by substituting female for male workers. They are cheaper. Often, though, male workers have resisted this strategy.

Employee strategies

This brings us to the third factor that helps explain the patterns of women's work. Many occupations and professions have attempted to exclude women from their ranks but with more or less success. By and large, it was the skilled trades that were most successful in excluding women altogether, backed by strong unions. When this strategy failed, women have entered but have often been segregated from men, put in lower grades where they are paid less. We might even think of the profession of medicine as structured by this gender segregationist strategy. Women's demands to enter medicine in the nineteenth century were partly accommodated by the development of nursing as a separate occupation for women, where even now no progression through training and experience to the ranks of doctor is possible. Here again, as with teaching, there is a gendered division of labour between the 'caring' and 'curing' sides.

A further factor involves the baneful interaction of the strategies of both employers and employees. Given the construction of women's labour as cheap, this means that employers have acted to de-skill (and cheapen) male occupations by attempting to recruit women, and other forms of cheap labour, notably migrants and young people. Cynthia Cockburn's (1983) study of the London newspaper print industry documents these strategies in detail. However, male workers have not remained passive in the face of this strategy. Cockburn goes on to explain how they have all too often responded by attempting to exclude women or segregate them into less skilled jobs, rather than asserting women's (or migrants') right to equal pay for the work. The entry of women into what had previously been defined as *men's* jobs was a definite threat to the printers' hard-won status and relatively high wages. In one sense, this is a struggle between labour and capital, but it is also a struggle between men and women. Cockburn reports that though other types of 'unskilled' labour have also threatened the printers' status and pay, such as young not fully trained men, the conflict between labour and capital cannot be reduced to the single dimension of class. Women were only a threat because they were cheaper:

> Had nothing but class interest been at stake, the men would have found women acceptable as apprentices, would have fought wholeheartedly for equal pay for women *and* for the right of women to keep their jobs at equal pay. As it was, the printers and their unions sought to have women removed from the trade.
>
> (Cockburn 1983: 151)

Women's labour as cheap and less skilled

Related to all the above is a recurring theme; that women are not the same kind of workers as men. They bring different skills and qualities to the workplace and present different advantages (and threats) to employers and to male workers. Many of these qualities *and* their assumed need only for a secondary wage are closely related to their location in the domestic division of labour. Typically, the skills that women learn in the household are invisible, undervalued when they exercise them in employment. They are assumed to be naturally 'there' in women. Conversely, the skills that men acquire in their early years, through a differential process of socialisation, are valued, and men are able to put them to work. Again typically, these skills include greater physical strength and greater technical know-how. Furthermore, men have organised to ensure that 'the attributes of strength and skill have also been deployed competitively in the manoeuvring for status between men in the male hierarchy that dominates women' (Cockburn 1983: 204).

Cockburn continues to spell out the implications of these assumptions. Men's career achievements, the long hours they work, their readiness to move around the country for promotions, and generally devote themselves to their jobs, are predicated on women's domestic labour:

> By this time-honoured family structure a man obtains hard economic advantages. He is free to build up a remunerative career, which his wife is not. He gets domestic service on the cheap – he would have to pay far more to have a living-in housekeeper. He also of course obtains many emotional and physical advantages – an unmarried or widowed man, after a certain age, is an outcast in a hard world organised around the nuclear family.
>
> (Cockburn 1983: 202)

Theories of women's work

All the factors mentioned above refer to two basic structures that underlie 1970s feminist theories of women's employment: capitalism and patriarchy. We will be considering feminist uses of the concept of patriarchy in a later chapter in more detail, as it has been so important and influential. The basic premise of these approaches was that women's position couldn't be understood without reference to their location in both the social and domestic divisions of labour. For many feminists in the 1970s, Marxism already appeared to offer a comprehensive theory of the social division of labour that could and should be expanded to explain also the gender division of labour. In practice, this proved impossible. Marxist accounts remained locked into an economistic concentration on class relations, and a focus on the conflict between capital and labour. Feminists wanted to insist that women's subordination was not simply a by-product of this major split, that it was not capital alone that profited from it, and that women's oppression was more far-reaching than economic disadvantage.

However, working independently, radical feminists were arguing that it was the system of patriarchy that explained women's subordinate status, not simply in contemporary societies. The problem with their approach was that it tended to lose the historical dimension of Marxist accounts, suggesting patriarchy is an unchanging structure. They were also unable to agree on its basis, though men's control over women's sexuality and their use of violence were highlighted.

These positions and arguments are comprehensively covered in a number of books. Readers who are interested can refer to Bradley (1989) and Walby (1990). Without going into all the details of these positions, we can say that in the 1980s the consensus among feminist sociologists was that both capitalism and patriarchy were equally significant. This is often referred to as 'dual systems theory', although there were minor disagreements about whether there were two systems, capitalism *and* patriarchy, or one system of 'capitalist patriarchy'.

Most of the productive debate concentrated on the ways that this dual focus illuminated the analysis of particular relations and practices, notably in the field of employment. When put to analytical use in this way, many emphasised that the 'capitalism/patriarchy' pair was in effect a feminist perspective. It taught us to see the world in a particular way. As Cockburn wrote: 'Feminism, like Marxism, is a world view and its subject is the world itself: a totality. The two systems are, at bottom, conceptual models, each explaining different phenomena. We need them both' (Cockburn 1983: 195).

However, as we shall see, this working consensus was seriously upset by recognition that a third system of racism had to be added, and the feminist perspective expanded considerably. Whether the concept of a system or *structure* of patriarchy would remain a workable concept will also be covered in the later chapter. For now, we will return to feminist analyses of employment.

The feminisation of the labour force

So far, this has been a fairly static picture, but we need to consider the recent feminisation of the labour force too. This is by no means peculiar to Britain, but is also apparent in other European countries and North America, where women now make up nearly half of the labour force (Crompton 1999). One of the most important factors accounting for this is the de-industrialisation of the West, the decline in manufacturing and the rise in the service sector. Insofar as these sectors are associated with men and women's employment, respectively, then this is a major factor. By itself, however, it does not explain either why more women *are* entering employment.

Although fewer children and more domestic appliances may seem to 'free' women from the household, it could well be that the relation works in the opposite direction. Women are having fewer children in order to find jobs, and their wages allow them to buy the washing machines and microwaves. Financial pressures are of considerable significance. The increasing levels of consumption, rising costs of accommodation, rising levels of male unemployment and the growth of single mother households often make it imperative for women, who a generation ago would have been at home, to look for a job. These pressures appear to impact especially on Black and ethnic minority women who have higher rates of full-time employment than white women (Phizacklea and Wolkowitz 1995). In addition, the restructuring of the global economy has also lead to an unprecedented increase in rates of migration by women across national borders in search of work both in the formal and informal sectors (Marchand and Runyan 2000). We will look at this in more detail in a later section. This brings us to a major omission in many studies of employment: ethnicity. Jobs are not only divided along gender lines but also ethnic ones – though these of course overlap. Black and

---

Case study 3.2 Women and ethnic minority businesses

Many ethnic minority women are found employed in small family businesses such as restaurants, corner shops and clothing production. Annie Phizacklea, in a study of small business clothing manufacture in Britain, argues that minority men are pushed into these enterprises largely due to the racism and discrimination they encounter in the 'host' economy. In addition, the jobs they originally came to fill in manufacturing industries are fast disappearing. A redundancy payment may be enough to set them up in business. Their 'choice' is over-determined. In turn, they tend to employ family members, or at least members of the same ethnic background, many of whom are women. Such labour intensive enterprises are 'characterised by social structures that give easier access to female labour subordinated to patriarchal control mechanisms' (Phizacklea 1990: 86).

Not all ethnic minorities are as likely to engage in this strategy. It is much less often found among Irish, Afro-Caribbean and Hong Kong migrants. The difference may relate to the conditions under which women migrate, whether as dependant family members or as independent workers. Afro-Caribbean women, for example, often came to Britain independently, with aspirations to gain financial independence. Many were directly recruited to work in the health service. These women were much less likely to be dependent on a sponsor who could show evidence he (overwhelmingly) could support them. Dependence on sponsorship puts minority women in a far more subordinate position. Because of the family and ethnic ties between the male bosses and female workers, the relation between them is more than a purely economic one. Moreover, some employers undoubtedly take advantage of women's dependence and loyalty. Phizacklea often found wives and daughters working unpaid in the 'family' business. Although sons may also work on similar terms, they could look forward to the day when the experience allowed them to set up in business in their own right. This prospect is reserved for men. It makes it hard, though not impossible, for women to recognise and resist this exploitation.

ethnic minority people not only have to contend with barriers and assumptions relating to their gender but also to their ethnic background. The 'attractive demeanour' referred to in the section on gendering jobs, for example, is often interpreted to exclude ethnic minority women from positions where they will be dealing with 'the public' face to face unless they are selling their 'exotic difference'. Sociologists argue that the 'choices' people make about employment are made in a context where structural factors constrain them. Case study 3.2 illustrates how some ethnic minorities respond to racism they encounter by entering the small business sector.

Case study 3.2 also points to two further trends: the advent of a global market, and the feminisation of a new labour force in world-market factories. The existence of this British clothing manufacture sector that Phizacklea researched can only be understood in the context of both these trends. First, though, it is necessary to sketch in some of the historical background.

Moving beyond the 'West': gender and colonialism

This account of gender and employment trends, with the exception of Phizacklea's case study, is overwhelmingly a Eurocentric one. It describes the situation of white women and men including, with some modifications, those who migrated to colonies in North America and Australasia. It is less relevant to the experiences of non-European men and women, whose lives were as profoundly and often violently affected by the changes both preceding and accompanying industrialisation. In many parts of the world, it was colonialism that interrupted older patterns of labour and household relations, most notoriously in the growth of the slave trade which provided labour for plantations and mines in the colonies which European powers were establishing.

Examining these other parts of the world is not simply an exercise in increasing the geographical range of sociology: the class and gender relations that were emerging in Europe were closely related to the growth of colonialism and the wealth it generated for a certain class. We cannot fully understand these relations without also analysing this wider context. Very few feminist researchers have, however, until recently attempted to put together pieces of this jigsaw and have, instead, tended to work in geographical isolation.

The histories and analyses of gender relations in North American and European societies are now extensive and are, to an increasing extent, complemented by a rich body of material about various slave and colonial societies, where 'racial' as well as class and gender dynamics were obvious. The German sociologist, Maria Mies, in particular has done much to draw these together (Mies 1986).

Again, part of the impetus in the 1980s for moving beyond a narrow Eurocentric perspective came from forces outside the academy. 'Race' was becoming a serious political issue across Europe and, with the rise of neo-fascist groups, racist attacks and far-Right politicians, academics were prompted to respond. Black women's critique of feminism, as we saw in the previous chapter, was well established too by now. In many European countries, debates and campaigns around 'race' took the form of arguments about immigration: how many was 'too many'? Who had what rights to migrate? Who had what rights once they had arrived? What was 'their' presence doing to 'our' culture? Consequently, it was no longer possible to bracket off the history or the current situation of Europe from its relations with the rest of the world, because many of 'them' were only 'here' because 'we' had been 'there'.

The particular contribution of feminist researchers to this radical rethinking was to insist that colonialism was not only a project by which the West exploited and colonised the 'Rest's' resources, human and natural. The making of the modern world as an interlinked system, was also a project that made and remade new categories of people. It was fairly obvious that one axis along which this was done was by a system of 'racial' classification and hierarchy, and sociologists were also arguing that there were parallels with emerging class categories in the West (Balibar 1994). If the poorer areas of the cities of nineteenth-century Europe were often likened to 'jungles', dark and alien places, it was a short step to seeing their inhabitants as alien 'races' too, brutish, ignorant and irredeemably different. But these ideologies were also gendered. Women were typically placed at a lower stage on the evolutionary scale than men. Although a few 'ladies' might be thought to be more delicate, sensitive and spiritual than men, they were all prone to be more governed by instinct and emotion which was particularly evident in those women who 'fell' sexually. We will examine the complexities of this intersection of racial and gender categorisations in a later chapter on The Body.

In *Patriarchy and Accumulation on a World Scale*, Mies argues that two processes, colonisation and housewifisation, were interlinked in the nineteenth century. By 'housewifisation' Mies means not only turning women into economic dependants of men, but also a process by which their labour becomes invisible as real work. In addition, their role comes to be seen as primarily one of consumption. Mies argues that this process was one engineered by the (European) state and churches, by laws designed to promote marriage, decrease illegitimacy and decrease legitimate employment opportunities for women. The reproduction of the working class, Mies claims, contrary to Marx's belief, could not be left to its own 'instincts': they were not producing enough future labourers. For a while, as long as the industrial working class was being replenished by numbers of dispossessed peasants migrating to towns, this did not particularly matter. But as this supply dried up, the working class had to reproduce itself, and this was achieved by turning adult women into housewives who would bear and care for children as their main 'work'. All the many other forms of work they did was to supplement a man's wages, was both real yet officially invisible. So was born the idea that housewives do not 'work', and if they are employed, only work for 'pin money'.

Mies' originality, however, lies in the links she makes between these developments and what was happening in the colonies. First and most obviously, it was the wealth generated by various colonial exploits that powered and financed the industrial revolutions of Europe and North America. And it was this wealth that enabled the rising bourgeoisie to 'keep' their wives and daughters in the non-working style to which only aristocratic women had previously been able to aspire. The household, with the wife at its centre, was also an important market for a whole new range of goods. Even some of the working class was able to enjoy the trickle down fruits of this enterprise, in the form of cheap imports of consumables such as cotton for clothes, tea and the sugar to sweeten it.

Second, the position of women in the colonies was entirely different, unless they were of the slave owning class. There was no ideal of separate spheres for native and slave women, no notion that they were too delicate for hard labour. Their place, like that of men, was in the fields or relieving planter wives of the burden of childcare and housework. After the introduction of large-scale sugar plantations around 1760, slave women were even actively discouraged from forming families and bearing children. It was cheaper to import new slaves, though this began to change in the early nineteenth century. Now, 'local breeding' was the economical

olition became a reality. But as Mies records, basing
the work of historian Rhoda Reddock on Caribbean
e women often resisted this new demand to become
a new generation of slaves, by resorting to abortion
de, producing acute problems of labour shortage for

thesis here is that the colonial process had apparently
t inevitable consequences for women of the colonised
nising classes: the first were brutalised while the second
ticated: 'This creation of "savage" and "civilised" women,
and the polarisation between the two was, and still is, the organising principle also in other parts of the world subjected by capitalist colonialism' (Mies 1986: 95).

A few qualifications to Mies' broad picture are necessary: not
all European women proved capable of becoming 'civilised', and
some colonised women were also to enjoy the fruits of civilisation.
Education was the means whereby women were to be raised though,
as we shall see in the next chapter, the education offered to
future wives of the middle class and future wives of the working
class was often different.

The gendering of the global economy

By 'global economy' sociologists, economists and political scientists
refer to a process of growing integration in capital and labour flows
in the world especially since the 1970s. Associated with this are
growing numbers and influence of transnational corporations
(TNCs). These do not simply trade internationally, but actually
manufacture goods in different countries. To an increasing extent,
services are also being relocated. The voice you hear on the other
end of the telephone when you contact a customer service department of a major company may well come from someone in India.
Large American hospitals are now 'outsourcing' their record
keeping to clerical departments in the Philippines. Strategies both
in the developing and the developed world contribute to this.
Developing countries have attempted to trade their way out of
economic crisis. Instead of relying on the export of raw materials
that the West then transforms into consumer goods, they are now
manufacturing goods, such as clothes, electronics and toys for
export to the developed world. In turn, in the face of increased

competition and rising labour costs, many Western companies are now relocating production sites to developing countries where labour costs are significantly lower. This phenomenon has been called 'the First World in the Third World' (Mitter 1986). Many developing countries are offering advantageous deals to TNCs, to attract them to Free Trade Zones, waiving taxes and providing the necessary infrastructure. In many of these developing countries, the national state prohibits or fails to enforce labour legislation on a whole range of rights: minimum pay, length of the working day, redundancy and sickness benefits, and the right to join a union or to strike. The TNC provides the working capital, often specifies the design of the finished product, and markets it in the developed world. Although often formally autonomous, the local factory is closely tied to the demand of the 'customer' company. Indeed, many of the big companies, like Levi-Strauss, now manufacture absolutely nothing and hire no workers directly: they subcontract, place orders with as many as ten companies that produce the jeans. They have become 'corporate shoppers' (Klein 2000). The preferred labour in many of these factories is often, as it was in nineteenth-century Europe and North America, young and female.

There has been some debate about whether, or how far, the experience of labour in the new factories has been liberating for women. By and large, the consensus is that it has not, but occasional dissenting voices insist that employment can mean the disintegration of traditional patriarchal control and can expand women's horizons (Lim 1983). Although she recognises that the workers are paid far less than those in developed countries, Linda Lim also points out that working for a local or foreign factory is for many women at least marginally preferable to the previous alternatives of staying at home, early marriage and childbearing, prostitution or unemployment: 'Factory work provides women in developing countries with one of the very few channels they have of at least partial liberation from the confines and dictates of traditional patriarchal social relations' (Lim in Visvanathan et al. 1997: 225).

This new form of factory work has attracted a lot of attention from sociologists but we should not forget that it is only a small part of the picture of women's employment in developing countries. Employment in the formal sector is simply not available for many women who have been forced to find other ways of earning enough to survive. Many find work in the informal sector, and create self-employment opportunities especially in the preparation and sale of goods (food, beer and clothes), in domestic and sexual services, and home production. Many of the world market factories referred to above are further attempting to reduce costs by subcontracting production to outworkers, in their homes and small workshops.

Although economists distinguish between the formal and informal sectors of the economy (and often have problems in estimating the size of the latter), women move into and out of these over the course of their lives. A young woman may first find employment in one of the world market factories then later move into market selling or home work. Older women may be the ones producing the food sold by their daughters on the street. In the course of these varied experiences, women also develop a range of self-help activities, more or less formally organised. One of the best known is SEWA, the Indian Self Employed Women's Association, a union that helps to organise women across a huge range of informal income generating activities, such as agricultural workers, pottery and basket makers, street cleaners and traders, wood and refuse collectors, and street entertainers as well as those who perform piece and out work in their homes for subcontractors (Rose 1992).

So far, this picture fails to connect the patterns, processes and transformations in the developed and developing worlds. Since Mies' work there has been some progress not simply in identifying common elements and experiences (the feminisation of the labour force), but in explaining how we are all now subject to the process of global restructuring (Moghadam 1999; Marchand and Runyan 2000). This is not to say that all women experience global restructuring in the same way, or that we can generalise across national boundaries. Global restructuring produces new forms of inclusion and exclusion along the axes of gender, class, ethnicity and sexuality.

Returning now to Phizacklea's example of the clothing businesses in Britain, this is the other side of 'The First World in the Third' phenomenon of capitalist relocation. It is, conversely, the phenomenon Swasti Mitter calls 'The Third World in the First' (Mitter 1986). This can have several meanings. It refers both to:

- Multinationals from newly industrialising countries (NICs) locating production in declining peripheral areas of Europe – a Hong Kong based textile company in Ireland, a Japanese semi-conductor plant in Scotland;

- Parallels in the conditions of employment and composition of the labour force in these factories with those in the Third World factories, whatever the national origin of the multinational.

These parallels include:

- The local availability of cheap and flexible (often young, female and non-unionised) labour to fill the basic assembly line jobs;
- The provision of incentives and infrastructure by the 'host' country to lure foreign investment.

Further, the same capitalist logic that has operated to see a rise in subcontracting in Third World factories has also operated in the First. As the big corporations shed directly employed workers, there has been a corresponding rise in small businesses tied to them. Both the electronics and textile industries, for example, are out-sourcing many of the basic production processes to the type of small 'ethnic' businesses Phizacklea researched. As Mitter comments on these developments:

> The concepts of core and periphery are no longer used simply to describe the differentiation between the metropolis and the ex-colonies, but also to describe an emerging dichotomy between the core (elite) workers and the peripheral (casual) workers within a national boundary. In this new division, as in the case of the global division of labour, race and gender provide the most effective grounds for stratification devised by corporate managers.
>
> (Mitter 1986: 105)

At the time Mitter was writing, the global feminisation of the labour force was well underway. What was less apparent was the way that women were also (in small numbers) beginning to enter the core workforce.

Numbers of feminist sociologists have since commented on this aspect of feminisation and women's use of the qualifications lever, referred to above (Walby 1990; Bradley 1999). Bradley, for example, identifies two factors that have contributed to a significant change in women's attitudes to their employment. First, there is now a 'climate of equality', a refusal by women to accept their subordination as natural or inevitable. It is in large part a legacy of second-wave feminism, an acceptance of its basic message even by women who would never call themselves feminists. This has also worked its way into many equal opportunities initiatives and policies in workplaces everywhere. The second factor is the influence of the New Right economic policies, apparent in many Western governments in the 1980s and 1990s. Although New Right policies contributed to the polarisation of women's and men's fortunes, it also legitimised and encouraged a career-focused, ambitious and individualistic ethos. Bradley is careful, however, not to overstate the extent to which gender boundaries are falling. Gender segregation remains a feature of the occupational division of labour: 'The rules and norms of employment are still laid down by men, largely policed by men, and reflect the practices of dominant masculinities' (Bradley 1999: 211). Successful women often have to adopt the attitudes and work norms of male peers.

Work and non-work

Whether we look at women's employment patterns in the First or Third Worlds, there are certain similarities. Gender segregation persists, even in the face of the feminisation of the labour force. Although a few women are breaking through what was a glass ceiling to a previous generation, most women are concentrated in poor work. A number of factors have been identified as serving to maintain gender segregation in employment. First, many employers continue to fill the less skilled, casualised and insecure jobs with women, jobs that are more vulnerable to technological advance (Rubery and Tarling 1988). Second, male and white employees and employers continue to resist women's and ethnic minorities' progress and equal opportunities policies, more or less covertly (Cockburn 1991). This means, of course, that white women can be as racially discriminatory as white men.

But a third factor that all the above and other feminist writers cite is women's continuing responsibility for domestic work and childcare. It is this form of labour, of 'non-work' in the limited and conventional sense, that is crucial to understanding women's 'work' in the conventional sense. If the years when children are young typically match a dip in the numbers of women in full-time employment, this time is matched with a *rise* in the number of hours that fathers work (Moss 1980). Thus the gender pay gap contributes to the persistence of the domestic division of labour which in turn reinforces differential opportunities in employment.

Case study 3.3 The patriarchal contract

Cynthia Cockburn carried out an intensive study of four large British organisations noted for their commitment to equal opportunities policies. Although she concentrated on their impact on women, Cockburn acknowledges that 'women' are not a single category: class, ethnicity, sexuality and (dis)ability also divide them. In assessing the policies' effectiveness, how both individual men and the companies interpret, implement and impede them, Cockburn recognises that although individual men may be striving to change their personal lives, institutional change requires more: 'Though it is hard for men to see it, they have an interest in doing so' (Cockburn 1991: 8). Later, she explains what men's interest is in challenging and changing patriarchal practices:

> Many men feel a sadness and an anxiety over their alienation from women and domestic concerns. . . . They suffer from the increased independence of women and the growing volatility of marriage, which often removes their children from them. Increasingly too men are recognising the costs they pay, tied to the rat race to earn their breadwinner wage. . . . What in the long run has to change is the pattern of men's lives. A forty-five hour week, a forty-eight week year and a fifty year wage-earning life cannot be sustained by both sexes. It should be worked by neither.
>
> (Cockburn 1991: 103–4)

The American writer Barbara Ehrenreich (1983) has identified that behind this division of labour, domestic and social, lay a particular patriarchal contract based on (an ideal of) a family wage. But even by the mid-1970s it was breaking down, when less than half of American men's jobs paid enough to support a family. The old family wage pact was between both employers and workers, and between men and women:

> To the working class, it seemed to offer dignity and a certain gentility. To far-seeing capitalists and middle class reformers, it seemed to offer social stability: men who were the sole support of their families could be counted on to be loyal or at least fearful employees. And for decades the system worked. More or less. . . . More and more people entered the mainstream culture centred on the breadwinning husband and devoted themselves to the consumption of better houses, cars and leisure activities. . . . Personal consumption helped fuel general prosperity,

> and the domestic order seemed to be eternally stable
> and even 'natural'.
>
> (Ehrenreich 1983: 174–5)

This was a system that bound women to men, and men to their employers. But by the 1970s, this pact was under threat, evidenced by the growing numbers of female-headed single parent families, and by the related phenomenon of the feminisation of poverty. This could be interpreted as a 'male revolt', an abdication by men of their traditional roles as protectors and sustainers of women and children in favour of individualism and consumerism. But this is not, by and large, the interpretation Ehrenreich favours. What happened to this pact was the phenomenon of 'runaway capital' (Mitter 1986):

> The family wage has become a less attractive investment to the men who control corporate wealth. Money that might have sustained individual workers as sole breadwinners has gone to other uses: to overseas investments, to six-figure incomes for the managerial elite.
>
> (Ehrenreich 1983: 174)

Which is where we came in, in the section on the Gendering of the Global Economy.

The demise of the male breadwinner

As Ehrenreich points out, the family wage pact referred to above is disintegrating, as more women enter the labour force, and as male wages decline and their unemployment rises. This has been called 'the demise of the male breadwinner' (Crompton 1999). So, how are families coping? How far are traditional patterns of the domestic division of labour changing, whether under the impact of male unemployment and/or female employment? *Are* men changing? This has not happened on a wholesale basis. A recent survey by the Office of National Statistics, *Social Focus on Men*, reveals that men living in households with children still do less work around the house than their partners. They report, for example, spending an average of three-quarters of an hour a day caring for and playing with their children, just under half the time that mothers do (Carvel 2001).

In the case of male unemployment, we might suppose, if the functionalists and human capital theorists are correct, that when men are forcibly 'freed' from the labour market while their wives and daughters can find jobs, that they might 'reverse' their domestic roles. Luxton's study, referred to above, indicates that there is no single response. Others have concurred (Wheelock 1990). Overall, internationally, Britain and Canada seem to fall midway between countries where the domestic division of labour remains extremely segregated and men perform hardly any domestic and childcare tasks (Japan), and others where there has been a considerable equalising of the tasks (China) (Stockman et al. 1992). These differences do not, however, emerge in a vacuum. It is also necessary to identify the factors that enable or inhibit changes in the domestic division of labour.

One of the most extensive comparative studies of the 'demise of the male breadwinner' examined patterns in a number of European countries (Crompton 1999). Two factors that the authors identify as having a major impact on the domestic and social divisions of labour are the role of the state, and the nature of particular occupations. Crompton suggests that we can conceive of a range of gender relations and the social and domestic divisions of labour, along a continuum, from most to least traditional. Crucial to the differences reported between European countries, is the role of the state and how far it establishes 'family friendly' policies, or leaves care work either to families or to private market provision.

The pattern that has emerged in Britain, of the dual earner/ part-time female carer, has not been associated with any significant change in the domestic division of labour, while full-time female employment does make more of a difference. But when women work full-time, care still has to be organised: it may be shared, it may be provided by the state or by the market. State provision has been associated either with (ex)socialist states, or the Scandinavian welfare states that have been active in establishing 'women-friendly' policies, encouraging women to fill the postwar labour shortages while meeting their maternal responsibilities. Although this was also the case in Eastern Europe, public provision failed to continue after the collapse of state socialism and gender attitudes remain highly traditional. Crompton points out that in contrast, the Scandinavian countries have experienced a greater transformation of gender relations, and she links this to active feminist involvement in developing state policies.

Apart from the role of the state, Crompton identifies occupational differences *within* countries that produce different typical domestic divisions of labour. Of the two occupations examined across the countries, medicine and banking, women doctors are more likely than women bankers to have the major responsibility for housework and childcare. Different jobs, in other words, within and across countries make it easier or harder for women to plan ahead and combine motherhood and careers. The women doctors were able to enter specialisms such as general practice that gave them greater control over hours worked, and many of the respondents had made this a conscious choice at a relatively early stage in their careers. In banking, by contrast, the organisational and managerial practices are far less compatible with family life, and women bankers had not been able to plan ahead: 'Under these kind of pressures, many of the women bank managers who had children had been "forced" to involve their partners in childcare' (Crompton 1999: 211). The location of these two occupations in the public or private sectors appears significant. Generally, occupations in the public sector are more 'women friendly' and family friendly. This factor appears to override state welfare policy differences. In Norway, for example, although there are generous leave and reduced working hour provisions for parents, few in the private sector take them up. Competitive private sector employment cultures act against taking advantage of the various benefits since employees fear it would have a negative impact on promotion prospects.

One final issue that Crompton raises is that of connections between gender inequality and more general social inequality. There is no necessary connection between greater feminisation of the labour force and a diminution of class inequalities. Indeed, the opposite may be apparent; there may well be polarisation, a widening gap between dual earner households and no-earner households especially where care is provided by the private market rather than the state. Only dual earner households can afford it. In the Scandinavian states, for example, there is greater income equality than in Britain. Several other sociologists have also commented on growing polarisation in free-market economies such as Britain and America. Bradley, for example, points out that although the term 'polarisation' originally came from a Marxist vocabulary referring to a trend towards the concentration of classes at opposite ends of the class spectrum, it has been broadened (Bradley 1996). It can now also refer to polarisation between the developed and developing worlds in the global economy, and to polarisation within countries between social categories based on gender, ethnicity and age. In both Britain and America, there is growing evidence of a polarisation between women that also involves dimensions of class, age and ethnicity. In short, although a minority of women may be achieving equality with men, the older, working-class and ethnic minority women are not seeing their lives and opportunities improve.

The 'family-friendly' public sector?

As Crompton's study suggests, how 'women friendly' or 'family friendly' various occupations may be, appears to be related to their location in the public or private sectors. The public sector in Scandinavian states is still characterised by less of an emphasis on narrow cost–benefit criteria and, influenced by a vigorous feminist and trade union movement, has developed a culture with more flexible employment patterns and options. Insofar as many women have found employment in expanding welfare services, this has undoubtedly benefited them.

For women in other, often contracting, welfare states, the picture is far less rosy. The restructuring of the global economy, referred to above, has often meant that states in the less developed and developing worlds have been forced to cut public expenditure and welfare services. Structural adjustment programmes (SAPs) have exacerbated this trend. SAPs were introduced into many debt ridden countries in the 1980s as international lenders such as the World Bank and International Monetary Fund insisted on the privatisation of state-owned services and resources. This was in order to enable these countries to generate money to pay off their debts, or at least keep up with interest payments. As feminist development specialists have pointed out, women are particularly dependent on the provision of free or cheap welfare and education services and have seen their and their children's lives severely compromised as the services become accessible only through the private market (Aslanbegui et al. 1994). Further, women's reproductive labour remains invisible to the economic planners who assume either that women are 'free' to move into employment and/or that women will continue to perform these tasks in the face of competing demands on their time and labour (Elson 1989). The demands increase, as public service provision drops. The demands on women are twofold: demands both to cover for this erosion with their reproductive labour, and demands on their productive labour, to find money to pay for schooling and health care. There is considerable evidence from Africa that subsistence agriculture, traditionally women's responsibility, is declining with grave implications for women and children's health (Turshen 1994). Hoogvelt points out that:

> Even if the structural adjustment programmes have achieved little or nothing from the point of view of . . . the improvement of standards of living of the masses in African countries, the programmes have been a resounding success when measured in terms of the acceleration of the process of **globalisation**. Structural adjustment has helped tie the physical economic resources of the African region more tightly into servicing the global system, while at the same time oiling the financial machinery by which wealth can be transported out of Africa and into the global economic system.
>
> (1997: 171)

This shift entails a reconsideration of the role and nature of the state. The state has often been the focus for feminist activism, for demands it should provide full citizenship rights and services geared to women's and family needs. But if this 'public' sphere has been, as in Scandinavia, significant in improving women's lives, it may well now be of diminishing significance. The welfare state, at least, is being subordinated to 'private' capital or to those parts of the state that are concerned with financial and economic policies. National politics too is changing. Just at the moment when women are beginning to make inroads into 'public' politics, as elected officials and administrators, this sphere too is becoming reduced simply to matters of economic 'efficiency'.

It is in this context that we can better understand the variety of ways in which women's, environmental and labour activists have been attempting to 're-politicise' the 'neutral' world of economics. It includes work both within and outwith national and international governments and organisations, lobbying and direct action, education and transnational coalition building, and the provision of alternative self-help services. We will examine one initiative, on violence against women, in the chapter on Patriarchy. Here, feminist activists have been relatively successful in pointing out the links between global restructuring and violence against women, using the United Nations and its associated organisations as their forum. Not only does violence increase in times of economic crisis, but also the support services dry up. But although this work has been relatively successful in the case of 'public' national and international

organisations, demands for accountability and responsibility have
so far had little impact on 'private' TNCs and financial institutions.
Many have, though, been put on the defensive by consumer and
worker campaigns that have revealed the damage their activities
wreak (Klein 2000).

Summary

- Feminists have made an original contribution to
  sociological analyses of the division of labour by their
  insistence that we have to expand the concept of 'work'
  to look at both reproductive and productive labour.
- The domestic division of labour is a historical and social
  construct emerging with the industrial revolution, though
  the breadwinner/dependent wife model remained an
  unattainable ideal for many working-class families.
  Moreover, it was never intended to apply to the majority
  of non-white subjects in the colonies.
- Feminists have made a strong case for the view that
  women's responsibilities for reproductive labour have
  severely disadvantaged them in labour market competition
  with men. In effect, they are not 'free' labourers.
- However, women's relative disadvantage can be capital's
  advantage, and employers have constantly used women as
  cheap unskilled labour to fill the inferior, poor jobs that
  are always being created. Male workers have often
  colluded with this strategy.
- All over the world capital is increasingly reliant on
  women's labour and that similar patterns of gender
  segregation are evident. It is not simply that the capitalist
  labour process creates jobs into which workers are slotted.
  It is also a gendered labour process, and capitalists create
  jobs appropriate for either men or for women. In doing
  so, they use the characteristics socially ascribed to men
  and women – men's strength, women's nimble fingers.
- Patriarchy and capital alone, however, are insufficient to
  explain the patterns and changes. Racism also operates to
  label workers as more or less suitable for certain jobs, and
  to compel people into particular occupational choices,
  notably into self-employment. This strategy has also been

over-determined by global restructuring, by the trend towards subcontracting by companies all over the world.

- In all cases, women occupy a distinctive labour market position that can only fully be understood by analysing their place in the matrix of domination constituted by gender, class and ethnicity.

Further reading

Bradley, H. (1996) *Fractured Identities: Changing Patterns of Inequality.* Cambridge: Polity Press.

Kofman, E. (ed.) (2000b) *Gender and International Migration in Europe: Employment, Welfare and Politics.* London: Routledge.

Walby, S. (1997) *Gender Transformations.* London: Routledge.

Chapter 4

Patriarchy: public and private

Chapter outline

In the previous chapters, the term 'patriarchy' has come up from time to time. It is now time to examine the term in more detail. The term is feminism's most original, if controversial, contribution to the sociological vocabulary.

- Since its adoption by feminists, the term patriarchy has proved both valuable and contentious. It identifies a system of domination, but has also been used in vague and even contradictory ways.
- It served to inspire feminist sociologists to research relatively new areas, such as sexuality, or to review old ones, such as employment, in order to analyse patriarchal relations and structures.
- In spite of its limitations, 'patriarchy' has also offered an essential way in which to conceptualise the complex working of many institutions such as the state that had previously seemed 'ungendered'.

'Patriarchy': radical and Marxist feminism

It was the German sociologist Max Weber (1968) who first used it in sociology, to refer to a traditional system of authority in households. Literally it means 'the rule of the father', a rule that is not only over women but also over younger men. In contemporary sociology, however, it usually refers to a system of male domination more generally and as such has been particularly useful to feminist analysts. Although originally used by radical feminists such as the American writer Kate Millett (1970), it is no longer associated with this feminist perspective alone. However, Veronica Beechey (1979), a British feminist sociologist, while acknowledging that Millett's work introduced the concept of patriarchy into contemporary feminism, claimed it offered a description rather than an analysis of it. In particular, Millett failed to explain why patriarchy varied in intensity between societies, and failed to analyse the relations between patriarchy and other social relations, especially class and production relations. Other feminists around this time tried to fill these gaps, more or less successfully.

In the 1970s, two major positions were evident among feminists. Radical feminists continued to emphasise the significance of men's domination of women, its persistence over time, and its independence from any other system of inequality. Although they differ as to the basis for male supremacy, radical feminists typically emphasise how patriarchy penetrates and shapes even the most seemingly private and personal relations. It is in part because of their influence that sociologists began to investigate areas such as domestic labour, sexuality and violence. Heterosexuality, for example, began to be seen as an institution that is at the heart of women's oppression. In a paper from 1981, the Leeds Revolutionary Feminist Group explains this argument:

> Only in the system of oppression that is male supremacy does the oppressor actually invade and colonise the interior body of the oppressed. Attached to all forms of sexual behaviour are meanings of dominance and submission, power and powerlessness, conquest and humiliation. . . . The heterosexual couple is the basic unit of the political structure of male supremacy. In it each individual woman comes under the control of an individual man. . . . In a couple, love and sex are used to obscure the realities of oppression, to prevent women from identifying with each other . . . and identifying 'their' man as part of the enemy. . . . Before the sexual revolution there was no mistake about penetration being for the benefit of men. The sexual revolution is a con trick. It serves to disguise the oppressive nature of male sexuality and we are told that penetration is for our benefit as well.
>
> (in Evans 1982: 64–5)

In sharp contrast to this approach, Marxist feminism attempted to incorporate an analysis of women's oppression into the analysis of modes of production, especially capitalism. Various existing Marxist concepts, such as the reserve army of labour, and 'productive' and 'unproductive' labour were reworked to try and encompass women's position, both in the labour force and the household. In sum, this approach tends to explain women's oppression as an effect of and for the benefit of capital, and a way of dividing the working class within itself. Although Marxist feminism appeared to provide a historical materialist analysis its major problem was precisely its reductionism and its unwillingness to recognise that it was not only the ruling class that was benefiting. It was also an economistic analysis, one that tended to neglect all the ways, especially the personal and sexual relations which radical feminists had identified, in which male domination was evident. The arguments around these issues eventually ground to an unproductive halt, although a broadly materialist analysis continued to have an important influence on many feminist sociologists.

By the early 1980s, though, many feminist sociologists recognised that there are two systems of inequality in contemporary societies, economic and sexual. Drawing on both Marxist and radical feminist perspectives, they argued that we had to analyse both patriarchy *and* capitalism, without giving priority to one or the other. Since the analysis of capitalism was in a more developed state, the focus was initially on clarifying the term 'patriarchy'.

The debates about patriarchy focus on a number of questions. I will look at four of them. First, what kind of system of power is it? Is it material, is it ideological? If it is material, what is its basis? Second, where do we find it? At home? At work? Third, does it have a relation to other systems of inequality? And finally, is it a system at all?

Patriarchy as ideological or material

Analysts disagree between those who emphasise patriarchy as a materially based system of power, and those who regard it as an ideology. Since most feminist sociologists come down on the material side, we will first look at the argument that it is primarily ideological. Of these, the most influential in the late 1970s was Juliet Mitchell (1975). The point of seeing patriarchy as ideological is that it appears to deal with the deeply rooted hold of ideas, desires and forms of behaviour that continue to influence us. Without going into all the theoretical background, Mitchell pulls together a mix of psychoanalytic and anthropological theory to argue that patriarchy is an ideological mode of production that, working on our unconscious, turns us into gendered individuals subject to the law of the father. For her, patriarchy is a universal system resting on men's exchange of women in marriage, to avoid the incest taboo. However, there is an undoubted tension between seeing patriarchy as a universal structure, and Mitchell's desire to integrate it with a Marxist analysis of *changing* modes of production. She does attempt to deal with this by arguing that capitalism has now evolved to such an extent that it no longer 'needs' patriarchy and the exchange of women. The feminist revolution therefore consists in a cultural struggle against the outmoded ideology of patriarchy, although Mitchell holds back from saying we may also need to abandon the incest taboo!

Part of the reason for Mitchell's insistence that patriarchy is an ideological system is due to her desire to claim that there is a separate basis for women's oppression apart from the economic structure. She does not want to reduce this to an effect of economic relations. Her analysis therefore implies that there are two related but separate systems and that we need to analyse the ideological system of patriarchy if we are to discover the basis of women's oppression. By implication, however, existing analyses of the economic system can tell us little about this. Mitchell therefore is what we could call a dual systems analyst.

In contrast to Mitchell's position, but still within the dual systems approach, is the argument that patriarchy has a material base. Another influential theorist adopting this line is the French feminist sociologist Christine Delphy. Delphy (1976) provided one of the most detailed accounts through her work on French farming families. Her argument is that a domestic system of production in households coexists with the capitalist system in industry. It is, according to Delphy, the former that accounts for women's subordination, established through the marriage contract that gives men control over women's labour in the family. Delphy further insists that the marriage contract is, in effect, a type of labour contract. Wives, in the domestic mode of production, are the producers while husbands are the expropriators, and this justifies describing them as two **sex** *classes*. All wives are in the same sex class in opposition to men. Apparent differences between women in different social classes are no more significant than the differences in wages between different members of the proletariat. What matters is that they all share the same relation to the means of production. Divorce, Delphy argues, impoverishes all women and reveals that membership of a superior economic class is provisional, dependent on marriage.

There are three problems with this analysis. First, it would seem that women could escape subordination to men by not marrying. Related to this is the second problem. Not all women *are* wives; not all men *are* husbands, so the explanation fails to account for the subordination of women more generally. The third problem is the implication that the two systems are unrelated, except in historical times, and that women's exploitation and subordination occurs only in the domestic mode of production, that patriarchy is only to be found within the family. Although Delphy concentrates on non-employed wives, many women do take on paid work too, and they are not somehow immune there from patriarchal relations. Of course, analysts such as Delphy may well recognise that exploitation also takes place in the industrial mode of production, but a thorough feminist analysis also needs to examine the special position of women here. They are *not* ungendered members of the proletariat, occupying the same position as men.

Another materialist, the American feminist Heidi Hartmann (1979) attempted a formulation that would recognise both relations within and outwith the household. Patriarchy, she said, was based on men's control of women's labour. Patriarchy may have originated in the household where men controlled the labour of women and children, but this control was transferred to workplaces with the industrial revolution. Here, men organise to ensure that the best-paid jobs are reserved for them. Although Hartmann insisted that there are two systems, that patriarchy pre-dates capitalism and so cannot be reduced to an effect of it, she also argued that they are closely interrelated. In an influential formulation, she says 'Capitalist development creates the places for a hierarchy of workers, but traditional Marxist categories cannot tell us who will fill which places. Gender and racial hierarchies determine who fills the empty places' (Hartmann 1981, cited in Crompton and Sanderson 1990: 15). In Hartmann's scenario, there is a kind of unholy alliance between capital and men of the proletariat, both benefiting from women's subordination. Hartmann also argues that the two systems, capitalism and patriarchy, largely operate in harmony, each reinforcing the other. In a qualification to this Sylvia Walby (1990) argues that tension and contradiction is also evident. Indeed, the history of women's labour under capitalism is 'one in which there is endemic conflict, but in which there are historic political compromises hammered out after moments of crisis' (Walby 1990: 11).

Although many feminists agreed that patriarchy had a material basis, they disagreed over its basis, some (Hartmann 1979) emphasising men's control over women's labour, and others (MacKinnon 1989) emphasising control over women's sexuality. Almost all, however, agreed that it was *not* biological and could therefore be changed. As Millett argued, though, the *belief* in a biological basis legitimates patriarchy by appearing to give it a grounding in nature.

A Canadian writer, Shulamith Firestone (1972) did, controversially, argue that it was the reproductive biological differences between men and women that provide the basis for women's oppression. Firestone did not use the term 'patriarchy', preferring instead the 'sex class system'. This preference indicates Firestone's debt to Marxism, in her attempt to outline a materialist history of sex difference. Although biological difference may seem to mean that women can never be liberated, Firestone instead argues that women have the means to transcend nature, through access to modern fertility control and reproductive techniques. Indeed, Firestone foresees a time when what she calls 'cybernetic communism' will prevail, meaning that technological 'fixes' will liberate us both from reproduction and production.

Other feminists were far less sanguine than Firestone about the benefits of technology, especially reproductive technologies (Rose and Hanmer 1976). Currently, government and industry, through the allocation of research and development funding, increasingly control the form and direction of science and technology. Some reproductive technologies have allowed women greater control over their fertility but the latest sex selection techniques are far from women friendly (Kulkarni 1986). This argument also highlights an issue that was both a demand of the wider British and other feminist movements, and also was becoming a key topic for feminist sociological research: biological reproduction and childbirth.

Where is patriarchy?

The preceding discussion has already indicated some of the debates about patriarchy's location, but by the 1980s most feminists agreed that if it had its origins in the household, it was no longer to be found only or even primarily there. The divisions and relations in employment are profoundly gendered, to women's relative disadvantage. Whether we look at the overall patterns of job segregation and pay levels, or at the day-to-day interactions in offices and factories, there is such systematic structuring that it makes sense to describe these too as evidence of sex power. It is, however, not possible to call these relations and practices simply patriarchal: they are also as deeply shaped by their location in a system of class power. The British sociologist Cynthia Cockburn (1983) explained how we had to learn to view matters through two perspectives, a class and a **sex**/gender one. Capitalism is not in one place and patriarchy in another, where class relations are not. Our families, our workplaces and our schools are at once class and gendered institutions.

To those Marxist feminists who argue that women's relative disadvantage in employment can be explained by their class position, Cockburn (1986) points out that men do not just passively enjoy a relative advantage, but actively organise to perpetuate it. Although employers might gain an advantage by dividing their workers, by attempting to lower the pay levels through the introduction of cheaper labour, this does not explain why male workers have so often responded to this strategy by fighting to exclude women. She concludes her argument by insisting that we also need to expand on the notion of 'material', to include not only economic relations (such as men's control of women's labour) but also sociopolitical relations, ideology *and* physical power. The inclusion of the last may seem controversial, since sociologists have usually rejected the suggestion that men's power rests on a natural basis.

Cockburn points out that men, by and large, stronger, taller and heavier than women, do have a physical advantage. They are also more at home with technology than the majority of women. Bodily differences and technical competencies are social products, acquired in infancy and childhood through various training and socialisation processes. For the feminist sociologist what is significant about this is 'the way in which a small physical *difference* in size, strength and reproductive function is developed into an increasing relative *advantage* to men' (Cockburn 1981: 44). Using the example of the printing industry, Cockburn points out that the traditional tools and machinery required a degree of bodily strength to lift and use them that most women lacked. Pride in the job was also pride in the printer's manliness, his job and his gender appeared indivisible. But the machinery could, of course, have been designed to be lighter and smaller if men had not been the assumed users. The design of tools is political which, combined with men's greater size and strength (on average), make men appear capable and women incompetent.

Cockburn's work also provides an addition to the well-established claim that definitions of skill are gendered (Phillips and Taylor 1980). Those workers doing jobs defined as 'skilled' have traditionally been able to command higher wages, but Phillips and Taylor point out that achieving or holding onto this label for your work has often been a consequence of greater union strength rather than the actual content of the job. Typically, men have been better organised than women have and this accounts for their monopolisation of the 'skilled' jobs. But Cockburn points out that there often *are* things which cannot be acquired overnight, and that 'skill' is more than just a piece of ideological justification for men's higher wage rates.

Cockburn's detailed analysis of the job of printing also allows us to see why the printers have reacted so badly to the introduction of electronic photocomposition. The print union's resistance is not simply because the technology is a way in which capital can deskill and cheapen their labour. The new technology requires little more than a good typing ability, a 'feminine' skill, and so it is the printers' very understanding of themselves as skilled *men* which is under threat.

Interestingly, although Cockburn offers one of the most comprehensive and thorough accounts of what patriarchy is, and where it is located, she also expresses some doubts about the term. It is, she says 'too specific an expression to describe the very diffuse and changing forms of male domination that we experience' (Cockburn 1981: 55). In a later article she concludes 'Let's admit that the term patriarchy is now and always has been used by feminists not because it is ideal but for lack of another' (Cockburn 1986: 82). This raises some of the points that we will look at in relation to the final question.

Patriarchy's relation to racial domination

As we have seen, there appeared to be a consensus by the 1980s among feminists, that there were two systems to be analysed, patriarchy and capitalism although there was disagreement about exactly how they were related. Black feminists who insisted that, again, not enough attention was being paid to a third system – racial domination – raised a more profound problem. When racism had been referred to, it had very much been treated as an afterthought, a relatively minor detail which could simply be added on by, for example, noting the particularly disadvantageous position of Black women workers.

Some of these issues come out clearly in relation to two articles published in 1985 and 1986. In the first, Michele Barrett and Mary McIntosh (1985) reviewed some of their own work, especially on the family, in the light of criticisms by Black feminists, while Kum-Kum Bhavnani and Margaret Coulson (1986) review this attempt to rewrite elements of their analysis. The articles demonstrate both the key points Black feminists were making as well as how often White feminists simply did not – initially – understand them.

Barrett and McIntosh begin by recognising their relatively privileged position as White middle-class women, and the failure of too many feminists like themselves to listen properly to Black feminists. They also agree that their book *The Anti-Social Family* (1982) showed their ignorance of racism and ethnocentrism in a failure to consider whether or how far their analysis applied also to ethnic minority families.

Barrett and McIntosh begin the substantive part of their argument by attempting to document some of the empirical differences between the situation of Black and White women. They also note that the categories Black and White are problematic, apparently excluding ethnic minority and migrant women, but justify this broad division since anti-Black discrimination appears to be the major cleavage in British society, and they want to give priority to antiracist struggles. Barrett and McIntosh then go on to recognise that family forms and relations and labour market situations are quite different for Black, Asian and White women and must be taken into account in future feminist analyses. They also review the concepts of patriarchy, ideology and reproduction in the light of a greater understanding of the impact of racial divisions. Already attuned, as socialist feminists, to the effect of class divisions on simple generalisations about male domination, they point out that racial hierarchies can also reverse a sexual hierarchy. White women have, in many societies, by virtue of their racial status, dominated Black men. They cite various examples of laws and practices such as the White Women's Protection Ordinance enacted in colonial Papua New Guinea which made even the attempted rape of a White woman by a native man a capital offence. The rape of a native woman by a White man was not a capital offence. Such considerations further weaken any claims about the existence of a single system of male dominance – patriarchy.

On ideologies of femininity and masculinity they state that we have to recognise that these are multiple, and are different among different ethnic groups. They begin to confront the possibility that these are not simply multiple, however, but some are in dominance in relation to constructions of White women's purity as against the myth of heightened Black sexuality.

In the case of reproduction, Barrett and McIntosh confine their discussion to reproductive rights. They recognise that there has been a move, correctly, away from campaigns around women's right to abortion to those focusing more broadly on reproductive rights. Black, Third World and ethnic minority women have been subject to a host of reproductive abuses, such as compulsory sterilisation and the promotion of dubious contraceptive drugs, which a focus on abortion alone cannot encompass.

Reflecting on the consequences of these points for feminist analysis, they go on to ask whether 'the introduction of a third system (racism) must necessarily fragment an analysis that was already creaking at the seams' (Barrett and McIntosh 1985: 41). They offer no answers, but an earlier comment on the usefulness of the term patriarchy is indicative: 'We are still of the view that it is not a very useful noun . . . [but] the adjective "patriarchal" has a specific and illuminating quality as a description of certain types of social relations' (Barrett and McIntosh 1985: 39).

Although this is undoubtedly an honest attempt to rethink their earlier work, both from the point of view of empirical and theoretical adequacy, there are still some issues that troubled other feminists. Bhavnani and Coulson (1986) argue that Barrett and McIntosh side-step the issue of racism and instead focus on ethnocentrism. Barrett and McIntosh do, however, refer to racism but as an external struggle to which they may lend support, not as something which is a problem *in* feminism. The ethnocentrism which Barrett and McIntosh identify as a problem in their own work is seen as a cultural bias, something that could be eliminated by more information. It is, thus, another kind of 'add women' approach, rather than the transformation of feminism which Bhavnani and Coulson deem necessary.

As an example of this transformation they examine the role of the state in its support of family life that, Barrett and McIntosh reassert, is profoundly damaging and oppressive, especially for women. But this is far from being the case if we look at Black families in Britain. Not only do immigration policies often try to split up Black families, or prevent them from reuniting, but such families are often the source of important political support for their members against racism. The supposed patriarchal assumptions of the state must therefore be considered within a dynamic of state racism. They also note that this dynamic places Black and White women in a very different relation to the state.

Two further points emerge from a close reading of the two articles. First, Barrett and McIntosh seem to be working, implicitly, with a particular academic division of labour in the effort to reconstruct feminism. White feminists like themselves depend on the research and writings of Black women to inform their theories but largely confine these to the level of empirical and experiential observations. As they say in relation to Black women writing on ideologies of femininity, 'it is still possible for us to familiarize ourselves with the many accounts and analyses of these socialization processes that have been written from a basis of experience' (Barrett and McIntosh 1985: 40).

Second, by focusing on ethnocentrism, as Bhavnani and Coulson rightly point out, Barrett and McIntosh tend to reduce the issue to a matter of difference whereas racism is a matter of inequality. It is not simply about attitudes and prejudices, about discrimination, harassment and violence experienced by Black and ethnic minority people. If this is how racism is understood, then it would be possible (for White people) to stand outside it, as long as they are not prejudiced. Ruth Frankenberg's research adopts a different way of looking at systems of racialisation in her study of some White American women's experiences of growing up in a racially divided society (Frankenberg 1993). Unusually, for the time, Frankenberg's focus was on Whiteness, which is also a socially constructed racial category. Whiteness, she explains, consists of three dimensions:

- A position of structural advantage, associated with material benefits such as higher wages, better access to health care and education. Naming it as a structure means that not every White person will have higher wages, necessarily, than every Black person.
- A standpoint, in the sense of a place from which to look at oneself and the world.
- A set of cultural practices often not named as 'White' but simply seen as 'normal' or 'American'.

Collapsing racism into ethnocentrism avoids confronting questions of power, and the awkward question (for some feminists) of confronting power inequalities between women. This is an issue to which we will return in the chapter on Living in a Post World.

In concluding this section, it appears that feminists in the 1980s were struggling to juggle a three systems analysis. The list of questions still to be resolved which Barrett and McIntosh identify indicates the problems:

> Should we concentrate on the relations between race and gender and ignore for the moment the consequences of class analysis? . . . Can we argue that racism, like women's oppression, has independent origins but is now irretrievably embedded in capitalist social relations?

> (Barrett and McIntosh 1985: 41)

The difficulties had become so pressing that some feminists were considering abandoning the idea that patriarchy *is* a system or structure, which brings us to the final question.

Is patriarchy a system?

This question refers to the considerable doubts that some feminists have expressed about the usefulness of the term. This may seem odd when, as we have seen, despite some disagreements about its definition and location, it has proved a massively influential concept, almost a marker of a feminist perspective. As Cynthia Cockburn said, 'we cannot do without a concept of long-term male self-interest, of systematic male dominance: patriarchy' (Cockburn 1986: 80). But by the mid-1970s, some feminists were wary. The American anthropologist Gayle Rubin (1975) was one of the first to express her reservations. She explained that to use the term patriarchy to label all societies was analogous to using the term capitalism to label all class societies: 'Sex/gender system, on the other hand, is a neutral term which . . . indicates that oppression is not inevitable . . . but is the product of the specific social relations' (Rubin 1975: 168). Rubin did not want to extend the term to encompass all societies in which there is male domination, only those in which men's power is based on their role as fathers.

Throughout the 1980s, numbers of other feminists repeated and developed Rubin's points (Beechey 1979; Barrett 1980; Rowbotham

1982; Crompton 1986; Bradley 1989). Although all agreed that there was a pattern to gender relations, often involving male domination, the term patriarchy was not helpful except in very specific cases. It was either too general, as Rubin had explained, or if reserved for the specific cases it left unexplained how male domination operated in non-patriarchal societies. Taken, moreover, with the criticisms of Black feminists examined above, it looked as if the concept of patriarchy as a system or structure had to be abandoned. However, the British sociologist Sylvia Walby (1990) attempted another formulation designed to deal with all the problems raised by the critics. She identifies a number of ways in which we need to go beyond existing definitions in order to clarify the concept. These include recognising ethnic variation and racial inequality, exploring the role of the state, specifying the various substructures in which patriarchy is secured, and acknowledging historical change. Walby identifies six substructures where patriarchy is found: in the household, employment, the state, culture, sexuality and in violence. She also makes a distinction between two basic forms of patriarchy that she calls private and public, marking a transition around the turn of the nineteenth/twentieth century.

In the system of private patriarchy, the central site of men's domination is the family/household and what she calls the domestic mode of production. It is patriarchy in the more classic sense, with individual patriarchs expropriating women's labour. What Walby calls public patriarchy was emerging at the turn of the nineteenth/twentieth century, and here the central sites are the 'public' arenas of employment and the state where women confront patriarchal institutions rather than individual patriarchs. She also states that the typical strategy of subordination changes in each type. In private patriarchy, women are excluded from participation in public life, from employment and formal political participation. In public patriarchy however, the strategy changes to one of segregation and subordination. Women are no longer formally excluded from participation but either segregated – as in the case of employment – and/or subordinated – in the case of the relations of sexuality.

Although the two forms of patriarchy are distinguished, Walby is careful to note that there is a continuum rather than an absolute divide. In particular, she states that there are different degrees of private and public patriarchy among different ethnic groups in Britain, with Afro-Caribbeans at the 'public' end, Muslim Asians closer to the 'private', with Whites in the middle. Walby also says we should recognise that in some countries in the industrialised world, such as the former Soviet bloc, it is the state that has brought women into public life, whereas in other economies, such as the USA, it is the market which has played an equivalent role. What she offers us is a model for analysing gender relations, and it is empirical work that will tell us which is the central site and what is the key strategy in any one particular case.

There are three further points of interest in Walby's model. First, she avoids the arguments over which is the central site of women's subordination by including pretty much all the contenders. No a priori statement can be made; each case (in a particular country, at a particular time) has to be evaluated individually. Second, she places the transition in gender relations later than many previous analysts who tied it to the industrial revolution. The third point is that Walby credits first wave feminist campaigns for helping to bring about the shift from private patriarchy.

Persuasive though her argument is, there is something that may strike readers as a little odd. Classically it is, after all, the pre-industrial period that has been identified as patriarchal, though Walby has no name for this pre-'private' epoch.

Improved though this is, Walby's model has also come in for criticism. In particular, Bradley (1989), for example, says it remains at the level of a description rather than an analysis. Patriarchy, Bradley explains, is not a structure of gender relations in the way that class is. Class relations are grounded in a set of production relations, from which others are built up, but gender relations pervade all aspects of life, there is no 'base'. Walby tries to avoid this problem by identifying the domestic mode of production as the central site, for private patriarchy, but adding other sets of relations. But this only serves to make her account 'vague, un-bounded, all-inclusive, fuzzy and ultimately descriptive rather than explanatory' (Bradley 1989: 60).

Crompton and Sanderson (1990) have similar reservations, centring on Walby's idea of a system of patriarchy based on a mode of production. Her account of this mode, of the domestic division of labour, is one of typicality rather than necessity. In many house-holds, it is overwhelmingly women/wives who perform domestic labour and men/husbands who bring home wages, but this is less and less true today. Dual earner and pensioner households are *not* implicated in a patriarchal mode of production. Even in those classic housewife/breadwinner households, the wife could retain the greater part of the husband's wages, she could work fewer hours than her husband, or they could even reverse this division of labour entirely so that the man becomes the 'househusband'. Walby's model, therefore, is one of typicality, and also one based not on gender but on 'market' versus 'non-market' labourers.

They do not, however, want to abandon the concept of patriarchy entirely, but instead regard it as one aspect of gender relations, one possible type of the way power relations between men and women are organised, as in pre-modern times. It is, they insist, possible and necessary to analyse gender relations but they prefer the model devised by the Australian analyst Bob Connell (1987). He argues that there are three interrelated structures of gender relations, the overall division of labour, second power relations, and particularly the association of masculinity with authority, and third what he calls cathexis. By this Connell means the construction of emotionally charged relations with other people. Together these structures make up what he calls the 'gender order', while a 'gender regime' describes these patterns at the institutional level. Connell's model also adds a significant dimension to Bradley's comments on 'structure'. Structure is, he says, not only a constraint on action but also an object of practice: we *also* maintain or sometimes challenge it through our actions. Readers will almost certainly recognise this view as an updated version of Marx's famous line that we make history but not in circumstances of our choosing. For a fuller discussion and evaluation of Connell's work, readers can consult Maharaj (1995).

Both they and Bradley demonstrate the effectiveness of their alternative approaches, omitting reference to a system of patriarchy, by proceeding to describe and analyse gendered patterns and relationships in employment.

The state and patriarchy

One issue that the sociologists mentioned above do not raise, that seems to me to be problematic in Walby's model, is the question of the state. The state is a curious institution in relation to discussions of the private and the public spheres since, in certain of its manifestations, although it is a public institution it also invades and regulates private life. It is very important to raise this as a matter for analysis, and indeed there is now a considerable literature on feminist theories of the state. The state is, at the very least, significant in helping to explain different configurations of gender relations between countries, both in its role as law and social policy maker and also as provider of various forms of welfare. These can have an obvious impact on women's lives.

Within classical sociology two models of analysis – Marxist and Weberian – have prevailed, each equally problematic for feminist theory since neither pays much attention to gender relations or power, although the models do emphasise its coercive and regulatory aspects. In contrast to this, the Liberal model, which is also probably most people's view, is that the state is a neutral institution that can be a vehicle for change. If we read popular accounts of first wave feminism such as Ray Strachey's *The Cause* (Strachey 1928, reprinted 1978) we can see that they are underpinned by an emancipationist view of the state. Basically this means that if once the state's laws were oppressive and exclusionary, women have changed its character through various campaigns; they have demanded and acquired the same citizenship rights as men. Indeed, many formal barriers have fallen, and health and welfare services have undoubtedly benefited many women. But what many other feminist commentators, including Walby, have emphasised is that these changes have been double-edged swords. As, for example, Mary Evans says, 'at the same time as the state extended a degree of assistance to women, so it demanded a degree of acquiescence in its expectations about women' (1997: 29). There are various ways the state does this, by education (such as school classes in home economics and domestic science), by direct intervention into 'problem' families, and by the way the various legal, penal and welfare systems are constructed around certain ideologies of proper family life and gender roles. In the case of schooling, for example, the historian Anna Davin (1979) argued that the British state only extended state schooling to girls in order to pass on to them a particular view of their future roles, as responsible wives and mothers.

Although Walby argues that the state is a patriarchal one, in the sense that its actions are more often in men's than in women's interests, she adds two qualifications to this broad picture. First, the state is not only patriarchal but also capitalist, and second its actions are the result of competing political interests and campaigns. This means that the way the state represents patriarchal interests has changed. Key changes affecting women include political representation, the extension of voting rights to women; laws regulating women's employment which have progressively become less exclusionary; laws on marriage and divorce; and in the provisions of the welfare state. In all of these areas, changes have often been the result of feminist campaigns though the actual provisions have rarely been precisely those for which women campaigned. To examine these arguments in more depth, it is helpful to look at some specific examples of issues.

Case study 4.1 Reproductive rights and the state: Britain and China

In Britain, although women's access to contraception was an important campaign in the first decades of the twentieth century, in the second half feminists focused on women's rights to abortion. In Britain, the 1967 Abortion Act significantly improved many women's access to safe, legal abortions for the first time (though the law was different both in Scotland and Northern Ireland where the Act did not apply). But it was not 'on demand' as feminists had hoped, it was instead dependent on two doctors' judgement about possible harm to the woman if the pregnancy proceeded, and was subject to time limits. This has meant that women's access has been conditional on the attitudes of doctors that lead to considerable regional variations, and on medical advances which have reduced the time limits on abortion. These provisions have been due to effective campaigning on the part of the medical profession to keep control in their hands.

But there are not just two players in the game, women and doctors: there is also the state. It is the state that makes the laws and its changing priorities, for more or fewer children, can put women's gains at risk. Whether the matter is phrased in terms of women's rights or of population control is crucial. The changes in policy in China are a case in point. The first centrally co-ordinated family planning campaign started in 1971, promoting birth control as a way of freeing women from outdated 'feudal' thinking and also improving their health. But the rhetoric of women's emancipation was not the main motive. By 1979, the first hints that something more drastic was needed, to halt rapid population growth, were evident. First, in the province of Sichuan, then in others, incentive packages were introduced for families who limited themselves to one child.

Another pregnancy resulted in the loss of benefits. Although nearly 60 per cent of couples had signed one-child pledges by 1981, and the birth rate was dropping, the rate of increase was still too high for officials' liking. Enforcement of the policy began, in the form of insertion of IUDs for women with one child, abortions for women who became pregnant for a second time, and sterilisations if they had two children. Within a few years, there was worrying evidence of the abandonment and drowning of girl babies since having a son is traditionally more highly valued (Hillier 1988). The 'missing girls' issue, and the skewed sex ratio at birth, have been much commented on in the Western media, but commentators have also been identifying other consequences such as an increase in violence to wives who fail to bear a son (Dalsimer and Nisonoff 1997). This skewed sex ratio is, according to some, already having consequences in the growth in practices of selling and abducting brides, illegal marriage and child betrothal (Kristof and Wudunn 1994). The consequences of the policy probably vary for different groups of women. Middle-class, urban, educated women may benefit; their households are less dependent on sons for agricultural labour or their willingness to support parents in old age (the traditional duty of sons). But those on the fringes of society, the urban and rural poor, are more likely to become victims of the policy and the increasing dangers of a male dominated society that has a shortage of women. Although some emphasise the benefits that the one-child policy may bring to women in reproductive health (Hall 1997), overall the policy does not serve to enhance women's choices or serve as a tool for empowerment when control over women's bodies is transferred to the state.

Case study 4.2 Immigration and the state

The second example is the case of immigration and citizenship laws, although they may not appear directly to target women. Women now make up around half of the world's migrants and 80 per cent of the world's refugees (Phizacklea 1996). Their movements and rights, like those of men, are controlled by the policies of the states in which they arrive. There are, of course, many qualified professional migrants, but a significant number are people who, through poverty and war, seek a living in a new country. Overwhelmingly, this migration is from a poor to a richer country, from what we used to call the Third to the First World. Women migrants may be looking for work or refuge on their own behalf, or as the wife of another migrant. In both cases, a woman's rights are severely limited, to a particular kind of employment or even employer in the first case, or by the continuation of the marriage in the second. As well as regular industrial or service sector employment, more and more women over the last twenty years are migrating as domestic and sex workers, or as 'mail order' brides. Whether or not they are legal migrants, there are parallels between their situations. Their status is distinctly disadvantaged, even within an overall picture of migrants' partial rights. Sex tourism is now big business in many countries, an industry from which their governments profit, but the rights of foreign workers are non-existent, even when there are laws against trafficking. Many sex workers are illegal migrants, sometimes deceived by traffickers about the job they expect to do, some are little more than bonded labourers, 'sold' by indebted parents to traffickers. Any attempt to break away could result in their deportation.

Although domestic workers may well be legal migrants, performing legitimate work, they very often have no immigration rights on their own behalf. They are, instead, subsumed into the family that employs them, and if they leave it are again subject to deportation (Arat-Koc 1992). In this respect, they are similar to the mail order brides who have no rights to residency if they wish to leave the marriage or are divorced by their husbands. In all three cases, the state's laws render women dependent on the 'protection' of husbands, individual employers and pimps, which is in effect to return them to the private sphere in which the law is reluctant to intervene.

Commenting on this evidence, Annie Phizacklea (1996) points out that especially in the case of domestic workers it reveals the persistence of inequalities, not only between countries but also between women. Maids relieve relatively affluent women of the need to perform household and childcare tasks; such women can buy their way out of this work though often, it has to be said, in the context of declining or inadequate state provision of services caring for children and the elderly. Phizacklea reminds us that differences between women, of class, ethnic group and nationality are not just differences, they are hierarchies of power and inequality. This is a theme to which we will return.

These two cases may well illustrate Walby's claim about the patriarchal nature of the state, but other evidence is less conclusive. First, it seems odd to locate the state as the main site of women's oppression when our rights *have* been extended, compared with the high point of private patriarchy in the mid-nineteenth century. These rights may well be conditional, not fully or effectively upheld in practice, but there is a world of difference between now and a time when we were excluded from entry to universities, government and the professions, when we could not divorce husbands or have rights to the custody of our children, and when they could beat and rape us. Women have successfully campaigned, and continue to campaign, to extend such rights and to make them meaningful. If we look at another issue and series of campaigns, we can see how the state *can* be influenced positively and also what sorts of factors have a bearing on the success of campaigns.

Violence and the state

Male violence, like reproductive rights, is another issue of concern to feminists. Much of the inspiration for academic work came from campaigns in which the wider feminist movement has played an important part. Until the 1970s, the question of violence had largely been the province of psychologists in the twentieth century. They were concerned with identifying what kinds of personalities, what kinds of 'dysfunctional' families generated violent behaviour.

Russell and Rebecca Dobash carried out the first major sociological study from a feminist perspective on Scottish data. In the first sentence they shifted the focus from 'family' or 'domestic' violence to male violence, and proceeded to tie it to the institution of marriage, which is the formal expression of the hierarchical relation between men and women. They insisted that this violence had to be studied not in the context of 'dysfunctional' families and psychology, but socially. This meant looking at community and institutional reactions to the problem, how wider institutions and processes continue to support patriarchal domination in general and the use of violence in particular. They also acknowledge their debt to feminist activists and members of women's refuges. The Dobashes' study was a meticulous investigation of the experiences of battered wives, of police records and procedures and the reactions of doctors and priests. Their conclusion to this survey is that:

> the entire community . . . is responsible for the continued assaults on women and in some cases their deaths: the friends and neighbours who ignore or excuse violence, the physician who does not go beyond the mending of bones and the stitching of wounds, the social worker who defines wife beating as a failure of communication, and the police or court officials who refuse to intervene. The violence is meted out by one man but the responsibility for that violence goes far beyond him.
>
> (Dobash and Dobash 1980: 222)

They present a powerful case for the centrality of the institution of marriage to the understanding of wife beating. On marriage, traditionally, a wife lost all sorts of rights: to own property, to personal credit and guardianship of her children. She came under the control of her husband who had the legal right to use force to ensure she carried out her obligations – consummation of marriage, cohabitation, sexual fidelity, and general obedience and respect. To become a wife meant taking on a special legal status, like that of children and servants whom a man also had a right to 'chastise'. The phrase 'rule of thumb' apparently derives from the ancient right of a husband to punish his wife reasonably, with a stick no thicker than his thumb. Gradually, the husband's right was questioned and modified, as part of a more general social unease with the private right to exercise violence. In 1853 an Act was passed that made it possible for a wife to divorce her husband for excessive and repeated cruelty, though this was only available to rich women who could afford to pursue such an action. Then, as now, this change also owed much to the intervention of women. Notable in the campaign was Frances Power Cobbe whose essay 'Wife Torture in England', based on her experiences, identified many of the same problems later feminists saw, such as under-reporting, and blaming the victim.

The Dobashes thus give wife beating a social context, a history and an explanation: patriarchal marriage, and a patriarchal state which upholds this form of marriage and fails to intervene except to limit, not prohibit, violence. It is interesting, however, to compare their analysis with that of Gordon (1989). She offers a rather different picture of the 'patriarchal' marriage from the Dobashes'. The 'rule of thumb' she sees as evidence of women's not men's power to limit, by communal sanction, men's use of violence towards their wives. It was men who overstepped the mark to whom women objected. She also claims that wife beating arises not just from subordination but from contesting it. To take into account wives' 'provocations' and husbands' 'grievances' is not to condone male violence but to uncover evidence of wives' resistance. Gordon's picture is also one that provides a historical and social context to family violence, but she also adds a political element. Violence among family members arises from conflicts that are political. It arises from power struggles in which individuals are contesting for real resources, for husbands' rights to dispose of their wages, for their rights to wives' sexual and domestic services. Her study also marks an important shift, from presenting women as victims to active agents attempting to influence their destiny.

Both studies, however, agree that if we now see wife beating as a social problem and abuse of male power, not a phenomenon of violent individuals or relations, this was one of the great achievements of feminism. Women have always resisted it, and in the last 100 years or so, they have also resisted it politically and ideologically, by offering other explanations for it and, increasingly in the second part of the twentieth century, providing refuges for women who want to leave violent partners.

This brings us on to the question of state intervention, the state's relation to autonomous women's support services. In the periods the Dobashes and Gordon were investigating, although men could be prosecuted for assault, they rarely were. But now we have government, both local and national, campaigns not just against wife beating, but male violence in general. There can be little doubt but that these were the result of years of feminist campaigns, and the provision of refuges and crisis counselling. Feminist sociological research, like the Dobashes', into the prevalence of various forms of violence, and the consequences for those assaulted, also contributed. The spread and type of services has, however, been patchy (see Abrar 1996 in Lovenduski and Norris for details).

Explaining this variation, Fiona Mackay (1996) identifies three different feminist models of the state.

- Liberal: the state is seen as a neutral arbiter, an institution that can remedy gender inequalities.
- Socialist, radical: in the early 1970s, feminists had regarded the state as little other than an institution that reproduced capital and patriarchal and racist relations. They concentrated on building alternative autonomous structures such as women's refuges and crisis lines. By the late 1970s and early 1980s the situation was changing, for two main reasons. First, the employment of a generation of feminist activists *in* the state, trade unions and political parties, especially the Labour Party. Second, there was a profound disaffection with Tory central government policies, so that Labour local authorities came to be seen as possible bastions of relatively progressive policies. This was especially true in Scotland.
- Poststructuralist: this resulted in a more complex conception of the state, arguing that it cannot be understood as a unified entity. Rather, different branches and levels can be seen as more or less open to intervention, possibly due to internal tensions between its

capitalist and patriarchal elements. In this view, the state is also seen as a *site* of struggle. The local state is particularly 'open' to interventions.

This third view has parallels with the perspective adopted by Gordon, cited above, of women as agents. The model also had resonance for the ways feminist politics was changing in the 1980s and 1990s. Now feminists felt they could identify places within a no longer monolithic state where change was possible. It is different from the liberal model in that feminists recognised the deeply rooted assumptions and practices, of racism and sexism that they were up against.

Mackay focuses on one intervention that has seemed to be remarkably (relatively) successful, the case of the Zero Tolerance (ZT) Campaign, first in Edinburgh, then throughout Scotland. She asks why this campaign seems to be an exception to the generally more dismal picture of feminist intervention in the state. In the most progressive local authorities, including Edinburgh, there has been a strong women's committee or unit (also the result of past campaigns), that is backed both by autonomous women's groups and by feminist officers or councillors. The relative success and the lack of a backlash (so far) to ZT are due to a number of factors. They are the specific Scottish and Edinburgh political contexts, the groundwork carried out by anti-violence women's groups, the salience of the issue with women and the diffusion of feminist ideas, and also the penetration of the local state by official and unofficial feminists. Mackay warns, however, that there is no room for complacency, the possibility of a backlash is always present.

Feminists have also been successful on the international level, have worked and lobbied to make the issue of violence a high priority one. In 1993, the United Nations General Assembly adopted a Declaration on the Elimination of Violence Against Women. It used a wide definition of violence against women as:

> any act of gender-based violence that results in, or is likely to result in, physical, sexual, or psychological harm or suffering to women, including threats of such acts, coercion or arbitrary deprivation of liberty, whether occurring in public or private life.
>
> (United Nations 1994)

It encompasses, but is not limited to:

> physical, sexual and psychological violence occurring in the family, including battering, sexual abuse of female children in the

household, dowry related violence, marital rape, female genital mutilation and other traditional practices harmful to women, non-spousal violence and violence related to exploitation; physical, sexual and psychological violence occurring within the general community, including rape, sexual abuse, sexual harassment and intimidation at work, in educational institutions and elsewhere; trafficking in women and forced prostitution; and physical, sexual and psychological violence perpetrated or condoned by the state, wherever it occurs.

(United Nations 1994)

We have seen that both the Dobashes' and Gordon's studies have emphasised the importance of the way problems are named. Renaming acts of violence is more than a semantic issue. The name given to an act of violence determines whether it is a culturally acceptable act, such as killing an enemy soldier during war, or a crime punishable by law. Campaigners and women's groups throughout the world insist that we must use women's perspectives and experiences when defining such acts. While 'violence against women' accurately describes the problem, the term 'gender based violence' used by the United Nations emphasises the power relationships that lead to violence. Different agencies and bodies also put the problem in different contexts: the UN highlights violence as an issue of human rights, the WHO as a health issue and so on. Renaming acts puts them in a more general context, not of isolated and unrelated incidents. Another example is the case of feminist human rights activists who have successfully lobbied for the International Criminal Court to recognise rape and sexual violence in war as a crime against humanity.

These numerous campaigners have also argued for the need for research that will persuade the general public and governments of the extent of the problem, and of the ways it adversely affects their societies. In 1994 the UN Commission on Human Rights appointed a Special Rapporteur on Violence Against Women whose mandate includes seeking and compiling data. Research that documents women's experiences contributes to developing projects that will meet their needs. It is also a powerful advocacy tool at the national and international level and has been used effectively to engender the International Criminal Court.

Not all campaigners have been as successful, not all governments are in fact implementing the declarations they have signed. The case of rape demonstrates some of these contradictions. As noted above, women have been successful in having this recognised as a war crime, and the International Criminal Tribunal for the former Yugoslavia has now convicted the first three men, Bosnian Serbs, for rape, torture and enslavement. Whether women are forced into 'rape camps' or raped in their homes, whether they are raped by regular soldiers or by militias, systematic rape has been used as a weapon of war in a growing number of conflicts around the world, especially as an instrument of 'ethnic cleansing'. There are, of course, continuing violations of women's rights and these raise questions about the international community's willingness to enforce the law without distinction.

Although the United Nations and other international bodies are taking the issue of gender related violence seriously, these are not 'top-down' changes. As in the case of ZT, these are responses to considerable effort by feminists at grass roots level, in NGOs, and in the agencies themselves. All the major agencies continue to work in conjunction with autonomous women's groups around the world and there is a continuous process of lobbying, negotiation and renegotiation between them. Undoubtedly also, feminists' effectiveness has been due to their establishment of global networks of information exchange. These links are, however, different from a simple notion of the universality of 'sisterhood' that characterised the early phases of second wave feminism. Women now take much greater account of differences and inequalities, there are fewer assumptions that White, Western feminists are either more advanced or are the ones with the answers that will liberate Southern women.

This brief survey indicates that a simple view of the state as a patriarchal institution is inadequate, even when Walby's qualifications are added. It may have patriarchal elements, it may uphold and reproduce certain family forms, certain ideologies that are oppressive to women, but it may also be the site of struggle that the poststructuralist model describes. And, occasionally, through struggle, it may even become a point of leverage for feminists to achieve change.

Summary

- 'Patriarchy' has proved to be an important addition to the sociological and feminist vocabulary. There have been problems in using it analytically, but it has provided a new sociological perspective on many areas.

- It has helped to focus attention on systems of domination in addition to those of 'race' and class, both in the private and the public sphere. It has enabled people to 'see' these institutions and practices in new ways, as parts of a hierarchically structured set of relationships between men and women.
- Identifying certain institutions and practices as 'patriarchal' has also had political uses, for example in campaigns against violence.
- Feminists have identified the role that the state has played in regulating men and women. But it is not only or always a patriarchal institution. Feminists (and of course many others) have been able to campaign for changes in policies and in practices that have benefited women.
- It is important not to generalise about 'women's' relation to the state. We must specify which women (and men) we are talking about, and different women will have different relations to the state. They will also have different priorities, and different opportunities to intervene or campaign.
- Although useful, the term has not proved indispensable to feminist analysis. It is not the only way to 'see', to analyse or to take action.

Further reading

Beechey, V. (1979) 'On Patriarchy'. *Feminist Review*, 3: 66–82.

Hester, M., Kelly, L. and Radford, J. (eds) (1996) *Women, Violence and Male Power: Feminist Activism, Research and Practice*. Buckingham, Philadelphia: Open University Press.

Mies, M. (1998) *Patriarchy and Accumulation on a World Scale: Women in the International Division of Labour*. London: Zed Books.

Murray, M. (1995) *The Law of the Father?: Patriarchy in the Transition from Feudalism to Capitalism*. London: Routledge.

Ollenburger, J.C. and Moore, H.A. (1992) *A Sociology of Women: The Intersection of Patriarchy, Capitalism and Colonization*. Englewood Cliffs, NJ: Prentice Hall.

Walby, S. (1990) *Theorising Patriarchy*. Oxford: Blackwell.

Chapter 5

Body politics

Chapter outline

Although not uniquely a feminist preoccupation, nevertheless another area of sociology that has recently been opened up by feminists is that of the body. The chapter will look at the 'return of the body' in the sense of a re-evaluation of feminist sociology's original emphasis on the social construction of gender (as opposed to the biological given of sex). The chapter will examine:

- Questions of domination and subversion with special reference to the sexed, sexualised and racialised body.
- The importance of 'body politics' in wider feminist movements, in relation to questions of beauty, health and eating disorders, for example. Campaigns around these issues contributed to the growth of the feminist self-help health movement.
- How far do certain practices such as female body building and athletic achievement challenge dominant norms? Does the commercialisation and commodification of fitness regimes render them *dis*empowering for women? How *do* women resist and subvert the technologies and discourses that manage bodies?
- How, more recently, the body has also been conceptualised as a site of struggle, which has led to an examination of the possibilities for subversion of meaning through, for example, dress and some forms of performance art.

- The main contention of this chapter will be that there is a distinctive feminist perspective on the body, through its emphasis on power relations.

The background to feminist interest in body politics

'Body politics' has taken a while to establish itself as an area of interest to feminist sociologists, though it has been of more significance in the wider feminist movement. Some of the earlier sociological studies, such as Ann Oakley's (1980) study of motherhood, did touch on women's experiences of embodiment, but women's bodies were mainly seen as ways women were dominated. It is also possible to read some of the campaigns, for abortion on demand for example, as demands that control should be returned to women. We can relate this initial lack of interest to two factors. First, to the insistence of one of the 'founding mothers' of second wave feminism (Simone de Beauvoir) that a woman's body was *not* her destiny, and second to the more general sociological neglect of the body – until recently.

Within sociology there has traditionally been little overt interest in the body but instead a focus on social relations. In part, this has been a reaction to naturalistic, common sense ways of thinking about people, their relations and behaviour, a way of explaining things by reference to supposedly natural qualities based on material differences or innate instincts. An example of this would be explaining racism in terms of a 'natural' hostility to those who are visibly different. Since women are often similarly 'naturalised' and differences between men and women explained by their reproductive differences, feminist sociologists have had an ambivalent attitude to thinking about bodies in their work. On the one hand, they did not want to contribute to this naturalisation by focusing on women's bodies, while on the other, many important campaigns were being waged *around* women's bodies in the wider movement.

Resisting naturalisation

A precedent for feminist sociologists' absence of attention to the body can be found in Simone de Beauvoir's famous opening line in *The Second Sex* (1963):

> One is not born but rather becomes a woman. No biological,
> psychological, or economic fate determines the figure that the
> human female presents in society; it is civilisation as a whole that
> produces this creature, intermediate between male and eunuch,
> which is described as feminine.
>
> (de Beauvoir 1963: 9)

This statement can also be read as an early formulation of the
sociological distinction between sex and gender, between biology
and culture. More recently, Ann Oakley provided what has
remained a highly influential definition of these terms.

> 'Sex' is a word that refers to the biological differences between
> male and female: the visible difference in genitalia, the related
> difference in reproductive function. 'Gender' however is a matter
> of culture: it refers to the social classification into 'masculine'
> and 'feminine'.
>
> (Oakley 1972: 16)

Until recently, most feminist sociology has concentrated on the
analysis of gender, while the existence of sex difference has been
taken for granted, with the minor exception of intersexed people.
This concentration on gender is understandable, given that so many
conservative arguments in the past have rested on assumptions
about women's nature and biology. The focus on gender returns
women to the social world. But later in the book, de Beauvoir
adopts a more complex perspective on women's bodily (sexual and
reproductive) difference. Her argument is that it is a combination
of two factors that produce women's secondary status: one is external, society's ideologies, and one is internal, women's complicity
with this set of beliefs. Woman's biology, especially her reproductive capacities, means she is always construed as 'Other' and so
it seems she can only escape this fate and reject collusion with
'otherness' if she chooses, as de Beauvoir did, to reject maternity.
She seems to argue that either biological differences between
men and women inevitably introduce ideas of domination and
subordination, and/or that biological differences are inevitably
oppressive to women. She accepts that maternity *is* simply biological
maintenance, there is nothing creative about this labour, unlike
men's capacity to transcend the merely biological and to be
creative. Although she provided a valuable corrective to the post
Second World War idealisation of motherhood, she went overboard
in condemning it as brutal, painful and degrading. Although she
looked forward to a time when women might be able to combine

motherhood and employment through the provision of public childcare services, de Beauvoir accepts that as things stood then, it would be impossible for women to be other than dissatisfied with and oppressed by motherhood.

Early campaigns

De Beauvoir's arguments clearly relate to feminist campaigns for the provision of state nurseries in the 1970s. In the absence of these, women in many areas in Britain began to open their own alternatives, although they ran into various problems of principle: should they be run on a voluntary rota of parents (overwhelmingly, mothers), that would exclude employed women? If properly paid nursery workers were employed, would this not put them beyond the reach of poorer parents? By the end of the decade the TUC, certain unions, the Labour Party and some local authorities recognised the importance of comprehensive childcare (at least in principle), although public expenditure cuts were already beginning to eat into the already meagre provision of nursery places (Coote and Campbell 1987). The issue did not go away, of course, and resurfaced in the 1990s, when the government began to recognise that it would have to cope with the needs of an increasingly feminised labour force. There are echoes here of the other time in Britain when there was something like an official recognition of women's needs both as mothers and workers: during the Second World War when many nurseries were established in order to allow mothers to take up 'war work' (Riley 1983).

To an extent, other campaigns at this time could be read as campaigns to free women from the 'burdens' of their bodies, such as the campaigns for contraception and abortion on demand, but feminists typically phrased these as campaigns to give women greater control over their bodies. The slogan 'Not the Church, not the state, women must decide their fate' associated with the abortion campaigns sums this attitude up well. Other 'body politics' campaigns also illustrate this demand, in campaigns for 'natural' childbirth, demonstrations at Miss World competitions, and criticisms of the pornography, media, fashion and advertising industries. Women were also concerned to develop alternatives that would enable women to have greater control over their bodies. This included setting up self-defence classes, self-help health centres and publishing such as *Our Bodies, Ourselves* (Boston Women's Health Collective 1976). All these influenced feminist sociology, producing important works on medically managed maternity (Oakley 1979, 1980), the beauty industry (Perutz 1970), reproductive technologies (Corea 1987; Stanworth 1987), the history of birth control (Gordon 1976) and abortion (Petchesky 1984), the fashion industry (Wilson 1985), advertising (Williamson 1978), women's magazines (Ferguson 1983), television programmes (Tuchman et al. 1978), and film (Kuhn 1982, 1985).

Many of these phenomena were characterised by feminists as instances of sexist stereotypes, propaganda for submissive femininity, and of masculine values and standards imposed upon women to their detriment. Some also emphasised women's agency in resisting these values as, for example, did Linda Gordon's (1976) study of the history of birth control in America who argued that women had always found ways of controlling their fertility whether or not these were legal. Black women and lesbians also pointed out that many of the practices, assumptions and stereotypes further discriminated against them within the category of 'women' (Abbott and Love 1972; Wittig 1975; hooks 1982a; Bryan et al. 1985).

What most of these studies had in common was a focus on gender, its cultural construction through practices and ideologies that were oppressive to women. There was some growing recognition among White, heterosexual feminists that 'women' was also a category in need of further deconstruction: the practices and ideologies also operated differently for women of different 'races', ethnicities and sexualities. What was still, at this stage, largely lacking was a focus on the body (the 'sex' part) of the sex/gender couplet, although the way apparently scientific arguments were drafted in to shore up justifications for gender inequalities (Sayers 1982) could and did come in for criticism.

Case study 5.1 Women and nature: a special relationship?

Other feminists instead emphasised the positive aspects of women's bodies, especially their sexuality and reproductive potential, and have taken a rather different approach. The problem, for them, was the negative ways these were valued in most cultures. One strand of this fed into eco-feminism in the 1970s and a growing interest in the relations between women and the environment. This has become a significant movement in development studies and has produced a reconceptualisation of women in less developed countries not as victims but as sources of strength, wisdom and resourcefulness.

Vandana Shiva (1989) has argued that while the dominant Western model of development has been destructive of nature and the environment, the traditional Indian system works in harmony with nature. It draws on Hindu religion and philosophy to see the feminine principle as the source of life. Women in less developed societies are thus particularly well placed to develop a sustainable mode of development because of their closer relation to nature both in their agricultural and reproductive activities. Colonisation destroys this balance, and men begin instead to take part in life destroying activities (Shiva in Visvanathan et al. 1997). Shiva goes on to explain that this vision is different from that of Western ecologists who tend to see women only as victims of the process of development. Embedded in nature and responsible for producing life, women often lead ecology movements in countries like India and provide alternative visions to what Shiva calls 'patriarchal maldevelopment' (Shiva in Visvanathan et al. 1997).

Other feminists working in the field of development and environmental studies are more sceptical, while recognising that approaches such as Shiva's have been important both as sources of inspiration and as guides for rethinking development practices. Rosi Braidotti (Braidotti et al. 1994) and her colleagues have pointed out that Shiva probably idealises a past that probably never existed, and that she fails to take into account exploitative structures of caste and class both in the past and present. Bina Agarwal (1992) warns that:

> By locating the 'problem' almost entirely in the Third World's experience of the West, Shiva misses out on the very real forces of power, privilege and property relations that pre-date colonialism. What exists today is a complex legacy of **colonial** and pre-colonial interactions.
>
> (Agarwal in Visvanathan et al. 1997: 73)

Sexed bodies and history

All this began to change as sociologists and historians began to investigate the nature of various natural sciences. As a result, sex – the bodies that biologists and anatomists investigate, label and explain – has become problematic.

One of the most important recent works about the history of the sexed body is that of the historian Thomas Laqueur (1992). Underpinning our ideas about the body is an assumption that it is nature, specifically biology, which holds the key to determining what sex is. In addition, it is science that most accurately describes and defines this sex difference *and* the purpose of sex difference: to reproduce. This is what it means to say that our ideas about bodies are about bodies that are sexed and sexualised, that nature made (most of) us this way, and it is science, biology, that has demonstrated this. The inclusion of this heterosexual assumption into biology is why Monique Wittig (1992) argued that lesbians were not 'women'.

First, historical analysis has revealed that the form and character of the sex/gender distinction cannot be taken for granted. The body, like gender, has a history. Laqueur argues that there is a clear break between pre-modern and modern conceptions of the sexed body. The pre-modern model is, he claims, a one-sex model of which there were two variations, male and female. Basing his argument both on European writings and anatomical diagrams, he argues that the two sexes were supposed to share the same basic set of reproductive organs, but men 'wore' them on the outside and women on the inside. The female model was, however, seen as a less developed and inferior version. This is what Laqueur calls a hierarchical model of sex difference. The model also assumed that female orgasm, like male orgasm, was necessary to conception.

However, there was a major change in the way sex difference was conceived in the late eighteenth century that stressed the difference between the two sexes. Women's reproductive biology was seen as the opposite of men's and although their natures were governed by their biology, this did not extend to sexual pleasure. The opposition of female/male is one of passivity/activity, of nondesire/desire. A key point of interest is that Laqueur points out this shift in the model did not happen because of any new biological knowledge but due to political reasons. Basic, total biological difference between the sexes becomes a politically useful argument against women's emancipation. Women are now seen as inevitably, unchangeably different from men and this natural bodily difference becomes the model for the proper relations between men and women, since 'nature' reveals the character and capacities of the two sexes.

Given this legacy, it is not surprising that feminists have been so suspicious of arguments about biology and its relation to character, because these arguments have so often been used conservatively. But Laqueur's point is not that there are no bodily, anatomical or reproductive differences; he does not argue against science in general. His argument is that the language of objective, naturalistic description does not exist in a vacuum, but is deeply embedded in the culture from which it comes. The 'facts' of biology do not simply present themselves to us, but are always mediated by cultural presuppositions. The impulse to fix the true essence of woman in a natural set of characteristics that differentiate her from man continues, even when what we imagine those characteristics to be has changed.

There is actually, Laqueur concludes, no scientific way of choosing between the one-sex and the two-sex model: 'The body does not itself produce two sexes' (Laqueur 1992: 21). It is *not* the case, he insists, that there is a real set of natural facts that is prior to and independent of the claims made about it; it is *not* the case that the pre-modern commentators just got it wrong, while 'we' got it right, that 'we' provided the correct description of the real natural differences between males and females. There is a political and cultural context to our preference for seeing difference or similarity, for deciding which features are significant. He also concurs with the opinion of some feminists such as Christine Delphy (1996) that what we say about sex is actually a claim about gender: 'Sex, in both the one and the two sex world, is situational; it is explicable only within the context of battles over gender and power' (Laqueur 1992: 11).

This does not mean, however, that the body is only discourse, the effect of naming, labelling and categorising things in particular ways. It does have a fleshy reality, even if there is no way of getting at it outside the language through which we apprehend it. In conclusion, Laqueur notes two omissions from his study: it is not possible to write a history of male bodies, he says, because the historical record was created in a cultural tradition where no such history was necessary. It is always *women's* difference – or similarity – that is being constituted. Women alone have to be explained, while the male remains the apparently unsexed norm. The second omission is that there is no sustained account in the documents he studies of experience in and of the body, or of how these different visions of the body shaped passion, friendship and love.

Subsequent feminist research has attempted to fill this gap, from Ann Oakley's study of first-time mothers that meticulously recounted their reactions to pregnancy and motherhood (Oakley

1979, 1980). She also argued that the many negative feelings women reported were a consequence of (largely male) medical professionals' takeover of childbirth. Unable to share the experience, their practices contributed to alienating women from their bodies.

One final omission that Laqueur does *not* note is the omission of 'raced' bodies that, incidentally, does help provide that missing history of the male body that Laqueur identified. This is partly covered in Gilman's (1985) work on the racialised construction of 'the Jew', that usually turns out to be of the male Jew, in European thinking.

Historical work reveals that bodies are always sexed. Women's bodies have been particularly prone to sexualisation, to the reduction of what woman 'is' to her biological and reproductive nature, which is of course a heterosexual model.

Women's experiences of their bodies: medicine

Many of us probably view medical discoveries and progress in a largely positive light (bar a few negative experiences of drugs that did not work or had undesirable side effects, or of incompetent practitioners). Some of the first feminist work on women's relation to medical experts in the nineteenth century took a very different view (Ehrenreich and English 1979). This account suggests medicalisation was basically a form of patriarchal control, turning women into weak, frail creatures to embody the stereotype of the age. Doctors had established that women are sick, that this sickness was innate, and stemmed from the very possession of a uterus and ovaries. Pale, on a couch, they would have been in no position to demand equal rights, or even take up a profession. Diagnosed as sick they might have been, but really they were sick with oppression. But this picture only applied to White, middle-class women whose fathers or husbands could pay for treatment. But the operations and cures that doctors devised were often arrived at by experiments on poor, ethnic minority women on the charity wards of public hospitals.

Another account by the historian Edward Shorter (1983) puts this into a different perspective, and interestingly links the history of medicine with the issue of women's emancipation. Shorter's is not a history of uninterrupted medical progress, but one of mismanagement and misunderstanding, especially in the case of women's bodies. Women, he says, for most of history, were often victims of medical incompetence, prejudice and ignorance, especially as regards their reproductive biology. The problems faced by women were compounded by other social factors such as poorer diet. The picture changed, however, in the early years of the twentieth century, as medicine became more competent, childbirth became (more) risk free, men more responsive and contraception easier. Only when the physical trials and tribulations of womanhood had been mitigated were women in a position to engage in the public sphere on something like the same terms as men. Only once women were freed from their bodies were they really free to pursue equal social rights.

This happy conclusion about the role of medicine is directly contrary to Ehrenreich and English's (1979), that the expertise that many men claimed to have, and exerted over women's lives and bodies, was highly problematic and had to be challenged by women themselves:

> The relationship between women and the experts was not unlike conventional relationships between women and men. . . . It was never an equal relationship, for the experts' authority rested on the denial or the destruction of women's autonomous sources of knowledge. . . . But it was a relationship that lasted right up to our own time, when women began to discover that the experts' answer to the Woman Question was not science after all, but only the ideology of a masculinist society, dressed up as objective truth.
>
> (Ehrenreich and English 1979: 4)

Bodies and physical activities: sport, dance and fitness

Another area investigated by feminists has been that of the relation between bodies and sport, or physical activities more generally. Typically, there has been a tendency to view men's bodies as more powerful, more competent and 'better' at sport and games than women's. We might easily dispense with the idea that men's bodies are naturally endowed with these capacities, but how are we to regard women's recent interest in developing their own strength, stamina and physical skills? Are these activities empowering for women? Or are women merely aping men?

In the nineteenth century, when women were very much seen as weak, frail creatures (except for those Black and working-class women who were expected to labour in fields, mines, factories and workshops for long hours), the prohibition on strenuous physical activities was undoubtedly seen by feminist pioneers as a barrier to women's equal rights. There was, though, one exception to the prohibition, dance, especially ballet. The long training, though, took place behind the scenes, and the physical exertion of ballerinas was invisible to audiences who admired the 'natural' and effortless grace of dancers. There was a cost, however, for female dancers. They were often seen as little better than prostitutes. There were several reasons for this: prostitutes were often found in the same areas where theatres were located, and they also frequented the promenades and bars inside the theatres. Both prostitutes and theatrical performers were working women, who made a living from their bodies, often at night when respectable women should be at home. In addition, dancers' dresses were extremely revealing by the standards of the day, loose, short and diaphanous, to give the impression of grace and delicacy. The pale colours of shoes and tights gave the impression of bare feet and legs, all of which meant that the 'visual message of the Romantic ballet was, therefore, that of highly contrived semi-nudity' (Davis 1991: 110).

More recently, more girls and women have been participating in sports and games (Dworkin and Messner 1999), often due to campaigns using equal rights legislation to improve their access to facilities in schools and colleges. Although men and boys continue to play more sports, and continue to enjoy the lion's share of funding and media coverage, 'the very existence of skilled and strong women athletes demanding recognition and equal access to resources is a destabilising tendency in the current gender order' (Dworkin and Messner 1999: 346).

But as women's sports expand, women are expected to emulate the characteristics of men's sports in their aggression and competitiveness. Even in the more 'feminine' sports of women's gymnastics, synchronised swimming and ice-skating, very young girls learn to continue in spite of injuries, and become prone to eating disorders to keep themselves fast and light: 'In short, as girls and women push for equity in sport, they are moving – often uncritically – into a hierarchical system that has as its main goal to produce winners, champions and profits' (Dworkin and Messner 1999: 347–8).

Picking up the issue of commercialisation, Dworkin and Messner examine the recent trend for some companies such as Reebok and

Nike to adopt the language of women's empowerment in order to sell shoes and other items of equipment. Their professed commitment to women, though, stops short at their employees:

> In 1996 when it posted its largest profits, and its CEO Phillip Knight's stock was estimated to be worth $5 billion, the mostly women Indonesian workers who manufactured the shoes were paid about $2.25 a day. Workers who attempted to organise for higher pay and better working conditions were fired . . . Nike's individualised and depoliticised 'feminism' ignores how individuals who 'do it' with Nike are implicated in an international system of racial, gender and class exploitation of women workers in less developed nations.
>
> (Dworkin and Messner 1999: 350)

Dworkin and Messner also consider the new emphasis on fitness and muscularity for women that largely takes place not in organised sports but rather in gyms. On the one hand, strong, fit women could be seen as challenging patriarchal norms, and undoubtedly many women do find these activities empowering. On the other hand, such women could be seen as conforming to the latest bodily norms in the service of patriarchal capitalism. These new norms have broadened from thin and slim to toned and tight.

Traditional norms of attractive heterosexual femininity continue to haunt women whose muscularity makes them particularly disturbing: women bodybuilders. Muscles have so often been seen as masculine attributes that women bodybuilders have often been seen as 'masculine' women, that is lesbians, in the popular imagination:

> Indeed the ways in which muscular women and the lesbian distress the heterosexual system are closely linked, and they therefore receive similar responses from the dominant culture. . . . Such charges have resulted in a sustained move to sexualise and wedge female muscle within a heterosexual frame. Her muscle is sold as sexy accoutrement and her heterosexuality confirmed to the point of exhaustion.
>
> (Coles 1999: 447–8)

Case study 5.2 Men's bodies and muscles

Body-consciousness is not an exclusively female preoccupation. Organised games and military training have long been used to shape and manage men's bodies, in ancient Greece and contemporary Western culture. In Classical and Renaissance art, the male nude has often been used to represent the virtues of a society: 'The young male body is the central image in Greek art . . . Naked Apollo embodies the most cherished cultural ideals of the Greeks. At once god and man, he is the dominating figure' (Walters 1978: 34). This image of the male nude expressive both of bodily and spiritual perfection continued to influence Western art for centuries, though sometimes in tension with the Christian counter-vision 'of man as a poor forked animal doomed to die' (Walters 1978: 106).

In the second part of the nineteenth century, organised sports and athletics were again seen as key vehicles for producing manly bodies and characters, and masculinity 'was defined in terms of vigour, competitiveness, bodily strength and assertiveness' (Peterson 1998: 47). Although originating in public schools, the lessons spread to state schools too, and were also popularised in organisations such as the Boys' Brigade in order to reach working-class boys. However, racist and nationalist values have also been evident in the promotion of a male body culture. Drill and athletics was also promoted in Nazi Germany as a means of developing the perfect 'Aryan race', and its cultivation and celebration eventually led to the attempted extermination of all the 'degenerate' bodies of Jews, gypsies and homosexuals.

More recently still, we have seen a revival of the idealisation of the muscular male body. He is not just confined to the pages of a few publications aimed at the body building fraternity either:

> He is everywhere. He's a movie star, action toy, model, pop star, TV presenter. He's staring at us from the sides of buses and buildings. He's on Top of the Pops. He's a regular in women's glossy magazines; even lad mags have sections or entire offshoot magazines dedicated to him.
>
> (Shabi 2001: 19)

Shabi also reports that, concurrently, men have an increasing obsession and dissatisfaction with their bodies. Men now make up around 10 per cent of those reported to have eating disorders (Shabi 2001) though generally men are more likely to resort to exercise and steroids to control body shape. In addition, men suffer from a new form of body dysmorphia, 'bigorexia'. 'No matter how muscular they are, bigorexic men have a chronically distorted perception of their own size, and feel ashamed of looking too small' (Shabi 2001: 20).

There are a number of explanations for this phenomenon. One is to blame the media for promoting unattainable ideals, in the way they have also been blamed for contributing to anorexia in women. Then there is the profit motive of companies that see men as a relatively untapped market, selling them body and 'health' products, and gym memberships. Others, such as Pope, Phillips and Olivardia (2000) and Susan Faludi (1999) relate it to a more general crisis in masculinity, which is what makes men vulnerable to these media messages:

> Stripped of other means by which to establish maleness, men are drawn to the gym as the final frontier as an arena in which women will never be able to exceed or even match male accomplishments. Muscularity, in this context, is important because it is so intimately tied to cultural views of masculinity, because it represents an assertion of discipline and command at a time when these qualities are no longer exclusive to men. . . . The trouble is that men who fall for the beauty myth aren't gaining a sense of control. Just like women, they're loosing it.
>
> (Shabi 2001: 26)

Getting 'the look'

Susan Bordo (1993) follows up some of these themes in her analysis of the modern cult of the slender body. She identifies a continuity of meaning between compulsive dieting and bodybuilding: both are united in 'a battle against the common enemy: the soft, the loose; unsolid excess flesh' (Bordo 1993: 191). Bordo locates this phenomenon in the contradictory demands of late capitalism. On the one hand, as producers we must sublimate desires, defer gratification and cultivate the work ethic. On the other hand, as consumers we are encouraged to buy and indulge ourselves. 'The regulation of desire thus becomes an ongoing problem' (Bordo 1993: 199) that is often played out in the arena of food and dieting:

> Many of us find our lives vacillating between a daytime rigidly ruled by the 'performance principle' and nights and weekends that capitulate to unconscious 'letting go' (food, shopping, liquor, television and other addictive drugs). In this way, the central contradiction of the system inscribes itself on our bodies, and bulimia emerges as a characteristic modern personality construction.
>
> (Bordo 1993: 201)

Although this is a general contradiction, it is usually most painfully apparent for women who are more tyrannised by contemporary ideals of beauty than men are. Rosalind Coward (1984) further notes that the language in which most adverts and women's magazines are now couched is that of 'health' rather than dieting, although promises that we will feel better are still linked to promises that we will look better. Coward also discusses the negative feedback loop that may operate. These body and fitness regimes are often sold to women as solutions to feeling bad about oneself which, in turn, may be tangled up with 'the narcissistic construction of women as objects for "the look" which may itself be a factor in causing women's depression' (Coward 1984: 25). 'The look' therefore has a double meaning: it refers both to the culturally desirable appearance and also to the way that women become objects of looks, their own as well as others'. Women learn to scrutinise their own bodies as if they were objects external to them, as they might be seen by other people.

Bordo also introduces the issue of racial differences between women. All women are subject to the same norms of what constitutes the ideal 'look' and are told that with the right diet, cosmetics and fitness regime they can acquire it. First and obviously, this ignores how getting the look demands material resources, time and money, that exclude many women. Second, not *any* look will do. The rhetoric of choice and self-determination actually hides the fact that some looks are better than others are: 'Does anyone in this culture have his or her nose reshaped to look more "African" or more "Jewish"?' (Bordo 1993: 25). The ideal is the slim, blonde blue-eyed woman.

Many Black women writers, including novelists such as Toni Morrison in *The Bluest Eye* (Morrison 1970), have documented how damaging this ideal is to Black and ethnic minority women's self-esteem. Patricia Hill Collins, for example, has written of the popular stereotypes of Black women in American culture, such as mammies and 'hot mommas' and has argued that challenging what she calls these 'controlling images' has been a core theme in Black feminist thought (Collins 2000).

Although in passing, Bordo refers to an apparently reverse phenomenon, that of White people adopting elements of black style, it is bell hooks (1992) who analyses it in most detail. By her metaphor of 'eating the other', hooks refers not only to Whites wearing cornrows (Bordo's example) and dreadlocks in their hair, she also includes the borrowing and consumption of 'tribal' art, Black music and ethnic dress. Part of this is a desire to value aspects of other cultures, to transcend a racist past, but it also often represents a romanticised vision of the other that 'denies accountability and historical connection' (hooks 1992: 25).

The phenomenon cannot be separated from the commodification of exotic otherness of which the Benetton ads are only the best-known manifestation. Difference sells: 'One desires "a bit of the Other" to enhance the blank landscape of Whiteness' (hooks 1992: 29). But hooks is also critical of certain types of Black and ethnic nationalist and revivalist movements, even when their initial impulse was to resist commodification and appropriation:

> Who can take seriously Public Enemy's insistence that the dominated and their allies 'fight the power' when that declaration is in no way linked to a collective and organised struggle? When young black people mouth 1960s' black nationalist rhetoric, don Kente cloth, gold medallions . . . they expose the way meaningless commodification strips these signs of political integrity . . . Communities of resistance are replaced by communities of consumption . . . even though a product like rap articulates narratives of coming to critical political consciousness, it also exploits stereotypes and **essentialist** notions of blackness (like black people have natural rhythm and are more sexual.
>
> (hooks 1992: 34)

But it is White artists like Madonna, even when they profess to admire and gain inspiration from Black culture, who come in for the fiercest criticism. On the positive side, hooks likes the way Madonna 'deconstructs the myth of "natural" White girl beauty by exposing the extent to which it can be and usually is artificially constructed' (hooks 1992: 159). But she goes on to add that only a White girl can play at being 'bad' in this way. Black women cannot play at being the sexual innocents, nor do they have the freedom to choose to act 'bad' since racist myth says this is what they always and already are.

Racialised bodies

As well as being sexed and sexualised, there is another major way in which bodies are classified by science, grouped with some bodies as 'the same', and distinguished from others. Like sexing bodies, this classification is also commonly considered to be immediately evident on inspection, natural and really 'there' in the bodies. Unlike sex, though, there is not just a two-category model but a multiple one whose precise numbers and labels have never been agreed. This form of classification is, of course, 'race'.

Sociologists are familiar with the idea that 'races' are not really natural categories, but social ones, largely produced by a now discredited science. However, the process by which one major category, 'White', has been produced is less well understood, and the intersections of 'racial' and sexed categories are only recently being researched. The focus of sociology has largely been on the construction of 'racial' others – in the same way that the focus of gender studies was initially on women. But if we now see that men are gendered, we now recognise that 'White' is a racialised category too. One of the points of interest of this intersection is that if we focus on 'racial' classification then sexual difference is less emphasised. Instead, the similarities between men and women within a 'racial' group are emphasised. I say carefully 'similarities' rather than identity because belonging to the same 'racial' group does not entirely override sexual difference within a group. It has rather the effect of muting, not obliterating it.

Alastair Bonnett (2000) makes a number of points about the category 'White'. It is, he explains:

- Not just a modern label. It certainly existed in pre-modern and even ancient societies.
- Not exclusive to European identities. Other people, especially in China and the Middle East have also described themselves as White. Indeed, they were quite likely to describe Europeans as grey, ashy or even blue. Conversely, in pre-modern Europe, Europeans also often described these others as White too, and early European settlers originally described even native Americans as White.
- Not necessarily a racialised category, in the sense of a naturalised category. Nevertheless, a gradual association of Whiteness with Europeanness, and a racialisation took place that displaced and marginalised what Bonnett calls non-European Whiteness. The Chinese took to describing themselves as yellow though this was still favourably contrasted with red and black people.

- As European Whiteness, an unstable category. Although in the colonial context, Europeans were all Whitened in contrast to non-White 'natives', *within* Europe not all were seen as White, not all managed to live up to the qualities associated with Whiteness.

On this last point, Bonnett reminds us that Europe was divided along many other lines, notably class, gender and ethnicity. The system of 'racial' classification developing in Europe as a scientific discourse was 'on a collision course with discourses of difference that subverted its claims of social equivalence' (Bonnett 2000: 22).

The cases of Irish and Italian immigrants, in particular, illustrate this, as historians have revealed how they were originally categorised as non-White, paralleling their social and economic exclusion. But the category of Whiteness can expand over time, depending on social and political factors. It expanded as these minorities were included in and mobilised for particular colonial and national projects (Roediger 1992; Ignatiev 1995). It was not only ethnic minority immigrants who might be excluded from 'Whiteness'. It was also true for much of the 'native' working class who were both literally and metaphorically seen as less 'White' than their 'betters'. From the point of view of the middle class, the act of moving from one part of a city to another could be seen as a kind of voyage into another world. As Charles Booth put it, 'As there is a Darkest Africa, is there not also a darkest England?' (quoted in Bonnett 2000: 23):

> Any undifferentiated application of racial Whiteness to all
> Britons would provide a profound challenge to class and ethnic
> hierarchy within that society . . . the rationale for their lowly
> position – their depravity, primitiveness, stupidity and darkness
> – would be placed in jeopardy.
>
> (Bonnett 2000: 23)

Moving on to gender, Bonnett sums up recent feminist work by stating that it shows how 'White' women have been assigned specific functions within the 'racial' ideal. Unsurprisingly, this is related to their supposed sexual 'function', as biological reproducers and guardians of the 'race'. They are the ones who pass 'racial' classification on to their children, giving added weight to the need for their chastity. This responsibility is cast as a privilege; it places them on a pedestal but demands they be protected from corrupting influences to which they are particularly prone in their ignorance/innocence.

This also means that sexual relations (or the fantasy of sexual relations) between 'White' women and non-White men was a hot topic. The struggle between the 'races' (that was also a fantasy masking anti-colonial and emancipation struggles) can therefore be, and often was, conceived of as a struggle over the bodies of 'White' women. Many Black feminists have researched the ways there were various panics over the imagined rape of 'White' women, notoriously in the Deep South of the United States, (J.D. Hall 1984; Collins 2000). Black men were imagined to be powerfully attracted to 'White' women. Meanwhile 'White' men were actually assaulting and raping Black women with impunity, and constructing an ideology of their greater sexuality (Davis 1982; Omolade 1984).

Not all colonial, racialised bodies were subjected to the same labelling, and battles in other colonial societies were fought out in different ways over women's bodies. In India, for example, the colonial project was often presented as emancipation for its women, from child marriages, purdah and the custom of *sati*. This missionary work, bringing enlightenment, was seen as an appropriate project for European women to engage in, a civilising mission carried out not only by missionaries but also by nurses and teachers (C. Hall 1992).

White, male bodies and deviance from the norm

We can now return to Laqueur's claim that we cannot write a history of male bodies in the way we can of female bodies. This may be the case if we focus on sex difference, but in 'racial' science men's bodies were very much the focus. Like studies of sex difference, 'racial' science was also an ideology that attempted to draw political lessons and justifications for social inequality from 'natural' facts. Considering the potentially revolutionary documents of the late eighteenth century such as the French *Declaration of the Rights of Man and Citizen* (1789) Londa Schiebinger (1993) points out that its appeal to 'natural rights' could only be held in check by an appeal to 'natural differences'. These related especially to sex and 'race'.

But the 'race' and the sex scientists often proceeded in ignorance of the work and theories of the other. Although these two sciences were pulling in opposite directions and had incompatible

assumptions, their intersections produced some interesting elabora-
tions of what they believed to be natural differences and similarities.
The 'racial' differences between women were phrased in terms of
their degrees of sexualisation, both in the sense of their reproductive and sexual capacities. Black, African women were supposed to
give birth more easily either due to their larger (more 'bestial'
pelvises), and/or the smaller heads of infants that passed through
the birth canal more easily. The imagined differences in Black
women's secondary sex characteristics were also supposed to
indicate their primitive, more bestial appetites.

Nineteenth-century European explorers and travellers often
liked to bring home and exhibit collections of foreign exotica,
including 'anthropological' human specimens. One Hottentot
woman, known as Sarah or Sartje Bartmann, was exhibited in
various European cities between 1810 and 1815 when she died in
Paris. The publicity served to fix both in the medical and popular
imagination the image and essence of the Black female that centred
on her sexual characteristics, her buttocks and genitalia, that
differentiated her from 'White' females. This buttressed 'racial'
science since if Black women's 'sexual parts could be shown to be
inherently different, this would be a significant sign that the blacks
were a separate (and needless to say, lower) race' (Gilman 1992: 180).

Commenting on Gilman's work, Evelynn M. Hammonds (1997)
adds that this idea of the Black women's uncontrolled sexuality
embodied everything that the White woman was not, or not supposed to be. This ideology is a perfect justification for the sexual
abuse and exploitation of Black women. However, there were
'White' women who also appeared, to the thinking of the time, to
embody uncontrolled sexuality: prostitutes. Analogies began to be
drawn between Black and some 'White' women, an analogy pursued
in detail by Sander Gilman (1992).

But putting aside this exception, the dominant idea of racial
difference between women meant that there was a **binary** opposition set up between respectability and sexual control, and promis-
cuity, that seemed to lock Black women outside true womanhood.
Hence the ex-slave woman Sojourner Truth's famous speech 'Ain't
I a Woman?' (see Spender 1982).

By and large, though, the 'race' theorists developed their
accounts by examining male bodies. Females were only a sexual
subset of any particular 'race'. The scientists did not consciously
focus on males; for them, the 'European' and the 'African' were
generic, universal types through whose study the scientists could

reveal the crucial features and distinguishing marks of 'racial' groups and hierarchies. But the features they chose to concentrate on revealed their underlying assumptions about sex difference too. Skulls (and male skulls at that) were a prime source of data since the brains they contained were associated with the capacity for reason that was, in turn, thought to be responsible for human superiority over animals. The ranking of skulls' capacity was devised to show the proximity of Africans and apes, and the gap between their and European brain capacity. But women, of course, were not imagined to possess the same capacities for reason and their skulls were proportionately smaller. Instead, as Schiebinger (1993) demonstrates it was the pelvis (and its associations with reproduction) that anatomists chose as the measure of female 'racial' difference. Unfortunately, African women's pelvises were larger than European women's, so bigger could not mean better in this context. Instead, it was the 'delicacy' of European women's pelvic anatomy that marked her as more evolved.

Sex scientists concentrated overwhelmingly on European bodies and anatomies. They were not much interested in the sex differences between members of other 'races', whether African women's skulls demonstrated *their* lesser capacity for reason than African men's.

But what does this hyper-sexualisation of Black women mean for politics? This brings us on to the final section.

The dominated and the subversive body

One important strategy for Black women, as Hammonds (1997) argues, has been to demonstrate the falsity of this belief. Many Black women reformers in the post-slavery era, often grounded in a strong Christian tradition, attempted to live up to notions of respectability and proper womanhood themselves and by policing examples of sexual 'deviancy' in other women as a threat to 'the race'. The reformers may, correctly, have seen that this kind of behaviour would rebound not only on the woman herself but also on Black women more generally. This does mean, however, that it was extremely difficult for Black women to articulate or express their sexuality at all in positive ways. One major way that Black women's sexuality *was* explored and expressed, though, was in the blues. But neither strategy, respectability nor defiance was able to overturn the negative stereotypes. Indeed, the strategy of defiance has become a highly marketable commodity for White audiences, as the case of Tina Turner indicates. 'Expressing yourself', even when Janet Jackson insists she is 'in control', may be personally satisfying, even profitable, but is rarely done on the woman's terms. There is, though, a process at work:

> Weaving throughout these historic and contemporary efforts at self-definition is the quest to move from silence to language to individual to group action. In this quest, persistence is fostered by the strong belief that to be Black and female is valuable and worthy of respect.
>
> (Collins 2000: 120)

It is also possible to look at all this in a Foucauldian perspective, of techniques of the discipline and surveillance of bodies. Important for this discussion is Michel Foucault's (1977) notion of anatomo-politics, of anatomical control as a form of power. From the late eighteenth century, various institutions began to target the mind, although the body might be the means of influencing and reshaping the mind. These would, it was believed, be more effective techniques of social control than force. The clinic and the prison were the characteristic forms of this new control mechanism, though they could also be seen in schools. The emphasis was on changing minds and characters both through surveillance (constant monitoring of progress) and discipline (cultivating the correct behaviour and attitudes). In the long term it was hoped that inmates, prisoners and pupils would internalise these lessons and become self-regulating and conforming, productive citizens. In the process, a new breed of professionals established themselves as the experts on diagnosing and treating various forms of anti-social behaviour or deviance from norms. The knowledge they elaborated became in turn a new form of control. Medical professionals are the archetypal example.

Case study 5.3 Disciplining wayward girls

As an example of Foucault's argument, we can look at Linda Mahood's (1990) account of the process of reform that took place in the nineteenth century in Scottish Magdalene homes, homes for 'fallen' women. Magdalene homes were established throughout the Western world from the seventeenth century, but dramatically increased in numbers in the nineteenth, as concerns about prostitution and venereal disease rose with urbanisation. Young women, who were seen as sexually wayward if not actually engaging in prostitution, were confined in these institutions possibly for their whole lives, but rarely for less than a year. The homes attempted to reform the girls through a mixture of Christian teaching, moral example and hard work. The labour both generated income for the home and was supposed to provide training for the girls' future in 'honest' employment. Apart from the confinement, the girls were dressed in uniforms, sometimes had their heads shaved, and were subjected to a highly regimented timetable and diet:

> On a typical day in the Glasgow asylum, inmates rose at dawn. Washers began work at 5.30 a.m., laundry workers at 6.00, and sewers at 7.00. Before breakfast, the 'sisters' gathered with the matron for 'family' worship. Breakfast (porridge) was between 8.00 and 9.00, after which the inmates resumed their revenue-generating employment in the laundry or sewing room. Dinner was between 1.00 and 2.00 and supper between 7.00 and 8.00. After supper there was 'family' worship again. It was not unusual for inmates to work an hour or two after supper. One hour was set aside for the education of inmates who could not read, and each girl was given her own Bible as soon as she was able to read it. The entire inmate population was examined regularly in reading and reciting portions of scripture. Bedtime was at 10.30. . . . It was against the asylums' policies to release anyone before she demonstrated that she was capable of a 'change in life' . . . Inmates who desired to leave before being formally discharged were required to give a month's notice and were frequently put in solitary confinement to think it over. . . . Inmates who were so anxious to leave that they ran away, were charged with the theft of their uniforms, forfeited any money they had earned.
>
> (Mahood 1990: 79–81)

The regime, however, only had limited success. Mahood calculates that only 40–50 per cent of inmates were placed in situations more or less acceptable to the directors of the homes after undergoing training and reform. Moreover, the figures do not include the many girls (24 per cent in Glasgow) who were sent to other institutions such as the hospital or insane asylum. But the girls who proved most troublesome were the third who were recorded as having left the home of their own accord or who were dismissed as intractable or insubordinate.

This dismal record, by the standards of the homes, brings us on to the issue of resistance that, Foucault teaches us, is always

there when power is exercised. Opposition to the homes and
their programmes was always apparent, from a range of groups
and movements, including the clergy who preferred to place girls
in private homes of good Christian families, some feminists such
as Dr Elizabeth Blackwell, who objected to the elements of
compulsion in the system, and at least in the first part of the
nineteenth century Owenite socialists who regarded the whole
question of prostitution as an index of the corruption and
exploitative nature of the 'old' moral order. In addition, we can
also reinterpret the homes' record not as failure but as resistance
on the part of those girls who refused to see themselves as guilty
subjects in need of saving:

> As we have seen there has been resistance, although
> unorganised and unarticulated, from all those recalcitrant,
> saucy and ungrateful girls who refused to submit to the
> asylums' efforts. . . . Opposition comes now, as then, from all
> the 'wayward' girls whose struggles evidence their resistance
> to a bourgeois (and patriarchal) moral code even when
> they are caught up in its technologies of power.
>
> (Mahood 1990: 166)

We can also give this a feminist slant by adding that some of
these are male techniques enacted on women's bodies, subject-
ing them to male control. Although Foucault does discuss the
'hysterisation' of women's bodies, the tendency to medicalise
women's bodies and attribute a whole range of symptoms to
hysteria, this is in the context of a more general politics and technology of sex (Foucault 1984). Generally, however, Foucault pays
little attention to gender, to the ways that power and knowledge
are gendered. Not only are male and female bodies and sexualities
constructed as different by these expert knowledges, these discourses are disembodied, not located in identifiable people or
groups whether classes, the state, men or patriarchy. From this
perspective, therefore Foucault:

> clearly denied that power can be a possession which one group
> can 'hold' over another. Women cannot then empower themselves
> in relation to men, because men (or classes or 'races') as a block
> do not 'have' power. . . . He did not, however, speak from
> women's experiences of having power exercised over them.
>
> (Ramazanoglu and Holland 1993: 240)

As Ramazanoglu and Holland (1993) go on to point out, by
contrast radical feminists have provided forceful analyses of the
body and sexuality that identify 'normal' heterosexual practices

and relationships as constructed in men's interests to control and subordinate women's bodies.

With this in mind, we can look again at some of the issues discussed above. Many of the forms of knowledge about sexed, sexualised and racialised bodies, many of the techniques enacted on bodies can be reread as instances of the dominated body. We can also look at opposition and resistance to this domination, the movements for choice, for natural childbirth, and of course for reproductive rights. The rhetoric that guides these movements is often one of choice and freedom, of a woman's right to control her own body. But we must not forget that choice is never free, always made within particular social and economic contexts. Choices to abort, for example, are always context bound: by the availability, cost, legality and method of abortion; by attitudes towards conception, the status of the mother (as married or not), and the social consequences of proceeding with the pregnancy.

Questions of choice become even more fraught if we look at the latest technologies of the body, not only in relation to reproductive rights. Are the new technologies to be welcomed because they give infertile women greater choice? Or do they simply serve to confirm the cultural understanding that motherhood is a woman's natural destiny and desire, and that failure to become a mother is a tragedy that any 'normal' woman would do anything (and pay large sums of money) to avoid? What of HRT therapies that keep menopausal women looking and feeling young? Are these liberating? Or damaging, since they operate on the assumption that a woman is only valuable, can feel good about herself, when she seems young(ish)? When the emphasis in our society is on youth and possible fecundity, the menopausal woman has no purpose in this heterosexist society.

One area where apparently increased choice may be no freedom at all is the question of disability. Forms of pre-natal testing may be seen by non-feminists as a way women can gain greater control over their bodies, but the technologies have serious repercussions, given the way most people regard disabilities in our society. The latest forms of genetic engineering and pre-natal testing only intensify the dilemmas. While there are issues relating to pre-natal testing that affect all disabled people, women, as the ones who give birth, face them in a particularly painful way.

Leah Wild who hopes to give birth to a 'designer baby' by PGD (preimplantation genetic diagnosis) has a chromosomal condition that makes it almost impossible for her to carry a baby to term. If

she did, the baby would most likely be born with severe, probably
fatal, mental and physical problems. The condition has no significance for Leah's own health. PGD allows doctors to test embryos
and select for implantation only those that do not also have Leah's
condition. But she does not welcome the technique wholeheartedly.
On the one hand, 'I either make this genetic selection, or risk
further multiple miscarriages or infertility' (Wild 2000). But she
also says:

> human genetic engineering is not, in the short term at least,
> about preventing and curing disease. It's about whom we want to
> be born. . . . It will increasingly be a decision that other people are
> going to make about us. . . . Why restrict testing to those who will
> be catastrophically affected by a chromosome disorder? Why not
> extend it to those like me who simply pass on such catastrophes?
> Why shouldn't I be eliminated?
>
> (Wild 2000)

This is an issue that is polarising opinion in the disability rights
movement, who are attempting to reconcile support for a woman's
right to terminate a pregnancy with fears that genetic testing could
be seen as an attempt to rid society of people with disabilities. In
part, this hinges on attitudes to what constitutes a disability. Sex
itself can be seen as a disability. At the moment, selecting the sex
of a child by screening embryos is forbidden in Britain by the
human fertilisation and embryology authority (HFEA), unless it is
to eliminate the risk of a baby who would inherit a gender-related
medical condition, such as haemophilia or muscular dystrophy,
which run in boys.

Challenging domination

Following the theme of the subjected body, we can examine how
far women contest or accept this disciplining, not only in relation
to issues of reproductive rights. One argument is that many women
have a kind of 'male in the head' as one book calls it (Holland
et al. 1998), are conscious of the way they are looked at and judged
by male standards, and turn themselves into objects for male
appreciation. This can also lead many women to disassociate from
their bodies, seeing them as separate from themselves, things to
be controlled, mastered and shaped. They dislike all those fleshy

aspects of their material bodies that do not conform to their ideal, sanitised bodies, all the things that threaten to leak, jiggle, wrinkle and disrupt. At its most extreme, this may lead to what are commonly considered pathological disorders, of dieting and resort to plastic surgery. Feminist analysis, however, asks us whether these are so different from the attitudes and techniques to which many women are subject.

Some kinds of female bodies are, by some feminists, considered to be innately disruptive to the gender order, with its implicit assumptions of White, able-bodied heterosexual femininity (Coles 1999). Other feminists even consider *all* female bodies to be threatening to patriarchal discourse (see Brook 1999 for a discussion of these accounts). But there is a difference between this kind of 'resistance' and conscious opposition. Sometimes, this takes the form of campaigns against particular practices, over medicalised childbirth, or female genital mutilation. At other times, it is more a celebration of precisely those aspects of the female body that are commonly considered to be 'disabling' or disturbing. Menstruation offers one example of this strategy. Some feminist artists have used menstruation in various ways in their work (see Parker and Pollock 1987 for some examples) such as Judy Chicago's lithograph *Red Flag* (1971) which showed her removing a bloody tampax from her vagina. Such work both breaks taboos of silence and attempts to 'validate female subject matter by using a "high art" process' (Tickner in Parker and Pollock 1987: 271). Such attempts to reclaim 'female subject matter' have also informed research programmes: into the medicalisation of menstruation in Western culture, and on young women's attitudes to menstruation (Martin 1987; Laws 1990; Grosz 1994; Lovering 1997).

Feminist sociologists have, though, been somewhat sceptical about the possibility of reclaiming and celebrating female difference. It may tend to return women to their bodies' nature, to confirm rather than challenge stereotypes. Judging something to be subversive or not, however, is too simple. We are not faced *either* with dominated *or* subversive and resisting bodies. It is more helpful to regard the body itself as a site of struggle, containing both elements. This is apparent whether we look at technologies and practices, campaigns or art works. Bodies in themselves do not have meanings: anthropologists may have argued that bodies are 'good to think with', that they can be used to symbolise other systems of relations, but we also have to ask whether the ways they are made to mean are good for us.

Summary

- There is a distinctive feminist approach to the sociology of the body through an emphasis on gendered power relations.
- If initial feminist emphasis was on male domination of our bodies, there is increasing interest in ways that women can take control of their bodies. This theme has inspired various feminist campaigns around reproductive rights, though women's 'freedom to choose' has also provoked dilemmas relating to issues of disability.
- Although much of the earlier emphasis was on the 'gender' part of the sex/gender couplet, 'sex' has more recently also been denaturalised. The body's construction as sexed, sexualised and racialised have been topics for investigation that have revealed how the male White body remained the norm against which other bodies were deemed different and inferior.
- Feminist 'body politics' has informed many of these analyses whether in the form of campaigns against particular practices and assumptions, or oppositional celebrations of female 'difference'.
- There remain tensions, however, between various strands of feminist analysis and practice. An emphasis on the body might be seen as a way of asserting or affirming something like a universal sisterhood, what women have in common with one another, or it might seem a way of denying crucial differences *between* women.

Further reading

Birke, L. (1999) *Feminism and the Biological Body*. Edinburgh: Edinburgh University Press.

Bordo, S. (1993) *Unbearable Weight: Feminism, Western Culture and the Body*. Berkeley: University of California Press.

Brook, B. (1999) *Feminist Perspectives on the Body*. London: Longman.

Price, J. and Sheldrick, M. (eds) (1999) *Feminist Theory and the Body*. Edinburgh: Edinburgh University Press.

Chapter 6

Living in a post world?

Chapter outline

Sociology has, from its foundations in Enlightenment thought, been conceived of as a modernist discipline, with pretensions to universalistic theories and explanations. The claims and certainties have, however, been under attack for a while, and there has been a shift from a concern with structures to a concern with discourses. This chapter will examine:

- How far feminist social theory and movements can be understood as part of **modernity**, or as part of its critique.
- What sense there is to the characterisation of some current thought as 'post feminist' in the context of debates over postmodernism.
- Whether postfeminism is simply a backlash to feminism.

Readers should be warned that this chapter will cover arguments between sociologists and between feminists that are particularly heated. Often, people take up strongly 'for' or 'against' positions that recognise no validity in an opposing analysis. As far as possible, I attempt to outline the various views and cover major disagreements, but as the chapter proceeds, readers will probably be able to identify my own position.

Gendering modernity

To understand all the arguments within sociology about the meaning and relevance of terms such as postmodernism and postfeminism, it is helpful first to clarify what is meant by modernism or modernity, and then more generally the significance of the prefix 'post'. Modernity, as Rita Felski (1995) points out, is one of a family of related terms including modernisation and modernism. Modernity, she says, designates a particular epoch in which the distinctive features of what we now see as 'modern' society came into being, marking it off from 'traditional' societies. Just what those features are, and just when they came into being is a matter of dispute: historians, political scientists, philosophers and literary critics each have their own view of what marked the break; the Copernican scientific revolution, democratic government, or a particular literary and artistic sensibility. For sociologists, however, modernity is part of the transformation of Western societies that took place in the nineteenth and early twentieth centuries. Central to these transformations was the new form of industrial production, capitalism and associated changes in social relations. The founding fathers of sociology were deeply concerned to identify and explain the transformations they were living through. Indeed Felski argues that as the quintessentially modern academic discipline, the frameworks and vocabulary of sociology 'were to have a powerful impact on common-sense attitudes towards the nature and meaning of the modern age' (Felski 1995: 36).

Within sociology too, however, there are different views on modernity's characteristics. Typically, what is modern is identified with a challenge to the past and a commitment to change and innovation. It may justify revolt against tradition and custom, recognising no authority except reason, but it was also implicated in domination over those supposed to be incapable of exercising this reason. Many feminist critics, for example, have pointed to a number of previously unnoticed features of modern life (Wolff 1990; Felski 1995). They point out that:

- Rationality was taken to be a masculine quality.
- Major public institutions (government) and spaces of modernity (the city streets) were largely closed to women who were associated with the private, the domestic sphere.
- The **modernist** artists, poets, architects and novelists were overwhelmingly men. And these are precisely the subjects and people that many commentators, at the time and subsequently, have taken as making up 'modernity'.

In sociology, as Felski comments, 'the equation of modernity with particular public and institutional structures governed by men has led to an almost total elision of the lives, concerns and perspectives of women' (Felski 1995: 16).

Felski's project, in *The Gender of Modernity*, is to write women back into modernity, and not simply in the sense of excavating a hidden history of women's contribution as neglected writers and artists, for example, though this is an important work. Rather, her analysis is motivated by a desire to reveal existing accounts' blindness to issues of gender.

First, she points out that these accounts are organised around a masculine norm – they concentrate on the changes that had the greatest impact on men's lives and relations. They do not pay attention to women's experiences, though she also adds that there is no single set of women's experiences; they are fractured by class position. For example, one of the archetypal figures of the modern city is the *flaneur*, one who strolls through the streets, taking in the changing sights and fleeting impressions of the modern city, with no particular purpose in mind other than enjoyment. But as Janet Wolff (1990) has pointed out, the city streets were off-bounds to respectable women; they were not at liberty in the way men were to stroll at will or frequent the bars and theatres that are so often the subject of modernist painters' pictures.

Second, Felski argues that the characteristics associated with 'modernity' and with 'tradition' are gendered, and the former is usually associated with masculine characteristics. Her third point is that feminism itself (which after all came into being as a mass movement during the period) has been both critical of and influenced by the concept of modernity. We will be examining this argument in more detail later.

First, though, certain aspects of modernity were actually coded as 'feminine'. Modernity is often also associated with the emergence of a culture of consumption and especially the development of department stores with a novel focus on the consumption of fashionable items. Shopping became associated with women at this time, and the new stores provided some opportunities for women also to engage in idle wandering as they browsed the goods on display. This allowed them, Felski suggests, to participate in modernity too.

But while this was happening, Felski notes that at this point the evaluation of modernity was changing. From being something that was welcomed by commentators at the time, modernity was coming to signify negative changes, and women (or femininity) epitomised this more pessimistic vision. Modernity came to be seen as excess and irrationality in the ceaseless quest for novelty, exemplified by the feminine consumer. Women consumers were seen as little more than buying machines, both driven by their own desires and manipulated by merchants who were persuading them to buy. Consumption, therefore, both reinforces male authority (it is men who engineer women's purchase of goods that men design and produce), and undermines it (women's appetite for novelty is never satisfied, and they may ruin their fathers and husbands in the process by excessive expenditure).

More recently, feminist critics have picked up on a point that Felski makes in passing. Feminist writers on consumption, she says, must pay attention to 'the limited alternatives available to many women as well as the economic, racial and geopolitical constraints determining the nature and extent of their access to commodities' (Felski 1995: 63). Angela McRobbie(1999) has developed this, pointing out, first, that this particular activity is limited to certain women. In the way that having leisure time – and money – is implicit in the figure of the *flaneur*, marking him as a member of the bourgeoisie, so too are these qualities implicit in the figure of the woman who shops in the new stores. Not all women were invited to consume. More radically, bridging the implicit divide between the sociology of consumption and the sociology of production, McRobbie explains that even feminist critics have failed to consider what she calls the female workforce of modernity, the myriad girls and women who served in the shops and bars, and produced and delivered the goods that were sold there. So, the attribution of masculine qualities to 'modernity' is, in fact, ambiguous, though there seems to be a tendency to label positive ones 'masculine'.

Gendering modernist movements

There is a similar argument about modernism as an artistic movement. Modernist art movements worked in reaction to classical traditions, and later to realist ones (in that constant revolution and rebellion), but there is a disagreement about their gender coding. Felski points out that avant-garde writers and artists, in their reaction against established conventions, would sometimes align themselves with what was coded as 'feminine', with traits such as intuition, and an emphasis on style and surface appearance.

Andreas Huyssen (1986), however, while agreeing with this, insists that modernist movements also set themselves against mass culture, which was implicitly identified with negative feminine qualities. The masses, like women, were merely passive consumers of mass-produced spectacles, exercising no critical imagination or cultured criteria of judgement.

Case study 6.1 Modernism in art

Although many conventional accounts of modernist artistic movements concentrate on male artists and designers, many women too were influenced and inspired by its principles. Yet they rarely appear in these accounts, or only as minor contributors. A number of feminist works, however, have challenged these omissions.

Griselda Pollock in *Vision and Difference* (1988) examines how this exclusion operated, both at the time, and in subsequent histories of the movement. Why, typically, do these histories refer almost exclusively to men, from Cezanne to Bauhaus.

> Is this because there were no women in the early modern movements? No. Is it because those who were, were without significance in determining the shape and character of modern art? No. Or is it rather because what modernist art history celebrates is a selective tradition which normalises as the *only* modernism, a particular and gendered set of practices? . . . any attempt to deal with artists . . . who are women necessitates a deconstruction of the masculinist myths of modernism.
>
> (Pollock 1988: 50)

Her argument is not simply that women's contributions have been undervalued – which they may have been. It is that the terrain on which male (principally the Impressionists) engaged with modernity was a very specifically masculine one. It's not just that the spaces and encounters they observed were often closed to (respectable) women – the bars and brothels – either.

> The territory of modernism . . . is a way of dealing with masculine sexuality and its sign, the bodies of women . . . [and the creators and viewers of these scenes are] men who have the freedom to take their pleasures in many urban spaces [with] women from a subject class who have to work in these spaces often selling their bodies to clients, or to artists.
>
> (Pollock 1988: 54)

Even when they occupied the public spaces, women had to comport themselves differently from men, who were free to look, without being watched. Men thus have a double freedom, to roam in public space and to observe, while women in public spaces are positioned as objects of this male gaze. The separation of spheres, in space and ideology, and the association of public space with masculinity made women's presence in these spaces problematic – the precise spaces and encounters which we associate with modernity.

In an earlier essay, the American art historian Linda Nochlin (1989) examined how a number of Impressionist painters treated the subject of work. Many were depictions of peasant agricultural labour, but some were of that 'workforce of modernity' that McRobbie alludes to, dancers and waitresses and barmaids. But this is not how they are typically seen by critics. Nochlin points out how often these paintings are read as illustrations of *leisure*. But what is leisure for some is employment for others. There is, she says:

> a tendency to conflate *woman's* work – whether it be her work in the service or entertainment industries . . . – with the notion of leisure itself . . . Men's leisure is produced and maintained by women's work, designed to look like pleasure.
>
> (Nochlin 1989: 42–3)

The concept of work, Nochlin explains, was generally understood to mean *productive* wage labour that served to exclude this type of women's work that is closely connected to their bodies and appearance. So,

> Women's selling of their bodies for wages did not fall under the moral rubric of work: it was constructed as something else: as vice or recreation. Prostitutes . . . are of course engaging in a type of commercial activity. But nobody has ever thought to call the prints from Degas' monotype series of brothel representations 'work scenes', despite the fact that prostitutes . . . were an important part of the workforce . . . and in Paris at this time, a highly regulated, government-supervised form of labour.
>
> (Nochlin 1989: 43–4)

Viewing modernist art movements from a feminist point of view indicates how deeply gendered the works and the writings have been. 'Modernism' in art and modernity more generally are socially constructed categories, constructed in ways that render the different experiences and concerns of women invisible.

Postmodernity

The prefix 'post' means, at its simplest, 'after' – in this case modernity. In some of its uses – such as post-operative complications, post traumatic stress – this is just what it means. In sociology and other academic disciplines, however, it implies something more, a break with whatever it qualifies, but also that its referent has not been fully overcome.

If there are disagreements about the timing and characteristics of modernity, the same is true also of postmodernity. Although the term is much used to label the current epoch (largely in the **developed** world), there is little agreement among sociologists about its characteristics. In a way, as Bilton and colleagues (Bilton et al. 1996) point out, that is almost inevitable and the point of the term. While it marks a shift from modern society, it does not clearly specify how or why it is different: 'The name does not give any clue to a *new* organising principle to post-modern society . . . Our world has no coherence, no totality' (Bilton et al. 1996: 607). This is, unsurprisingly, an opportunity for critics to attribute a wide range of features to postmodernity: Bilton and colleagues list fragmentation, diversity of social institutions, absence of clear structures, and a diversity of social institutions and social identities. While this list concentrates on features of the social, other writers focus on the cultural and emphasise instead that our world(s) is (are) now one of surface signs and images that endlessly refer to one another rather than to any underlying reality (Baudrillard 1988). While this may have some immediate recognition factor for readers whose world(s) seems saturated with mass media and advertising, its associated claim that there *is* no underlying referent inevitably causes problems for sociology. Traditionally, sociology has always aimed to go beyond immediate experiences and explanations, to examine the ways that our world is constructed to seem natural, inevitable and right. As Peter Berger memorably said, 'It can be said that the first wisdom of sociology is this – things are not what they seem' (1972: 34).

For writers such as Baudrillard (1988) there *is* nothing but appearance, but this is actually liberating. What postmodernists call 'grand narratives' (such as sociology?) or 'deep' explanations are inherently authoritarian and repress alternative subordinated voices and visions. Other critics, such as Jameson, attempt both to acknowledge the changes in social life, the dominance of cultural forms that is postmodernism, while holding on to a deep explanation for this shift. Postmodernity, Jameson (1991) argues, is actually the cultural logic of late capitalism. Capitalism has now moved into a new phase, one dependent on the production, circulation and consumption of images but the underlying logic, albeit a globalised and decentred one, remains the accumulation of profit.

Other critics (Davis 1988) remain sceptical about whether the concept of postmodernity can have any use beyond naming a particular artistic movement – as 'modernist' can be taken to label an earlier one. In this limited sense, 'postmodernism' can be taken to represent a reaction against the tenets of modernist movements in fine art, literature and architecture, for example. Modernist movements once represented a reaction to the dominant aesthetic norms of the nineteenth century, but subsequently became incorporated themselves into the art establishment, and so post-modernist ones represent the current rebellion against modernist practices and aesthetics. But can the features of postmodernist art – its playful jumbling of styles, its embrace of commercialism, and its denial of 'good' and 'bad' taste, of 'high' and 'low' forms – really be taken to characterise more than another transient artistic style?

Critique or condition?

At this point, it is useful to examine the term 'postmodernity' in two senses: as a condition and as a critique. As a critique, postmodernism can be taken as representing a reaction to, or break with, some of the certainties and values of modernism *and* of modernity. This can be interpreted as an artistic/cultural movement or style, or as a wider ranging reaction to modernity's principles and dynamics. Immediately, however, a problem arises for the latter interpretation, since what the constituent elements of modernity *are*, is disputed. Further, critiques of modernity are as old as modernity itself. From the start of sociological analyses of modernity, critics such as Marx and Weber identified both its positive and negative features. Auto-critique was therefore part of modernity from the start, and in a sense was made possible by its very nature. Reason and science, rather than belief and faith, were key values of modern society, and it was precisely these that enabled critics to dissect it with such power and vision, identifying, for example, both its progressive and its exploitative features.

One difference between the 'old' and new critiques may be whether they position themselves within or outwith modernity. Critiques that position themselves within modernity would be those that point out, for example, that its promises are unfulfilled or that its dominant features have undesirable consequences. Critiques that position themselves outwith modernity would be those that demonstrate that modernity is inherently unable to fulfil its promises, that the undesirable consequences are an inevitable and necessary part of it. The foremost example of the latter is, of course, Marxism.

Given the confusion and disagreements over the nature of modernity, and therefore of postmodernity, it is plausible, therefore, to suppose that some current 'post' critics of modernity will simply select those features that will most obviously appear as a contrast to those they label 'post'. Discussing postmodern culture Jameson, however, warns against such as deduction. The 'post' critics do not have to come up with an entirely new set of features. Breaks, even radical breaks, 'do not generally involve complete changes of content but rather a restructuring of a certain number of elements already given: features that in an earlier period or system that were subordinate now become dominant, and features that had been dominant again become secondary' (Jameson 1988: 27).

But even if we agree, it does not follow that the 'post' critics have identified a new(ish) *condition*. In response to Jameson's argument, Dana Polan (1988) warns against moving from an identification of postmodernity *in* culture to an identification of it *as* our culture. She goes on to point out that there are even huge disagreements about which objects, buildings, writers, or artists *are* 'post' ones.

Sociology and postmodernism

The debate among sociologists is still unresolved. Much time is spent discussing just which features of postmodernism (as condition) are those that signal a break, whether they can still be comprehended within a modified set of 'modernist' labels ('post-industrial', 'radicalised modernity', 'post-Fordist', 'disorganised capitalism' and the like), whether they see the changes as positive or negative, politically enabling or profoundly (by default) conservative, and where this might leave the sociological project. If grand narratives are suspect, if there are only surface appearances, what does this mean for sociology? What does a 'post' sociology look like?

Basically, there have been three approaches to this question, the first two of which accept that there have been changes that can usefully be understood using the label 'postmodernity'. The first option, and Jameson's analysis could be seen as an example of this, is to approach postmodernity as a condition to be examined and explained by fairly standard sociological procedures. It is a sociology *of* postmodernity.

The second option is to *do* a postmodern sociology, and this strategy is often associated with the 'end of class' arguments among sociologists. For these sociologists, there is no such thing as 'society' that has a structure, made up of classes for example, that can be analysed; there is no possibility of producing big theories, there are no ordering principles, but only chaos, instability and diversity. There is another consequence: since there is no position *outwith* postmodernity, there is no possibility of producing objective Truth about it, only small, contingent little truths that remain true only for the moment, only within a particular context. It is a pluralistic sociology that makes no great claims about itself, but is just one discourse among many between which it is impossible to judge. This has methodological implications, its proponents claim, that will allow for a greater diversity of voices to be heard and different viewpoints expressed, with the job of the sociologist simply being one of recording them. Along the way, sociologists should also be demonstrating the basis on which their own accounts rest, their translations of other views, without seeking to replace the originals but simply adding to them (Bauman 1990).

The third approach is quite different. Not all sociologists agree that either of the first two options is desirable or even necessary, as they dispute the existence of 'postmodernity' itself. All the assumptions of postmodernism are deeply suspect to Marxists such as Alex Callinicos (1989), and other sociologists. Anthony Giddens (1990), for example, while acknowledging that much, especially politics and personal relationships, has changed, argues that the new epoch in which we are living is not 'postmodern' but a new phase of (late) modernity.

Case study 6.2 Postmodern art: but is it 'feminist'?

Postmodernism is also a style, a reaction against modernist principles in art, design, literature, architecture and film. A number of women artists have sometimes been called 'postmodernists', and here we will look at the work of one in particular, and the critical reflections on it. First, I want to look at the developments in both feminist theory and art practice.

In the 1970s, in Europe and North America, feminists had come to the conclusion that many paintings and other visual images of women, created by men, did little more than objectify women, turn them into objects for men's pleasure. Feminist critics argued that this convention was so powerful that it was impossible for women artists to overturn or reverse it, by creating 'positive' or alternative images of women instead (Nochlin 1973). All they could do, it seemed, was refuse and disrupt the viewer's suspect pleasure in looking at images of women. There were various strategies such artists might use, such as abstraction, or conceptual art.

One of the best known examples is *The Dinner Party*, by American artist Judy Chicago. First shown in 1979 in San Francisco, this is a large installation, a triangular dinner table, set with embroidered mats and ceramic plates. Each setting represents a woman whose achievements had, Chicago felt, been neglected and/or trivialised (Chicago 1980). Although Chicago does not 'picture' women, she does aim to create a positive alternative representation, based on vaginal imagery. Her work was, however, criticised by other feminists on a number of grounds: for essentialising women through this vaginal imagery, and also for its goal of 'excavating' a list of overwhelmingly White, heterosexual and Western 'heroines' (Barrett 1982). (See http://www.judychicago.com/ for more information.)

Feminist art in the 1970s and 1980s was rarely figurative, and was more likely to use media other than painting and sculpture, such as photography, video and performance art. When the American photographer Cindy Sherman began exhibiting in the late 1970s, her photos, using herself as a model, attracted interest and acclaim from critics who had become used to feminist conceptual art. Since Sherman's first major exhibition *Untitled Film Stills*, she has rarely given interviews or written about her work, so it has been the critics who have made links between her work and feminist theories, both to praise and criticise her.

First, her black and white photos of herself, dressed up and posed to look like film stills, and her later restagings of 'Old Masterpieces', seem to link up with feminist ideas about the roles women have performed and been required to perform, to present themselves as spectacles. By deliberately presenting herself *as* a spectacle, by refusing to represent the 'real' Cindy Sherman in her work (or interviews), her work has been seen as a way of negotiating the male gaze while also exemplifying a postmodern sensibility in its depthlessness: her work is all surface and simulation, it does not refer to anything 'real', only to other images.

On the other hand, Sherman has also been criticised for getting too caught up in the spectacle, failing to maintain a critical distance from the way women's bodies have so often been presented. Another series of photographs, *The Sex Projects*, is particularly disturbing. She photographs parts of anatomical models, sex aids, plastic breasts and vaginas that she arranges into female bodies. Although this might be seen as an exploration of sexual sadism and the fetishisation of women's body parts, it seems that Sherman herself cannot do anything but repeat the masquerade for a fascinated voyeur. This line of criticism can be seen to link up with many feminists' concern over postmodernism more generally. Although there is an implicit critique of many modernist assumptions in Sherman's work – that art expresses the character of the artist, that it should distance itself from mass culture – there is also a refusal to engage critically with the issues of difference, sexuality and pleasure that it merely plays with. A more engaged work, such as *The Dinner Party*, at least explicitly takes up feminist issues, even if it fails to handle them in a way that satisfies all feminists.

(For examples of Sherman's work, and some critical reviews, see http://citd.scar.utoronto.ca/VPAB04/projects/ Helen_Papagiannis/introduction.htm And http:// www.temple.edu/photo/photographers/cindy/sherman.htm.)

. . . and feminism

But apart from wanting to take part in a current debate, just what does all this signify for feminists? Why should we be interested in it? Some sceptics have claimed that the debate around postmodernism is 'an attempt by disillusioned male academics, who feel they are no longer at the "centre" or have authority and control over knowledge, to win back credibility and influence . . . what we have here are theories that analyse the malaise of a particularly privileged group' (Skeggs 1991: 256). Or as Dana Polan puts it 'postmodernist discourse frequently functions to allow entrenched academics a new way of doing the same old work' (1988: 50).

Nevertheless, many feminists *are* receptive to postmodern ideas, variously claiming that this is a way forward for feminism and/or that feminism is quintessentially part of the postmodern enterprise (insofar as feminism has 'an essence'). Some of these arguments will be considered in more detail later, under an examination of the term '**postfeminism**' which is in many ways the (temporary) conclusion of the debate about their mutual relations.

Postmodernism, feminism and cultural studies

One of the areas of feminist sociology that has proved most receptive to postmodern influences is that of cultural studies. Here, Angela McRobbie and bell hooks have proved to be the most lucid and enthusiastic (though not entirely uncritical) commentators. What is it that they find useful, both in analytic and political terms?

McRobbie's argument takes two questions to be central: what place might feminism have in postmodernism's new conception of 'the social'? And what role might feminist academics have to play in feminist politics? (McRobbie 1994). She addresses these questions by an examination of the notion of 'the real me'. This 'me' has traditionally underpinned many sociological theories of **identity**, identity that has been given by the structures of class, above all. More of these discussions are reviewed in the chapter on Difference. Feminists have, of course, been demonstrating that this identity has really been male, and also White. Thus it is based on a series of exclusions, 'the hidden dimensions of subjectivity, those that arise from positionalities which, within modernism, had no legitimate place' (McRobbie 1994: 63). But a stable subject, even feminism's subject 'woman', can no longer be taken for granted; she has been deconstructed, in turn exposed as a fiction that itself excludes other ways of being a woman. Feminism, at least since the 1970s, has constantly been criticised by Black feminists for claiming to speak as and for 'women' when what they are actually doing is speaking as and for *White* women.

But lest this be seen as undermining the possibility of a feminist politics, McRobbie argues that a fixed and stable subject is not a necessary basis for a feminist politics: 'The feminist social self, it might be suggested, is an amalgam of fragmented identities formed in discourse and history' (1994: 71).

In more practical terms, feminist politics becomes a process of interaction and debate, and also of looking for new spaces where feminism permeates and helps shape new conceptions of what it might mean to be a woman, a feminist. McRobbie pulls back, however, from simple pluralism, a kind of 'live and let live' where each woman is free to go her own way and come up with an equally valid feminism. Debate, argument and negotiation between women and feminisms is the mark of this new politics, rather than the search for a single authoritative voice and position. A final point to note, for the moment, is the similarity between this and what came to be called a transversal politics. bell hooks begins her essay 'Postmodern Blackness' by calling attention to the exclusions in writings on and about postmodernity, exclusions both of gender and 'race' (hooks 1992). She finds this particularly serious, given that these writings claim to open up a space where difference and otherness are supposed to be of central concern. Like many other feminists we will be looking at, hooks also identifies a way of writing that directs itself to a very privileged and educated audience, using a language that assumes familiarity with the very 'master' theories it purports to challenge. hooks, however, sees a radical potential in postmodernism that *could* be significant for a new Black politics, though it must be linked with the politics of racism in American society.

Like McRobbie, hooks addresses the issue of whether the **deconstruction** of fixed identities means the end of politics. Like McRobbie, she concludes that current conditions, of despair *and* what she calls yearning, actually make room for the construction of new enabling political identities of Blackness. These identities would no longer be externally imposed definitions of Blackness, but would arise both from the diversity in Black experiences and from a shared history of exile and struggle. Making a point that leads onto her interest in popular cultural forms, hooks argues that the expression and circulation of radical ideas and critical thinking need not, and indeed must not, be confined to the academy. Equally, radical critics must maintain or develop ties to communities beyond the academy, must know about and be responsive to their lives, concerns and practices, including artistic and cultural ones. Although postmodernists often gesture towards such popular cultural productions, hooks claims that few have any deep knowledge of what Black and other minority writers, musicians and artists are doing. She cites rap as one such instance, a musical form that has enabled young Blacks to develop a critical voice and also a new identity community. She concludes the essay with a speculation, that popular culture may well be the central place where resistance struggles take place.

This is precisely a point taken up by Angela McRobbie (1999), in some essays on the meaning of 'girlie' culture and young women's magazines. The essays explore what, in the previously cited essay, she calls 'new worldly identities' (McRobbie 1994: 66) that have been brought into being.

While these magazines have traditionally been seen by feminists as little more than 'how to' manuals for turning girls into dependent, insecure, boy obsessed losers, McRobbie argues that they, and their readers, have changed significantly. It is not that they have become 'how to' manuals for turning girls into feminists, but that feminism (leaving aside for a moment what that means) *is* present in them, and that they are a way of popularising 'feminist' ideals. Blanket condemnation of the magazines simply creates a gap between feminists (who have seen the light) and 'ordinary' girls and women. The magazines are, McRobbie argues, contradictory: 'there is both a dependence upon feminism and a disavowal of it' (1999: 55). There is dependence in the sense of building on and expressing many of the ideals and achievements of the previous generation of feminist campaigns and consciousness raising:

> It has presence mostly in the advice columns and in the overall message to girls to be assertive, confident and supportive of one another. It is also present in how girls are encouraged to insist on being treated as equals by men and boyfriends, and on being able to say no when they want to.
>
> (McRobbie 1999: 55)

But there is also a desire, as she says, to be provocative to feminism, which is construed as a repressive, kill-joy, earnest adult kind of thing, to suppose that a younger generation has transcended the need for an explicit feminist politics. She concludes by suggesting that though there is no immediate identity between feminism as a political movement and the cultures of commercial femininity embodied in these magazines, nevertheless they share overlapping terrains and therefore offer a channel of communication among different women, of different generations.

These two examples suggest what feminists working within a postmodern framework in the field of cultural studies can achieve.

It allows them to explore, in substantive terms, what the new centrality of culture may mean for the future of a feminist and a Black politics. It may be, however, that in their eagerness to look for positive openings, they lose a certain critical edge, though they try not to engage with a simple celebration of the pleasures of the popular.

Postfeminism

For beginners to the 'post' world of sociology, it is important to clarify the two meanings of the term 'postfeminism'. In the first, and probably best known sense, it refers to the notion that we inhabit a postfeminist world. In turn, this has two variants: first, that feminism has achieved all its goals and is no longer needed (though it once might have been). Second, that feminism in trying to reach its goals went 'too far' and has reversed the 'natural' order of things, making both men and women profoundly unhappy. This is the postfeminism that the American writer Susan Faludi dissected in her popular book *Backlash* (1992). From there, the term **'postfeminist'** migrated to describe a woman who had seen through the false promises of feminism and realised that not only can't she 'have it all', but actually didn't even want to try. More recently, a 'postfeminist' may now be used to describe the young woman who is fun and sexy, bored with politics, and too busy picking out the latest lipstick to be worried about the pay gap.

Although Faludi's argument about a media-led backlash might seem dated, a recent article in *The Guardian* is still making this particular connection:

> What is a post-feminist? It's just a posh word for 'not a feminist', that's all. It's like calling Tony Blair a 'post-Marxist', or a dog a 'post-cat'. It's one of those words which assumes we live in a new post-modern times.
>
> (Steel 1999)

Case study 6.3 Postfeminism as backlash

The term 'postfeminist' probably reached most people's consciousness through media reports in the 1980s. Women were tired, we were told, of trying to juggle careers, partners, babies and households. They were burned out, exhausted and

---

frustrated. Many who had put settling down, finding a partner and having a baby 'on hold' in order to pursue a high flying career, found they were unable to find that partner, let alone conceive. They had left it too late.

As Faludi points out, the media try and have it both ways: feminism has 'won', in the sense that women can now take their equality for granted and don't have to go on about it, let alone do anything about it. Feminism has also 'lost' in the sense that women are now rejecting it as never offering them what they really wanted (Faludi 1992). She goes on to list the scare stories in the media of 'man shortages' and 'barren wombs', and of a backlash in politics, education and psychology. All were intent to put the clock back, to warn women of the costs of striving to be like a man. It is probably at this point that popular images of feminists as power hungry, sexually aggressive but ultimately lonely women in shoulder pads became established, exemplified by obsessive and murderous Glenn Close in the film *Fatal Attraction*.

One of the strengths of Faludi's book is, according to Imelda Whelehan (1995), that she never forgets the material effects of the backlash on women's position. Faludi documents with depressing and meticulous detail the continuing pay gap, in levels of violence especially sexual violence, the inequalities in education, employment and in reproductive rights.

Another point Faludi makes is that the 1980s backlash was not the first of its kind. Conservative reactions to the women's movement, its aims and its gains, have dogged it throughout both the nineteenth and twentieth centuries. Faludi also argues that a backlash is set off 'not by women's full achievement of equality but by the increased possibility that they might win it' (1992: 14). The latest movement has made a few gains, she acknowledges, but millions were left out too. The force of her attack on the media is a consequence of her argument that it is they who have worked to persuade women that it's feminism that is to blame for their ills, rather than the fact that feminism has been stalled as a movement for change.

Coming into the new millennium, the backlash has mutated somewhat. Imelda Whelehan has charted its progress in *Overloaded* (2000). In the book, she examines a host of new phenomena in the media, lads' magazines, 'girl power', and what she calls 'the Bridget Jones effect'. For Bridget and her friends in the novel, feminism has happened; she is *au fait* with its ideas (claiming to be reading *Backlash* when she first meets Mark Darcy – Mr Right) but really dreaming about good old love and romance (she is actually reading *Men Are from Mars*).

Whelehan goes on to discuss other manifestations of the effect, in *Ally McBeal, Sex in the City,* and *Sleepless in Seattle* among others. All these chart the pleasures and miseries of being single, sexually active, professionally successful woman, but who are 'desperate to find a life partner to the point of utter self-abnegation . . . or spinning out of control emotionally' (2000: 139).

American writer Susan J. Douglas (2002) goes further in probing continuing media obsessions with postfeminism, a repetition that she calls the 'manufacturing' of postfeminism:

> But to perpetuate this 'common sense' about feminism and postfeminism requires the weekly and monthly manufacturing of consent. Postfeminism is, in fact, an ongoing engineering process promoted most vigorously by the right, but aided and abetted all along the way by the corporate media. Postfeminism is crucial to the corporate media because they rely on advertising.
>
> (Douglas 2002)

Douglas also looks at glossy women's magazines' responses to criticisms that they constantly show models who are too skinny, and hence promote an unreal and damaging ideal for women. American *Vogue,* for example, responds that 'To be slim and fit is healthier than to be seriously overweight and out of shape', to which Douglas replies 'Our choices as women are anorexic versus blimp' (Douglas 2002). It is interesting, however, that magazines' language has shifted from appearance to fitness as a justification of dieting (now called 'healthy eating'), and buying more cosmetics, clothes and 'treatments' is now justified as 'pampering' yourself – because 'you're worth it'.

This reveals another backlash mutation: multinational companies have shamelessly co-opted various ideas and terms from feminism – freedom, independence, pleasure and self-esteem – in order to sell more things to women.

A further twist to the backlash is to revert to an apparent revelling in old stereotypes, which is also presented as two fingers up to 'political correctness'. Here, feminism is presented as a form of political correctness that young men and women know about, are bored by but delight in transgressing. Ironically, perhaps, postmodern insistence on how meanings may 'float', enables the producers of what were once considered by feminists to be offensive images to argue that they are using them 'ironically', in a 'post' kind of way. As Whelehan comments, this new irony 'makes it difficult to object to *anything* potentially offensive' (2000: 68). If you do, you just haven't got the joke.

Academic postfeminism

I want to examine academic appropriations of 'postfeminism' through an analysis of Ann Brooks' *Postfeminisms* (Brooks 1997). This is the book that probably has made the best known attempt to give 'postfeminism' a different meaning, one that is not a rejection of feminism but one that provides a new understanding of the feminism of the 1990s.

In her review of the themes and thinkers that go to make up postfeminism, Brooks distances herself from the popular meaning and attempts to locate postfeminism within the academic context of the post world. For her,

> Postfeminism . . . is about the conceptual shift within feminism from debates around equality to a focus on debates around difference . . . Postfeminism is about a critical engagement with earlier feminist political and theoretical concepts and strategies as a result of its engagement with other social movements for change . . . postfeminism facilitates a broad based pluralistic conception of the application of feminism, and addresses the demands of marginalised, diasporic and colonised cultures for a non-hegemonic feminism capable of giving voice to local, indigenous and post-colonial feminisms.
>
> (Brooks 1997: 4)

In this passage, several assumptions are condensed:

- First, as Steel suggests, it contains an assumption that we do live in postmodern times – many of the movements and currents she considers are 'post' ones.
- Second, that there has been a conceptual shift.
- Third, that it is postfeminism that critically engages with earlier theories.
- Finally, that it is postfeminism that facilitates a broad-based feminism and gives voice to local and other feminisms. All of these are suspect, or at least in need of qualification.

While we might agree that feminism has changed, it is not obvious that the changes within feminism can be labelled 'postfeminist', and even more dubious is the assumption that it is only something called postfeminism that has dealt with challenges from other social movements. We will look at each assumption in turn.

From equality to difference?

We have already seen that postmodernity is a highly contentious term, but leaving this aside, we can consider the other assumptions. Many feminist critics repeat the claim that while the women's movement used to be concerned with issues around equality (with men), it is now concerned with issues around difference (between women). However, this claim is rarely argued out carefully.

Certainly, as many feminist historians testify, equality was a prime concern of First Wave feminists, equality with men, in political, educational and legal terms (Spender 1984), and it was this goal that motivated their numerous campaigns, not least for the vote. But even by the 1920s, something was changing. Careful readers will note that I have used the terms 'women's movement' and 'feminism' interchangeably, but to do so is to gloss over an important shift. 'Feminism' is actually a term barely a hundred years old: nineteenth- and early-twentieth-century 'feminists' called their movement the 'women's', or in the USA 'woman's', movement.

The American historian, Nancy Cott (1987), has researched this moment in detail in America. She was prompted, she explains, by an apparent anomaly: the term 'feminism' was coming into common use *at the time* when the women's movement was supposed to be exhausted, in decline. Why was there this change in terminology? What could 'feminism' signify that 'women's movement' (or in the USA, 'woman's movement') did not? Cott argues that this moment (early twentieth century) when women *were* beginning to obtain the rights they had fought for as women puts the term 'women's movement' into crisis. The diversities between women began to be more apparent then. The shift in language and label represents a shift from an assumption of unity among women (which is easier when *all* women are, for example, denied the vote), of common cause, to a more problematic and modern conception of women as a social grouping: it is a shift from 'women' as a sex to 'women' as a gender. The term 'gender' had not yet come into use in this context but this is precisely the understanding that early-twentieth-century feminists were working towards. 'Feminism' represented another kind of unity among women, a unity that was not tied in a simplistic way to their sex:

> So long as 'woman's sphere' bound women, they had a
> circumstantial unity; once women were formally (though
> ambiguously) unbound, joining together on behalf of their sex
> required a new deliberateness and ideology, which the appearance

of the word Feminism symbolized. A new understanding was
needed, which Feminists proposed by making individuality and
heterogeneity among women their principles and yet holding
these in abeyance by acting in sex solidarity.

(Cott 1987: 7)

The women represented under the term 'feminism', for Cott, are
not essentialised women, but diverse and often divided ones. The
category 'women' is a social *and* a political identity. Nothing else
could explain the change in terminology. As she goes on to explain:

> The woman's rights tradition was historically initiated by, and
> remains prejudiced toward, those who perceive themselves first
> and foremost as 'woman', who can gloss over their class, racial and
> other status identifications, because those are culturally dominant
> and therefore relatively invisible. The privilege – or self-deception
> – of making gender more important than its attendant attributes
> has not been available, most obviously, to women of color in the
> United States, where race has been such a crucial marker . . .
> Nonetheless, that perception of 'womanhood' as defining one's
> identity has, at times in history, galvanized women of diverse sorts,
> and it has been the essential element of coalitions based on sex
> solidarity.

(Cott 1987: 9)

I have spent some time discussing Cott's account and analysis
in order to compare it with the claims of 'post' feminists such as
Brooks. Issues of difference were part of modern feminism from
its start, although Cott concentrates on class and racial differences
between women and others have subsequently surfaced. It may be
that in analyses and campaigns, feminists have not been attentive
enough to differences, and have chosen, as Cott puts it, to gloss
over their class, racial and other status identifications, but this is
different from an assertion that feminism has focused on equality
while only *post*feminism has focused on difference.

Conceptual shift?

Brooks' next assumption is that there has been this conceptual
shift, not only to a focus on difference, but a change in what sort of
things feminists want to analyse, and in the concepts they use to
tackle them. She refers to Michele Barrett's observation in 1990 on
the new interest among feminists in cultural theory, in issues of sym-
bolisation and representation, and a reliance on psychoanalytic

theory as well as host of 'post' discourses. Broadly, these shifts have marked a move from an analysis of structures to an analysis of discourses, a move from Marx to Foucault.

The book that Barrett edited with Ann Phillips in 1992, *Destabilising Theory*, explains and reviews many of these ideas and theories, suggesting that there has, indeed, been a paradigm shift within feminism. In terms of what gets published and debated, it may appear an uncontroversial statement. The bibliographies and indexes at the end of books such as Brooks' and Barrett and Phillips' seem to warrant it. There are far more references to the various 'posts' than to 'patriarchy' in Brooks' subject index, for example.

I do not want to take issue with the various trends these books identify at this point. Rather, I want to make a basic sociological point about the construction of knowledge, in this case knowledge of feminism. Academic books (including this one) are social constructions, selections (and exclusions) of issues, writers and theories that, of course, get labelled as 'significant'. What I am suggesting is that it is not a simple exercise to identify trends, or paradigm shifts, in any field. At various moments, feminists (among others) have taken issue with publishers, academics and critics for their exclusions – not least for the exclusion of feminist and minority writers, artists and scholars from what comes to be taken as important and valuable. So the identification of a paradigm shift, for example, could actually be the *construction* of such a shift, through opaque and subjective processes of selection and exclusion. If all writers and editors are constructing knowledge about a field, then the least they can do is to recognise and acknowledge this is what they are doing.

Perhaps readers will now (correctly) ask what is this writer doing? How are my selections and exclusions made? What are my biases? At various times in my academic career, I have found a home in departments of philosophy (from which I fled as soon as I graduated), of anthropology and of sociology. Placing myself now as a sociologist, writing (mainly) for sociologists, my selection is firstly motivated by what I encounter as central concerns for that discipline (though these cannot be unquestioned either). I also occasionally attempt to 'keep up' with some debates in anthropology – and through friendships – in social history, media/cultural studies, literary criticism, and art history. I still avoid philosophy, even feminist philosophy (except for Simone de Beauvoir), as far as possible, and like many social science students (judging by mine over the years) have some kind of blind spot when it comes to psychoanalytic theory. In recent years, however, the greatest intellectual influence on my feminist thinking has been my exposure to the field of development studies, with its own 'sister' disciplines of politics and international relations – but not economics. Most important here, have been the interests and perspectives that 'overseas' students have brought to the postgraduate course I co-teach.

My survey of the field of feminist sociology is, therefore, partial. Due to my own biases (or ineptitude at understanding and hence explaining), certain issues and perspectives are neglected. Unfortunately for Brooks' claims, these are largely precisely those 'new' ones that she and Barrett identify as now interesting feminists. For readers who want to explore them, then Brooks' book would be vital.

My point in this section is not to attack the issues and theories, but to question her insistence that this is where feminism is (or ought to be). Brooks' review is more than a simple description of a field, since she goes on to argue that there is a clear gulf between feminism and postfeminism, and that the former has been shown to be wanting by the latter.

> Second wave feminism was limited by its own political agenda and modernist inclinations . . . [postfeminism] has encouraged an intellectually dynamic forum for the articulation of . . . debates emerging from within feminist theorising, as well as feminism's intersection with . . . critical philosophical and political movements.
>
> (Brooks 1997: 210)

Presumably, 'old' feminism was able to do or be none of these, and that unless one is 'up' on these debates one's feminism is a limited and lethargic one.

Interestingly, this is not a claim made by Barrett in *Destabilising Theory*. Indeed, Barrett warns precisely against assuming that the more recent a theory is, the better it is (a surprisingly modernist assumption for a postfeminist like Brooks). Barrett notes that this can be an unintended and unfortunate consequence of chronological reviews of feminist theory (Barrett 1992).

Critical engagement?

To read Brooks' pronouncement above, one might at first think that feminists had, until recently, not thought critically about feminist concepts and strategies, or had not been involved with and influenced by other movements, other theories of social change. There are three ways one can understand this claim. Either this statement is simply untrue, or is true by definition (and hence vacuous). A third possibility is that only now are feminists *really* engaging critically with their ideas and strategies.

First then, it is untrue in the most obvious sense, both for the earlier and later-twentieth-century movements. Critical engagement with theories and strategies (both within and outwith feminism) has been a mark of feminism at all times. First Wave feminists argued and debated issues of equality with or difference from men constantly; they argued over whether birth control was a feminist or a separate issue; whether girls should be educated in the same way as men, and whether protective labour legislation was a positive or discriminatory policy. There were women who were part of and influenced by early sex reform movements and theories, were members of socialist, Marxist, pacifist, anti-colonialist and internationalist movements, as well as those who were nationalist and conservative in their political views.

More recently, arguments between liberal, radical and socialist/ Marxist feminists have filled the pages of books and journals; arguments there and in meetings and conferences continued over the 'domestic labour debate', '*ecriture feminine*', wages for housework movements, anti-pornography and anti-censorship campaigns, Reclaim the Night marches, whether one should work 'in' or 'against' the state, and whether heterosexuality was, in effect, sleeping with the enemy (to name just a few). Second, the statement might be a tautology, true by definition.

In the 1960s and 1970s, the post movements that Brooks mentions were not, of course, either established, or well known. So, necessarily, feminists could not be challenged by (or challenge) them. But soon after the works of various post and discourse theorists were being published, feminists who had access to them – and institutional, educational and geographic constraints operate here – began to analyse and review them. The attitude was not dissimilar from that which Nancy Cott identifies in the first feminists, in relation to the ideas that surrounded them:

> Women railed against the insufficiencies of liberal political discourse even as they seized it for themselves; they apprehended Protestant teachings at a different angle from that intended by most ministers; and they adapted socialist models to their own purposes.

> (Cott 1987: 17)

Similarly, *parts of* the Second Wave feminist movement had links to other emancipatory social movements, local, national and international. In particular, antiracist, gay and lesbian, disability rights, antiwar, and anti-apartheid movements all helped shape (and in turn were variously shaped by) feminist concerns at this time. Even a small acquaintance with history must lead to the conclusion that feminism has been *particularly* open and responsive, both as a set of theories and a set of (sometimes warring) campaigns. A view of feminism as a set of dogmas, as being *one* thing with *one* 'party' line is a gross caricature.

Finally, the third interpretation: Brooks does agree that 'feminism has always engaged with the "master" discourses with which it has found itself allied' (1997: 13), as Cott points out above. Apparently, Brooks supposes then that there is something different about this latest critical engagement. Just what is never specified, although she does refer to a 'fragile consensus' in Second Wave feminism (Brooks 1997: 16) that was challenged both from within and outwith feminism. She cites the political impact made by the critiques of women of colour, the issue of sexual difference, and the influence of poststructuralism and postmodernism as instances of these challenges. Dramatic as these challenges may be, it is not immediately apparent how or why they are significantly different from any other challenges.

Giving voice?

This is the one item on Brooks' list with which I have most immediate sympathy. I would, though, take issue with her contention that it is *post*feminism that has 'addressed the demands of' and 'given voice to' local, indigenous and postcolonial feminisms. For a start, these feminisms are quite capable of addressing their own demands, and finding their own voices, and with their own vocabulary. Brooks' mode of expression locates them, instead, in a passive voice, silent until postfeminism comes along. Indeed, I believe that these feminisms are so important that I will be considering them in more detail, at greater length in the next chapter on Postcolonialism.

For now, I will just say again that my objection to Brooks' argument rests principally on her characterisation of the various internal and external challenges as so profound that they warrant the invention of a new label – postfeminism(s) – for what feminism is now. It is certainly legitimate for feminists to qualify or clarify their particular kind of feminism – as is often done by adding 'radical/revolutionary', 'postmodern', or 'lesbian' to it, or by inventing a new term such as 'Womanist', as the Afro-American writer Alice Walker (1984) has done.

Others, like Brooks, also want to distinguish their feminism from what they see as a once dominant, but now rather old fashioned kind of feminism. Third wavers, Generation X feminists, or simply 'new' feminists also claim that their feminism and theirs alone offer new ideas for a new generation of young women. The Third Wave, for example, describes their movement as 'putting a new face on feminism, taking it beyond the women's movement that our mothers participated in, bringing it back to the lives of real women who juggle jobs, kids, money, and personal freedom in a frenzied world' (www.io.com/~wwwave/). The British journalist Natasha Walter wrote *The New Feminism* (1998) to identify both the changes that Second Wave feminists had made, and to produce a new manifesto that would speak to the lives and concerns of younger women. Interestingly, the Boston based Female Liberation organisation had previously described their magazine *The Second Wave* as a magazine of the *new* feminisms, when it ran between 1971 and 1984.

Both of these examples, however, although they appear to take account of changes to women's lives, changes that 'old' feminism had helped bring about, the 'new' feminism they herald is an overwhelmingly White, First World and heterosexual one.

To be fair, this Generation X or Third Wave feminism is not the feminism that Brooks writes for, and here, at least, her choice of the label postfeminist could be justified in order to distinguish her feminism.

Postmodernism and feminism

The final issue that I want to return to here is that of the relation between postmodernism and feminism. As we saw at the start of this chapter, there has been extensive debate about whether feminism can be seen as a modernist movement. As Felski (1995), for example, points out, women associated with the women's movement both adopted and criticised a language of modernity. They wanted to position their claims and movement as an intrinsic part of modernity, while also attacking its failure to recognise their legitimacy. A similar ambivalence characterises feminism's relation to postmodernity.

For some feminists, it is postmodernism as a critique that enables feminism to rid itself of dubious grand narratives and universalising categories, a legacy of its modernist provenance. Jane Flax (1987), for example, though recognising feminism's origins in modernity and also its critique of modernity, argues that feminist theory really belongs now within postmodernist theory. Feminism's critical understandings of knowledge and truth mean it cannot be contained within even a modified modernism, it has transcended its categories. Feminist meta-theories that claim to explain everything (such as a universal patriarchy), and the universal categories (such as woman), certainly came under attack. Postmodernism as critique generally is held to enable a philosophical criticism of these errors, and Marxism in particular became a target with its supposed meta-narratives of class struggle and the eventual emancipation of the proletariat. As numerous critics have pointed out (for example Montag 1988), this account of Marxism is somewhat of a caricature, and the claims of many postmodernists are themselves totalising grand narratives, of the 'death' of (all other) grand narratives. Rather than search for the single cause of women's oppression, rather than suppose that 'women' are a single and obvious category of humans, different from 'men', postmodernism tells us to look at the little local instances, at the differences within categories. In turn, feminists concerned about certain tendencies within main (male?) stream postmodernism, warn that it has to be subjected to a feminist critique itself (Fraser and Nicholson in Nicholson 1990). In particular, Nancy Fraser and Linda Nicholson highlight male-centredness and political naivety, although they believe these can be overcome through a feminist critique. As we have seen, both McRobbie and hooks also believe that postmodernism need not mean the end of politics, although it is often associated with nihilism and relativism. It would, though, be a different kind of politics, one attentive to differences – in this case between women – and one that does not privilege one kind of oppression over another.

One of the greatest enthusiasts for postmodern critiques is the American Susan Hekman. In *Gender and Knowledge* (1990), Hekman argues that feminism has much to gain from an alliance with postmodernism. She claims that it is postmodernism that challenges 'the fundamental dichotomies of Enlightenment thought . . . the homocentricity of Enlightenment knowledge and even the status of "man" himself. These are not issues on which feminism can be ambiguous' (Hekman 1990: 2). Indeed not, and feminism has not been ambiguous on them, nor – for that matter – has much critical sociology either. A central strategy of this postmodern approach is to obliterate any previous or alternative critical approaches in order to highlight the originality and profundity of postmodernism. Hekman's critical review of issues such as rationality and subjectivity aims to demonstrate a certain affinity between feminist and postmodern thought – an attack on Enlightenment thought – but only postmodernism 'can reveal some of the errors of contemporary feminist positions. The postmodern position reveals the futility of the attempt to define an essential female nature or to replace the masculinist epistemology with a feminist epistemology' (Hekman 1990: 8). The weight, therefore, is put on postmodernism as the ultimate critical apparatus, although feminism is allowed a minor corrective role to the occasional gender blindness of postmodernism.

Somer Brodribb, in a review of feminist approaches to postmodernism, argues that Hekman's project is to postmodernise feminism:

> It is no longer a question of extending post-modernism by adding gender; it is feminism which must be purged by post-modernism of Enlightenment, essentialist, absolutist and foundational tendencies. Cartesian epistemology, not class or heterosexuality, is the main enemy here . . . Indeed, Hekman's major target is not the sexism of social and political thought, but the 'women's way of knowing' literature.
>
> (Brodribb 1992: 308)

Many feminists are also sceptical whether we should wave farewell to grand narratives and generalised categories, as postmodernists do. The deconstruction of 'women' may suggest, for example, it is illegitimate to speak 'as a woman', since too many other identities – as a lesbian, a Black woman – can be submerged in it. But even more dangerous, perhaps, is the refusal to speak 'as a man': as Barrett and Phillips (1992) point out, the gender neutral speech, of postmodernism as much as modernism, has all too often disguised a masculine perspective.

Susan Bordo (1993) has dissected this particular conceit, calling it a postmodernist dream or fiction of speaking from 'everywhere'. If modernism she says, imagined it was speaking from 'nowhere', postmodernism 'remains animated by its own fantasies of attaining an epistemological perspective free of the locatedness and limitations of embodied existence' (Bordo 1993: 217–18). She also has some warnings about the lure of postmodernism for feminism on other counts too. Taking up the issue of difference, she warns that we can pay too much attention to it: 'But attending *too* vigilantly to difference can just as problematically construct an "other" who is an exotic alien, a breed apart' (Bordo 1993: 223). It was also precisely because of the work of feminists and other 'outsider' critics that postmodernists do now take account of difference: 'Could we now speak of the differences that inflect gender and race (and that may confound and fragment gender and racial generalizations) if each had not been shown to make a difference?' (Bordo 1993: 224).

On the question of feminism as a grand narrative, Bordo insists that there is a clear difference between feminism's grand narrative of gender inequality and:

> the meta-narratives arising out of the propertied, White, male, intellectual tradition . . . Located at the very center of power, at the intersection of three separate axes of privilege – race, class and gender – that tradition has little stake in the recognition of difference (other than to construct it as inferior or threatening 'other').
>
> (Bordo 1993: 224)

She continues by assessing the location of feminism as 'an outsider discourse':

> Feminist theory – even the work of White, upper-class, heterosexual women – is not located at the *center* of cultural power. The axes . . . give some of us positions of privilege, certainly; but *all* women, *as* women, also occupy subordinate positions.
>
> (Bordo 1993: 224)

In conclusion, Bordo warns that the danger for feminism is less in any totalising tendencies than in a paralysing anxiety over falling into ethnocentrism and/or essentialism: 'Most of our institutions have barely begun to absorb the message of modernist social criticism; surely it is too soon to let them off the hook via postmodern heterogeneity and instability' (Bordo 1993: 242).

Of the feminist responses to postmodernism, the most critical have been those of radical feminists. Denise Thompson, for example, claims that 'a "post-modernist" feminism is a contradiction in terms because, while feminism is a politics, post-modernism renders its adherents incapable of political commitment . . . post-modernism refuses to identify, and hence cannot contest, relations of domination and subordination' (1996: 325). Commenting on post-modernist feminists' claim that their position does not mean the end of politics, Thompson argues that just what this politics is, remains unclear, little more than a rhetorical flourish. They fail to identify what conditions might need to be changed:

> What is wrong with them, what is to be abolished, what retained and what transformed, in whose interests and against the interests of whom are the changes to be effected . . . And they never are addressed adequately because post-modernism's commitment to undecidability debars it from explicitly and unequivocally identifying the location of domination.
>
> (Thompson 1996: 335)

Kristin Waters focuses on three aspects of postmodernism that she finds deeply problematic, both in theoretical and political terms. First, she examines postmodern moves to 'destabilise the subject'. She explains what this means:

> Post-moderns hold that abstract general terms like 'women', 'men', 'Blacks' and 'Asians' wrongly attribute a single identity to widely diverse individuals. The singular form of these terms likewise wrongly attributes a signifying and misleading identity to selves that are in fact fractured and fragmented. Hence, a methodology which argues in terms of women and men, and other identity groups is bound to fail, since these groups, and indeed the individuals who comprise them, cannot be meaningfully characterised in such ways.
>
> (Waters 1996: 286)

Like many others (for example, Hartsock 1990), Waters points out that the 'deconstruction' of the subject takes place just at the moment when dominated groups are beginning to claim subject-hood for themselves:

> How is it that post-modernism is frequently called 'feminist' when the abstract general term under attack is not 'men' or 'western civilisation'. . . but 'women', a term that found broad political resonance perhaps as little as a decade before its 'deconstruction'?
>
> (Waters 1996: 289)

Second, Waters discusses the way the concept of 'reason' becomes transformed by postmodernism into the concept of 'desire'. She points out that the attribute of reason has traditionally in western thought been denied to women, from Aristotle on, and that women have fought over the millennia to claim they were just as capable as men of exercising it. This does not mean, however, that feminists have used 'reason' uncritically:

> In my view, women's struggle worldwide to be seen as rational individuals forms a fundamental stage in gaining political and civil rights. This is not because all cultures adopt the modern western notion of reason, but because western colonialism and imperialism have substantially exported our political systems and their intellectual detritus. Feminists, then, can and should explore reason and desire on their own terms wary of modern constructions which systematically exclude women, and Freudian and post-modern constructions which sexualise women according to masculine economies of desire.
>
> (Waters 1996: 292)

The final problem Waters identifies is that of the style of postmodern writing and theorising. Although she admits that the beauty of the prose of writers such as Judith Butler 'seduces' her, she also objects to it on a number of grounds. She notes that it is a style of writing, 'of dense discussion, and esoteric terminology' firmly located in the academy. It assumes a familiarity with western philosophy, and here 'what counts for salaries and prestige and position is what gets published, and what gets published and read depends on style' (Waters 1996: 294). It is a style, moreover, that resolutely prohibits concrete examples and personal experiences, and prohibits a feminism that starts from women's lives.

This is a criticism that the Black American critic Barbara Christian (1989) also makes for the particular example of Black women's fiction. In her essay, 'The Race for Theory', Christian says:

> I see the language it [literary critical theory] creates as one which mystifies rather than clarifies our condition, making it possible for a few people who know that critical language to control the critical scene . . . they [the critics] sought to 'deconstruct' the tradition to which they belonged even as they used the same forms, style, language of that tradition, forms that necessarily embody its values.
>
> (Christian 1989: 229–30)

Christian goes on to examine the current preference *not* for reading Black women's fiction, but for reading and cross-referencing theorists: 'Critics are no longer concerned with literature but with other critics' texts' (1989: 225). She warns that this orientation seriously risks neglecting the current and past writings of many 'minority' writers who have had trouble enough in achieving recognition.

Christian is at pains to make clear that she has no objection to theories or theorising, but only to this particular type of theory. Like Patricia Hill Collins and bell hooks, Christian also argues that 'people of colour' have always theorised, not necessarily in the forms of western logic but in other ways and through other forms. She is wary, though, of attempting to produce *a* Black feminist literary theory, since such a thing would legislate for how we *ought* to read: 'Instead, I think we need to read the works of our writers in our various ways and remain open to the intricacies of the intersection of language, class, race and gender in our literature' (Christian 1989: 227).

Waters finally considers postmodern feminists' argument that feminism should reject all modernist elements and ally itself firmly with postmodernism. She concludes by arguing that

> For feminist theory to leap-frog over the modern period because it is, after all, masculinist, is unfruitful. To fail to selectively appropriate the powerful theoretical tools of multi-faceted modern theories and readapt them for feminist analysis is a self-destructive move, especially if the reason is to create a more seductive style . . . to create a high style as an entrance requirement is contrary to everything for which feminism has always stood.
>
> (Waters 1996: 295)

Conclusion: last posts?

Summarising the arguments between feminists and postfeminists, we can note both agreements and profound disagreements about a number of issues. They agree that:

- Feminism began as part of modernist critiques;
- Feminism has also critiqued modernist assumptions;
- The homogeneity of the category 'women' has been disputed;
- This has put feminism as a political movement and analysis into crisis.

They disagree about:

- When the crisis happened (Cott says early twentieth century; postmodern feminists say late twentieth century);
- What happened as a result of this crisis (Cott says it precipitated a move from 'women's movement' to

'feminism'; postmodern feminists say it necessitates a move to postmodern feminism);
- Whether this means modernism must or can be revised or transcended;
- Whether postmodernism is now the 'natural' home for feminism;
- Whether postmodernism, in turn, can be adequately modified by feminist critique;
- Whether it is unmodifiable, and hence necessitates a move to postfeminism.

In particular, feminists disagree about how far it is possible to modify a dominant discourse (whether modernism or postmodernism), whether it is, as Waters argues, possible to pick and choose those elements that best accord with feminism's political and analytic strategies. Hekman, on the other hand, believes that it is impossible to preserve the positive aspects of modernity:

> feminists cannot overcome the privileging of the male and the devaluing of the female until they reject the epistemology that privileges these categories . . . [they] cannot escape from the inherent sexism of Enlightenment epistemology.
>
> (Hekman 1990: 8)

What has been less fully explored is whether it is possible, or desirable, to pick and choose from among the 'post' discourses. Brooks makes an argument similar to Hekman's, though her target is postmodernism, rather than modernism. Her response is to ditch postmodern feminism in favour of a new animal, *post*feminism. This, she argues, is the only feminism that is capable of responding to the other 'post' challenges, notably postcolonialism.

An essay by McRobbie, 'The Es and the Anti-Es' (1999), however, offers another option. It is 'a reconciliation of sorts between the post-structuralists and those who consider themselves on the side of studying concrete material reality'. But, and this is the importance of the essay for feminist sociology, it 'also envisages a return to the "three Es"; the empirical, the ethnographic, the experiential, not so much *against* as *with* the insight of the "anti-Es", that is anti-essentialism, post-structuralism, psychoanalysis' (McRobbie 1999: 75). In effect, McRobbie offers a way out of the paralysing anxiety that Bordo had argued was besetting some feminists, anxious about falling into essentialism, and so on.

First, she summarises what the 'anti-Es' had considered to be vulgar errors:

> Ethnography? That truth seeking activity reliant upon the (often literary) narratives of exoticism and difference? Can't do it, except as a deconstructive exercise. Empiricism? The 'representation' of results, the narrative of numbers? Can't do it either, except as part of a critical genealogy of sociology and its role in the project of modernity and science. Experience? That cornerstone of human authenticity, that essential core of individuality, the spoken voice as evidence of being and of the coincidence of consciousness with identity? Can't do it either, other than as a psychoanalytic venture.
>
> (McRobbie 1999: 76)

She goes on to present a history (acknowledged to be a history shaped by her own intellectual formation and hence familiarity with certain feminist and disciplinary ideas), of ideas about representation, language and discourse, as they affected feminist cultural studies. She also notes, in passing, that the 'post' ideas travelled far precisely because they were text centred, and hence devoid of local content and context.

She also distinguishes between 'materialism', as it is understood in the American and the British feminist contexts. For Americans, it is taken to be a bodily materialism, expressed in the works of feminists such as Dworkin and MacKinnon, and it is against this feminism that 'post' feminists such as Butler and Spivak argue. McRobbie, however, assumes that the labelling of this feminism as essentialist, neglectful of differences such as class and race, is correct. This may be how these writers are often described, but Andrea Dworkin, for example, has always been particularly attentive to issues of class and race. In a 1990 interview, for example, Dworkin says 'I think a lot of what people call the split in the Women's Movement is basically a class split . . . Is [feminism] going to be a movement for women who just want better career chances, or is it really going to deal with the way that poor women and women of colour are truly exploited?' (1996: 213–14). Feminists might disagree with her position that the battle against pornography is the key issue for feminists, or that it is the best way of tackling poor women and women of colour's exploitation, but Dworkin is clearly *not* neglectful of such differences.

Similarly, MacKinnon in an article on feminist theory/practice and the law, argues that in the work of 'post' feminists, race and class are not treated in the same way as 'gender', but simply used as a means of attacking supposedly essentialist thinking. These terms are not deconstructed. Equally, she insists that generalisations about 'women' are not necessarily essentialist:

> In its variations, the group women can be seen to have a collective social history . . . To speak of social treatment 'as a woman' is thus not to invoke any abstract essence . . . but to refer to this diverse and pervasive concrete material reality of social meanings and practices.
>
> (MacKinnon 1996: 47–8)

So, one of the lessons of this excursus is that you can't always depend on others, including feminists, to fairly represent the views of feminists! Use summaries (including this one) as starting points, but go and read the originals and make up your own minds.

To return to McRobbie's essay: materialism in the British context refers first, to the materialism of the economic (under the influence of Marx), and later to the materialism of discourse (under the influence of Foucault). British feminists, she suggests, under the influence of the latter, have come to see 'women' as a fiction, an effect of 'material' representational practices that constitute a group called 'women'. Feminists' use of the term, McRobbie says 'creates and gives an identity to a social group who might previously have been known as ladies, girls, housewives, or mothers' (1999: 81). I imagine Nancy Cott might think this is a bit of wheel re-invention, seen from the point of view of 1920s feminists.

She then proceeds to consider the ways that postfeminists such as Butler and Spivak have productively unsettled earlier feminist certainties. (I am not entirely convinced by McRobbie's reading of them, since I feel that Butler, at least, all too often operates by setting up 'straw women' to attack, attributing naïve essentialism where there is often complex constructionism – as in the MacKinnon example above – in order to allow her sophisticated deconstructionism to shine through.) McRobbie cites Butler's often quoted statement that she wants to 'expand the possibilities of what it means to be a woman' (Butler 1995: 50) as an example of the productive edge to postfeminism, that disrupts the confines of stable gender identities.

In relation to her own interest in popular culture, McRobbie sees it as echoing Butler's interest in demonstrating 'deviations from the deep binary divide of male and female' (McRobbie 1999: 87). Various forms of youth subcultures such as magazines and clubbing experiences offer young people new ways of being in the world, new more fluid identities that may seem like realisations of Butler's view of gender as performative. In conclusion, McRobbie argues for a 'strategic' use of both the Es and the anti-Es. Here, 'strategic' means both careful and self-conscious, and also politically justifiable. In other words, it means taking on board all we have learned from the post theorists, about the problems with empiricism, ethnography, and experience, but *not* jettisoning them from our analyses altogether. What would the Es look like now?

First, McRobbie suggests that empiricism (the language of results, data and statistics) could be used strategically in certain contexts, to inform and persuade. She mentions how cultural studies 'experts' are often called on to comment on debates in the media, about the effects of television violence, for example, while a more deconstructive approach is appropriate to other (intra academic) contexts.

The type of ethnographic work that has often been carried out by cultural studies researchers can also continue, in a modified way. McRobbie points out that questions about the right to speak 'for', in some way represent the realities of those being researched, have already featured in feminist arguments 'outside the direct influence of post-structuralism' (1999: 89). What would change, however, 'is the insistence that there can be no true and authentic account, that the lives and identities being chronicled are necessarily fluid, partial, performed and constituted in the context of that particular ethnographic moment' (McRobbie 1999: 89).

Finally, on the category of experience, she also acknowledges that considerable feminist debate has taken place on this issue (in relation to epistemological questions, as we saw in a previous chapter). If Foucault has taught us that 'experience' is socially produced, that we are taught to have and express certain experiences, this does not imply we have to abandon an exploration of subjects' or our own experiences. As with empiricism, the language of 'experience' can be strategically used, to 'humanize ourselves as feminist academics to speak the more popular language of experience where political goals can be achieved as a result' (McRobbie 1999: 90).

McRobbie concludes by making familiar criticisms of the post discourses too. She mentions how they challenge women's right to speak 'as women', and also cites the style and inaccessibility of their language. For feminists, 'this can seem like a real abrogation of political responsibility' (McRobbie 1999: 90). Her most original criticism, however, is that the anti-Es have largely failed to explore ways in which their ideas might be translated into more popular and practical forms. While they have sometimes analysed these forms – and we could mention Judith Butler's analysis of the film *Paris is Burning* in her book *Bodies That Matter* (Butler 1993) – they have been less interested in how their ideas are or could be taken up *by* these forms. Generally, however, Barbara Christian's judgement on the literary 'race for theory', its neglect of actual writers' work in favour of other theorists, seems true here as well. But as McRobbie comments, engagement and translation 'would demonstrate that high theory can have relevance to cultural and political practice' (1999: 91).

Given that Christian's argument is more than ten years old, I am not optimistic that McRobbie's plea will be heard, but at least she does make a strong case for a feminist *critical* interest in the arguments of the anti-Es. She also recognises that in many instances, feminists had arrived at similar conclusions, but following their own trajectories.

Summary

- Both feminism and sociology developed in modernity, though feminism had a more ambivalent relation to modernity. Feminists saw that women were often excluded from the rights that supposedly marked off modern from 'traditional' society. They also presented feminism as the epitome of a modern political movement.
- Feminist critics have pointed out that women were not so much excluded from modernity as given a special, and often negative, role to play. As consumers, of new goods, and of mass produced culture, women represented excess and irrationality.
- 'Modernism' in art and modernity more generally are socially constructed categories, associating men and masculinity with a set of features, and women and femininity with another. The categories are constructed in ways that render the different experiences and concerns of women invisible.

- Feminist sociologists and other feminists are in profound disagreement over the meaning and value of the various 'post' perspectives. Generally, the perspectives serve to focus attention on issues of difference, the end of grand narratives, and the impossibility of arriving at a single big truth.
- In sociology, 'post' approaches have had most impact in the area of cultural studies, especially popular and mass cultural forms.
- While some argue that 'post' perspectives overcome many of the problems and correct the errors of second wave feminism, others claim that they risk depoliticising feminism in the name of theoretical purity.
- The label of postfeminist has not, as yet, gained much credibility among feminists since it is easily confused with postfeminism in its popular and negative sense. Many feminists do, however, feel the need to mark a move beyond what are thought to be traditional feminist positions.

Further reading

Assiter, A. (1996) *Enlightened Women: Modernist Feminism in a Postmodern Age.* London: Routledge.

hooks, b. (1982b) *Black Looks: Race and Representation.* London: Turnaround.

McRobbie, A. (1994) *Postmodernism and Popular Culture.* London: Routledge.

Pfeil, F. (1995) *White Guys: Studies in Postmodern Domination and Difference.* London. Verso.

Seidman, S. (1998) *Contested Knowledge: Social Theory in the Postmodern Era.* Oxford. Blackwell.

Chapter 7

Postcolonialism and feminism

Chapter outline

The term 'postcolonialism' refers to more than simply the period after colonisation has ended. It also refers to a critique of colonialist practices and ideologies that can persist in changed forms. Although largely taking place in the context of literary and historical research, arguments about postcolonialism have also entered sociological analysis. In sociology, there has been a particular interest in connections between analyses of postcolonialism and of globalisation.

The term 'postcolonialism' may look the most straightforward of the 'posts' we have reviewed so far, and in one sense it does refer to a world *after* colonialism. We should remember, however, that the world is not yet a totally postcolonial one: conquest, invasion and colonisation are not in the past, as China's conquest of Tibet, and Malaysia's invasion of East Timor, remind us. Nor have all countries achieved political independence either, as the continuing struggle in Papua (formerly Irian Jaywa) for independence from Indonesia demonstrates.

But like the other 'posts', the term also signifies that some, at least, of the relations that characterised colonialism live on even when a country is formally, politically, independent. There is not a complete break with the past, but relations have changed enough to merit the use of a different term. The context in which these new relations develop is the changing world economy that is often called 'globalisation'.

Like the other 'posts', the term postcolonialism can refer both to a condition and a critique. First, though, it is useful to have some understanding of colonialism, the relations of dependence and domination between countries, and the changes in these in the later part of the twentieth century with particular regard to how these affected gender relations.

This chapter will examine and review:

- The concept of postcolonialism;
- The impact debates about postcolonialism have had on feminist thought;
- The impact that feminist thought has had on postcolonial studies.
- It will put this in the context of an outline of feminist approaches to colonialism and international divisions of labour.

International and sexual divisions of labour: colonialism

Most histories, from a variety of disciplinary and political perspectives, of the development of a world or global capitalist system in which colonialism was one phase are gender blind (Mandel 1973; Wallerstein 1979; Rodney 1982). One exception is the German sociologist Maria Mies' *Patriarchy and Accumulation on a World Scale* (1986). Drawing on a Marxist feminist framework, Mies aims to analyse 'the relationship between women's oppression and exploitation and the paradigm of never-ending accumulation and "growth", between capitalist patriarchy and the exploitation and subordination of colonies' (1986: 1).

The 'Woman Question' (a traditional Marxist expression) will never be properly understood, she continues, unless it is placed in the context of 'a global division of labour under the dictates of capital accumulation. The subordination and exploitation of women, nature and the colonies are the precondition for the continuation of this model' (Mies 1986: 2). Also, therefore, Mies argues that the form and development of this global capitalist system cannot be understood unless it is analysed from a feminist perspective.

Mies adopts a feminist standpoint as understood by Hartsock (1998), and further argues that women are best placed to 'develop a perspective of society which is not based on exploitation of nature, women and other peoples' (Mies 1986: 2). In particular, Mies recognises the contributions of Third World feminists in focusing on issues of violence, colonialism, work and politics, issues that have challenged 'old', Western, feminist theories. The basis of Mies' argument is her analysis of the sexual division of labour, between men and women. She affirms the fundamental sociological point that this is not a 'natural' division, but social. She also departs from classic Marxist analysis and defines productive labour as labour that produces things necessary for human needs and not only labour which produces surplus value. Productive labour in this narrower sense, she explains, is only possible because it rests on productive labour in the wider sense. And women largely do this non-wage labour – domestic labour, childcare and subsistence production:

> It is my thesis that this general production of life, or subsistence production – mainly performed through the non-wage labour of women and other non-wage labourers as slaves, contract workers and peasants in the colonies – constitutes the perennial basis upon which 'capitalist productive labour' can be built up and exploited. . . . It is not compensated for by a wage . . . but is mainly determined by force or coercive institutions.
>
> (Mies 1986: 48)

Although men's access to weapons (adapted from tools for hunting) may have been at the origins of men's power (over nature and women), Mies points out that it is more instructive to examine the present than to speculate about the past, in order to see how capitalism is even now integrating women, poor peasant and tribal societies, into the new international division of labour. 'Integrating women into development' – a euphemism for integrating them into capitalist accumulation – is a way of recruiting women as a cheap labour force, in agriculture, industry and the informal sector. The subordination of women to men, Mies explains, was also accompanied by the 'naturalisation' of women and their labour. Not only are parts of the world defined as 'nature' – in contrast to human culture – but people and their labour too may be defined as 'natural resources'. This is what happened to subjects in the colonies whose capacities and labour came to be defined, like nature, as raw material for exploitation. The produce and profits of this exploitation were largely consumed (although unequally) in the European countries: 'In fact, one could say that to the same degree that the workers of the European centre states acquired their "humanity" . . . the workers . . . of the peripheries . . .

were "naturalized"' (Mies 1986: 68). All women too, both in the centre and periphery, were subject to this process but women of the European bourgeoisie were defined as 'domesticated' rather than as 'savage' nature. By this, Mies means they were turned into housewives, that their productive and reproductive powers came under the control of the men of their class on whom they were dependent. This eventually became the model for all classes: 'The process of proletarianization of men was, therefore, accompanied by a process of the housewifization of women' (Mies 1986: 69).

The process of colonisation resting on the exploitation of land and labour depends on this naturalisation. The colonial subjects had to be rendered outside 'humanity', labelled as little more than savage, primitive animals. This was not only an ideological process in which racialisation was a key component, but also required the destruction of local industries. Many accounts of the colonial enterprise rest on a claim that many of the people coming under European domination were barely civilised, living in a state of barbarism, semi-naked, and subject to superstition and natural disaster. European domination would rescue them, civilise them, enlighten them and teach them how to make best use of their natural riches and would protect them from famine, flood and drought.

More recently, economic and social historians have exploded this picture. In the eighteenth century, differences of income and wealth between the major nations were relatively small, though class differences *within* countries were considerable. Indeed, it is likely that average living standards in Europe were lower than the rest of the world (Bairoch 1981). At the end of the century the largest manufacturing areas in the world were in India and China, not Europe or America, and India alone produced a quarter of the world's manufactured goods (Bairoch 1982). The turnaround did not happen until the middle of the nineteenth century when European production began to outstrip that of India and China. The common explanation is that Asian production stagnated, while the Industrial Revolution 'propelled Britain, followed by the United States and eventually the rest of Western Europe, down the path of high-speed GNP growth' (Davis 2001: 293–4).

But as Davis demonstrates, European success depended on the *de*-industrialisation of Asia, especially its textile manufacture: 'The looms of India and China were defeated not so much by market competition as they were forcibly dismantled by war, invasion, opium and a Lancashire-imposed system of one-way tariffs' (Davis

2001: 295). From being exporters, these countries became importers, not only of Lancashire cotton, but also Dundee jute and Sheffield steel. In parts of West Africa, where women had traditionally specialised in trading and had enjoyed a high status and accumulated great wealth, their networks were gradually destroyed and supplanted by British monopolies (Mies 1986).

A recent study by Mike Davis (2001) also discounts the claim that the Western technology and expertise that colonialists brought to the Third World at least rescued its inhabitants from drought and famine:

> A key thesis of this book is that what we today call the 'third world' . . . is an outgrowth of income and wealth   , inequalities . . . that were shaped most decisively in the last quarter of the nineteenth century, when the great non-European peasantries were initially integrated into the world economy. . . . By the end of Victoria's reign, however, the inequality of nations was as profound as the inequality of classes . . . And the famed 'prisoners of starvation' whom the *Internationale* urges to rise, were as much modern inventions of the late Victorian world as electric lights, Maxim guns and 'scientific' racism.
>
> (Davis 2001: 16)

There were indeed quite extraordinary climatic events in the late nineteenth century, in India, China, Brazil and northern Africa that brought unprecedented and successive droughts and famines and millions of deaths. But Davis accumulates impressive evidence to argue that famines on this scale are not natural disasters but 'man' made ones. It was actually the imposition of an unequal market economy and political domination that made these societies so vulnerable to the failure of rains. In the pre-colonial period, these regions had also been subject to rain and hence crop failure, but had devised social and technical mechanisms to cope which had been destroyed by the British. Indeed, in a terrible irony, the railroads the British were building across India were used to transport grain and other cash crops *out* of India even during famines. As Davis clearly demonstrates:

> We are not dealing, in other words, with 'lands of famine' becalmed in stagnant backwaters of world history, but with the fate of tropical humanity at the precise moment (1870–1914) when its labor and products were being dynamically conscripted into a London-centred world economy. Millions died, not outside

the 'modern world system' but in the process of being forcibly incorporated into its economic and political structures.

(Davis 2001: 9)

Gender relations in the colonial world

Men and women were, however, becoming incorporated in different ways. Many colonialists attempted to impose Christian, Western patriarchal notions of the proper relations between the sexes on their subject people – with the exception of slaves. This might mean 'rescuing' women from 'barbaric' customs such as child marriage, polygamy, or *sati*, or re-ordering property relations to vest individual ownership in male heads of households. In the process, women lost many of their traditional rights and roles (Etienne and Leacock 1980). Western colonialists often regarded women's proper place as in the household, as dependent wives and daughters, not working in markets and fields.

This ideology and its associated practices persisted well into the next century, so that when feminists first came to examine women's role in the development process they were struck by the fact that the benefits of modernisation had seemed to pass women by (Boserup 1970; Rogers 1980). Rogers, for example, called development 'the domestication of women', meaning that inappropriate Western notions had been imposed on women (and men), serving to exclude women from development. This largely liberal feminist argument became the basis for what has been called the Women In Development (WID) stage of policy making, that aimed to *include* women in development.

'Dependency' feminists who were closer to a Marxist analysis, in turn criticised this argument on two major grounds (Nash and Safa 1980). First, it assumed that development was a good thing that did actually bring benefits, and second that far from being *excluded* from development, women were already included, but on disadvantageous terms. It was women's reproductive and subsistence (unwaged) labour that contributed to their particular disadvantage since it provided a hidden subsidy to capital. Both approaches however, analysed situations in which women were not significantly engaged in employment, especially industrial production. The de-industrialisation of the nineteenth century that Davis examines had expelled women, as well as men, from local manufactures.

One exception to the de-industrialisation of the Third World was Brazil. This had gained political independence from Portugal in 1822, earlier than many other colonies, and the industrial sector was well established, and growing, from the latter part of the nineteenth century (Saffioti 1978). Although women were employed in certain sectors, such as textile production and food processing, the percentage of women employed in industry declined, especially after the 1930s.

Both the liberal and the dependency feminists agreed that development (as the liberals would call it) or capital accumulation (as the dependency feminists would call it) in general and industrialisation in particular excluded or marginalised women. But already, by the 1980s, patterns of employment, especially in industrial production, were changing in certain areas of the Third World.

International and sexual divisions of labour: postcolonial conditions

Colonial rule was not unopposed of course, and over the course of the twentieth century most of the European colonies gained independence, but it was an independence qualified by the global dominance of other countries, notably the USA after the Second World War.

In the colonial period, the international division of labour consisted of a broad division between raw material exporters (the Third World) and manufactured goods exporters (the First). With the end of direct rule, however, a new international division of labour was emerging in which certain Third World countries were themselves becoming producers and exporters of manufactured goods, often to the First World. In the drive to 'develop', former colonies attempted various strategies; first, to manufacture their own goods (import substitution) and decrease their dependence on expensive imports; and more recently to manufacture goods for export to the developed countries (export oriented production), to gain foreign currency. This strategy coincided with new imperatives in the old manufacturing core countries, to reduce wage costs while still retaining control over the overall production process and markets. It was possible to integrate these strategies since most of the former colonies were heavily dependent on the investment of foreign companies, to provide the necessary technology. Typically, research and development takes place in more developed countries, while the less skilled processes are carried out by cheap labour in less developed countries. Sometimes called the phenomenon of 'runaway capital' (Mitter 1986), the 'new international division of labour' connotes:

a changing structure of employment, globally, through the relocation of jobs from the high-wage countries of the West to low-wage, newly industrialising countries of Asia and Latin America. . . . As more and more countries are integrated into the expanding empires of the late twentieth century form of international business and capital, the workers of a nation state become vulnerable to the investment and procurement policies of the TNCs (**transnational** corporations). Even the government of a rich country can have only limited influence over the decision making processes of these giant corporations.

(Mitter 1986: 8–9)

A further phase, in parallel with this phenomenon of the 'First World in the Third', has been called 'the Third World in the First', or as Mitter calls it 'capital comes home' (Mitter 1986). The restructuring of First World industries created a reserve of cheap labour among the newly unemployed. Both in the clothing and electronic industries, production now often takes place at 'home' too, close to centres of final use. Regional grants often subsidise production in the 'peripheral' areas of Europe and North America in the way that Third World governments often tried to attract TNCs by offering attractive packages to encourage them to set up business in what are called Free Trade or Export Processing Zones (EPZs). In effect, these concessions and incentives are a form of welfare to capital, paid out of taxation by national states. They can reach astronomical sums. David Harvey (2000) offers one recent example in which the state of Arizona paid one quarter of a billion dollars to Mercedes-Benz in subventions in order to persuade it to locate there, equivalent to $168,000 per promised job: 'Welfare for the poor has largely been replaced, therefore, by public subventions to capital' (Harvey 2000: 65).

The significance of this export-oriented production in EPZs is that women, often young, single women, were the majority of employees. A number of key studies examined this phenomenon, arguing that employers' preference for female labour was largely due to women's cheapness and 'nimble fingers', though these features were constructed, not natural (Elson and Pearson 1981;

Elson 1983). The work on which they were employed is meticulous and repetitive, features that have often characterised women's work. It is conventionally also classified as 'unskilled', requiring little training, and also offering few prospects for further training and promotion. Another feature is that this is a 'disposable' labour force: the preference for young women rests on the assumption they will only be employed for a relatively short time, before getting married and leaving. It therefore offers employers a way of disposing of workers when orders are low. Finally, the 'cheapness' is partly based on the assumption that the wages women will accept are low because they are only earning a 'secondary' wage, one that is not enough to support dependants since they are not heads of households.

The 'skill' factor is, however, one that is also socially constructed – to women's disadvantage (Phillips and Taylor 1980). The women in factories like these may not have formal qualifications, nor be members of trade unions – factors that are associated with the official designation of a job as 'skilled' – but have acquired, through their socialisation, skills such as sewing that enable them to learn to perform the job quickly:

> Manual dexterity of a high order may be required in typical
> sub-contracted operations, but nevertheless the operation is usually
> one that can be learned quickly on the basis of traditional skills.
> Thus in Morocco, girls (who may not be literate) are taught the
> assembly under magnification of memory planes for computers –
> this is virtually darning with copper wire and sewing is a
> traditional Moroccan skill.
>
> (Sharpston 1976: 334)

Women's skills, learned in their households, are thus 'naturalised', constructed as simply part of their 'natural' capacities. Their knowledge 'can be projected as part of women's natural attributes, rather than as a skill or training which should be rewarded with higher wages' (Pearson 1992: 233).

Similar studies carried out within Europe revealed that women were also the preferred employees in small-scale clothing manufacture, especially ethnic minority women (Mitter 1986; Phizacklea 1990). Mitter's (1986) study also pointed out that women were being employed in large numbers in new electronics industries in places such as Scotland's 'Silicon Glen', though the sun is now setting on what were once hoped to be 'sunrise' industries for the economic regeneration of peripheral regions.

In the 1980s, a consensus seemed to be emerging that development (or at least industrialisation) in the developing countries was based on the employment of women. Given the dramatic rise in women's employment in the Third World, Mies (1986) argued that a division between women in the First and Third Worlds also marked this new international division of labour. What had been produced in the West was now being produced in the 'rest', often by women. First World women were meanwhile being mobilised as *consumers*, consumers of all the goods being produced elsewhere. Mies also notes that the privatisation of what were once public welfare services further shifts the burden of reproductive, caring, work back onto women who are assumed to have 'free' time in which to carry it out. First World women were the consumers, Third World women the producers. But this is only an appearance: 'housewifization' embraced them all. As we saw, the apparent cheapness of Third World women's labour is based on the, often erroneous, assumption that they are not major earners, not supporting households:

> By universalising the housewife ideology . . . it is also possible to define all the work women do – whether in the formal or the informal sectors – as *supplementary work*, her income as *supplementary income* to that of the so-called main 'breadwinner', the husband. The economic logic of this *housewifization* is a tremendous reduction in labour costs. This is one of the reasons why international capital . . . is now interested in women.
>
> (Mies 1986: 118–19)

But by the 1990s, this consensus was breaking down. For a start, industrial employment in the EPZs was only ever a small part of women's total share of jobs. Even if home based or informal sector production is included, it only makes up 5–10 per cent of women's employment worldwide (Pearson 1998). The focus on world market factory employment neglects all the various other ways in which *most* women are employed: in agriculture, in homeworking, in the informal sector, and in the growing service and sex industries. In the same article, Ruth Pearson also discusses the arguments 'for' and 'against' identifying this employment as emancipating. She refers, in particular, to the argument advanced by Linda Lim (1990) that factory employment has a positive impact on women, or at least is a less worse employment opportunity than others available, and provides the conditions for the development of collective and political consciousness. We will be looking in more detail later at the kind of politics that is emerging in this context.

Second, as Mitter and others pointed out, manufacturing work in certain industries was not necessarily disappearing from the First World. It may, though, have been taking a different, smaller, form, and one that was only part of a global chain. The third factor that led to the breakdown of the consensus was the *decline* in women's industrial employment in certain Third World areas, notably the Mexican border with the USA, although it was increasing in some Asian countries (Pearson 1998). It seemed it was not possible to generalise, to identify a single trend worldwide, or a dominant employment experience for women.

In a later work, partly as a result of changes in employment patterns, Mies modifies her thesis to propound that there has been a global feminisation of labour (Mies et al. 1988). This means more than simply women's employment is increasing. The claim is also related to arguments in sociology and economics about Post-Fordism. In flexible production systems, it is argued, smaller interlinked units may be more productive. With shorter production runs, they can respond more quickly to changes in consumer demand, and they also need a more flexible labour force. This means both that the labour force must be 'flexible' in its skills, and that it can be taken on and laid off quickly. It is only employed when needed, and produces the goods only when they are needed. The conditions of such labour, with no permanent status and employed on short-term contracts, are often associated with women's labour *whether or not* women are employed. This is one important meaning of the 'feminisation' of the labour force. As Pearson explains, the 'global feminisation of labour' thesis argues that 'industrialisation depends on the conversion of all industrial employment to the (inferior) conditions endured by female labour' (Pearson 1998: 176).

Postcolonialism as critique

The term postcolonialism (sometimes hyphenated) also identifies a critique that is a product *of*, engagement *with*, and resistance *to* colonialism and postcolonialism as conditions. The term post-colonial is a label both for a critique and for those who engage in it. It came into vogue among Third World scholars in the mid-1980s, in First World universities, who were there as émigrés, students, political exiles and refugees. They grouped around an identity that was not about nationality, but subject position. It is participation in the discourse that defines postcolonialism as critique. Subsequently, they defined a field of study and discourse in which others could participate. Most commonly, it identifies a field of literary and historical studies, rather than sociological ones. It examines the knowledge produced by the experts at the 'centre' about their subjects at the 'periphery'. This knowing 'underpinned imperial dominance and became the mode by which they were increasingly persuaded to know themselves: that is, as subordinates to Europe' (Ashcroft et al. 1995: 1).

Postcolonial critique, therefore, often focuses both on literature produced by the (ex)colonising culture about other cultures, and literature produced by (ex)colonised people about their experiences. It may include both the colonial and post-independence periods. In particular, postcolonial critique aims to rewrite forms of knowledge authored by colonialism and its legacies, reversing Orientalist thought, for example, and giving a voice to subordinated Others. This rewriting is not, however, the rediscovery of buried and authentic voices and experiences, but the forging of new hybrid identities that *must* bear traces of their past and present encounters with globalisation. As Ankie Hoogvelt explains 'The goal [of postcolonial criticism] is to undo all partitioning strategies between centre and periphery as well as all other "binarisms" that are the legacy of colonial ways of thinking' (1997: 158).

A couple of the terms may need clarification: 'Orientalist thought' relates to one of the founding texts of postcolonial studies, Edward Said's *Orientalism* (1978). Said defines **Orientalism** as:

> a style of thought based upon . . . a distinction made between 'the Orient' and (most of the time) 'the Occident'. . . . Orientalism can be discussed and analyzed as the corporate institution for dealing with the Orient – dealing with it by making statements about it, authorizing views of it, describing it, by teaching it, settling it, ruling over it: in short, Orientalism as a Western style for dominating, restructuring and having authority over the Orient.
>
> (Said 1978: 2–3)

'Hybrid' identity refers to the mixing of aspects of both the colonised and colonisers' culture. These identities are neither completely identical with those of the coloniser, nor completely different, 'authentic' original ones. The term emphasises that all identities that emerge out of the (post)colonial encounter are hybrids: neither culture, of the colonised nor the coloniser, is monolithic, nor unchanged. For some instances of the influence of the colonies on European cultures, see Codell and Sachko Macleod (1998). Finally, 'binarism' refers to a way of thinking and categorising experience and things into an either/or form, as Hoogvelt says in point three above.

As predominantly a textual analysis, with affinities with other 'post' discourses and critiques, postcolonial critique has been accused of political paralysis (Gewertz and Errington 1991; Udayagiri 1995). It deals with the lives and experiences of non-generic others only as representations in texts, disconnected from the world 'we' (who perform the textual analysis) inhabit (Gewertz and Errington 1991). As Udayagiri argues, 'The disjunction between "their" lives and "our" lives created by textual analysis renders political projects impractical' (1995: 166). At best, post-colonialism as critique has to be conducted alongside an analysis of postcolonialism as a condition: 'I believe theoretical strategies that show the interconnectedness of lives in a world-system are needed before coalitions can be envisioned and attempted' (Udayagiri 1995: 167). Mridula Udayagiri also enjoins those seduced by post theorists' claims that they and their criticism alone can confront universalising tendencies in writings about the **Third World** to be more modest. What she calls 'on the ground' accounts from activists and policy oriented researchers, as well as political movements, already 'constitute a powerful strike against essentialist or colonialist understandings' (Udayagiri 1995: 176). Feminists working in the area of development studies have produced many of these accounts.

Postcolonialism and feminism

There are certain similarities between the position of women and (post)colonial subjects (some of whom are women). Both have been seen as 'other' to the Western, White male norm. Both have had to develop a language of their own in opposition to the language of the dominant group, to rename their experiences and rewrite their histories. We cannot, however, push the parallels too far: the modes of exploitation and oppression suffered are too dissimilar, and the parallel neglects how White western women were often also part of a ruling racial category.

Sara Mills (1998) explains that postcolonial feminism arose out of two critiques, of the gender blindness in much postcolonial theory, and also of certain universalising tendencies in Western feminism. But as well as critiques, Mills claims that 'post-colonial feminist theory has begun to be established as a form of analysis in its own right . . . [and] has developed both a position from which to speak, and set of issues to be addressed' (1998: 99). More particularly, Mills' article addresses two issues; the gendered nature of colonialism and its legacy – including its literature – and 'an interrogation of the nature of "woman" and "universal" statements about what women want' (1998: 99).

In relation to the Western literature and paintings of empire and colonialism, Rana Kabbani, in a feminist commentary on Said's *Orientalism*, argues that 'the Orient' was seen as a feminised space, beguiling and seductive:

> The Orient, then, is caught in a state of timelessness, crammed full of incidents remarkable for their curiosity and exoticism, hushed into silence by its own mysteries, incapable of self-expression, mute until the Western observer (who is of course a man) lends it his voice. It is the seraglio of the imagination disclosing itself, with its veiled women, its blind musicians, its black eunuchs and jealous princes; it is the impossible other, the bourgeois gentleman's secret foil.
>
> (Kabbani 1988: 73)

This sexual metaphor or set of images also lay at the basis of Western political domination:

> All Easterners were ultimately dependent in the colonial power balance, but women and young boys especially so. Thus they served as the colonial world's sex symbols . . . Since the Victorian imagination could not conceive of female eroticism divorced from female servitude . . . the spectacle of subject women (and boys) could not but be exciting. The Western male could possess the native woman by force of his domination over her native land . . . She was his colonial acquisition, but one that he pretended enjoyed his domination and would mourn his departure.
>
> (Kabbani 1988: 81)

In a similar study, Anne McClintock (1995) has explored some of the ways in which a more domesticated, but equally gendered, set of images and metaphors saturates Victorian representations of Empire in advertising. McClintock also analyses the ways commodity advertising in Britain spread ideas of 'scientific' racism, of the inherent evolutionary superiority of the 'White race', among classes that had no access to the academic form:

> Late Victorian advertising presented a vista of Africa conquered by domestic commodities. In the flickering magic lantern of imperial desires, teas, biscuits, tobaccos, Bovril, tins of cocoa and, above all, soaps beach themselves on far-flung shores, tramp through jungles, quell uprisings, restore order and write the inevitable legend of commercial progress across the colonial landscape.
>
> (McClintock 1995: 219)

In the conclusion however, McClintock draws back from the label of 'postcolonial' for her analysis:

> The uncertain global situation has spawned a widespread sense of historical abandonment, of which the apocalyptic, time-stopped prevalence of 'post' words is only one symptom. . . . Asking what single term might adequately replace 'postcolonialism', for example, begs the question of rethinking the global situation as a *multiplicity* of powers and histories that cannot be marshalled obediently under the flag of a single theoretical term, be it feminism, Marxism or postcolonialism. . . . Without a renewed will to intervene in the unacceptable, we face the prospect of being becalmed in the empty space in which our sole direction is found by gazing back spellbound at the epoch behind us, in a perpetual present marked only as 'post'.
>
> (McClintock 1995: 395–6)

With this warning in mind, let us, for now, examine further the ways postcolonial feminism has claimed to advance new analyses.

First, as a First World current, feminist postcolonialism has largely been concerned with historical analysis, with rereading and rewriting histories of Western women's ambiguous position in colonialism (Ware 1992), and in the case of the USA, slavery (Fox-Genovese 1988). This is a different exercise from a simple excavation of women's (neglected) role in imperial and colonial regimes, or of their participation in anti-colonial or anti-slavery movements. There is, though, valuable historical work being done about the even more neglected role of Black women in anti-slavery movements in the USA that challenges the idea that this was largely a White movement (Yee 1992).

White women were both part of the Western systems and its ruling class, but not full equals to men within it. To an extent some, such as the anti-slavery campaigners, placed themselves on the side of 'native' or Black women, but invariably saw themselves as defenders of women even more oppressed than themselves. They spoke and campaigned on behalf of 'native' women, rather than making a space for other women to speak and campaign on their own behalf (Midgley 1992).

This is a point forcefully argued by Chandra Talpade Mohanty in a much-quoted essay 'Under Western Eyes' in which she points out that Western feminists still often continue to speak 'for' and about Third World women (Mohanty 1988). They also often speak as if this was a homogeneous category, made up of poor, illiterate, backward and oppressed women, who need the enlightenment that only Western feminists can bring. Mohanty also criticises assumptions that Western feminists therefore know what is best for this Third World woman, can impose their agendas in precisely the ways that earlier generations of colonialists and current development planners claim to know what 'natives' need in order to become civilised.

This is indeed an important issue, and one that has haunted not only feminist writings, but also political campaigns. One such campaign has been that against female genital mutilation (FGM). This is a practice carried out in many African and Arab countries in which young girls and women have parts of their external genitalia removed in order, so it is said, to make them 'clean' and initiate them into womanhood. Many international organisations now condemn the practice as harmful, a form of violence and a violation of women's human rights. It is grounds, in some countries, for a woman to claim political asylum if she establishes that she (or a daughter) is at risk from it (although only a handful of cases have been successful). The issue was taken up by a number of Western feminists in the late 1970s and early 1980s but women in the countries where it is practised, in turn condemned some of the ways the practice was depicted and publicised in the West. It was not that these women condoned the practice: far from it. What they objected to was a reduction of 'other' women to the status of victims, of their oppression to their sexuality, an ignorance of the campaigns in which indigenous women were already involved and a belief that Western intervention was necessary to 'liberate' their 'sisters' (Davis 1985). All of these expressed an underlying racism which, as Davis says 'such a campaign evokes in countries where ethno-centric prejudice is so deep rooted' (Davis 1985: 326).

This example, and the following case study on veiled women, raises questions about the possibilities and problems for feminist organisation in a global framework.

The next chapter, therefore, will consider how this has proceeded. It brings together the critical feminist perspectives on globalisation and postcolonialism reviewed above, and places these in the context of feminist development studies.

Case study 7.1 Veiled women

There has been a long-standing western fascination with the image of the veiled 'Eastern' woman. On the one hand, she seems to represent the most oppressed of the oppressed, not allowed to move outside her home without covering herself, and punished if she fails to do so. On the other hand, she can be the epitome of 'Eastern promise', Salome slowly stripping off her seven veils, a princess from the Arabian Nights.

The veil (variously called the *hijab, chador* or *burqa*) and ranging from a headscarf to a totally body enveloping garment that just leaves a slit for the eyes, also has a politics: twentieth-century nationalist leaders, such as Ataturk in Turkey, Reza Shah Palavi in Iran and Nasser in Egypt, saw the *hijab* as a symbol of their country's 'backwardness' that they wanted to prohibit. In the later part of the century, there was a reaction against this, and a 'return' to the *hijab* in some countries, sometimes voluntary, sometimes enforced, as part of a rejection of westernisation. What is now called the *hijab* is not, however, a revival of traditional dress; it is a modern interpretation of Islamic dress (El Guindi 1999).

More recently, the strict enforcement of the *burqa* by the Taliban in Afghanistan came to stand for the extreme subordination of women there and also the repressive nature of the regime more generally, particularly in western eyes. Western media use of the image of the veiled Afghan woman might have been well intentioned, a way of raising consciousness or, in the case of human rights groups, money for campaigns, but it risks reinforcing dangerous stereotypes of all Muslim women as powerless victims of gun toting terrorists (Reif 2000).

Feminist anthropologist Lila Abou-Lughod has also warned against the strong appeal of 'saving' Afghan women that justifies American intervention and dampens criticism of this intervention: 'The problem, of course, with ideas of "saving" other women is that they depend on and reinforce a sense of superiority by westerners' (Abou-Lughod 2002). This does not, however, entail that common campaigns are impossible:

> We might still argue for justice for women, but consider that there might be different ideas about justice and that different women might want, or choose, different futures from what we envision as best. Among the most difficult things for American feminists to accept is that these futures might involve women in developing within a different

religious tradition, or traditions that don't have as their primary ideal something called 'freedom'.

(Abou-Lughod 2002)

In the way that there is no single way of veiling, there is no single meaning that it has for the women who wear it. It may, for example, in the case of minority Muslim women in the Philippines and Indonesia where believers are under attack, be a way of asserting their religious convictions and identity. It may, as in Palestine, be the assertion of an alternative religious and nationalist identity in the face of an aggressive Zionism; or – as in Saudi Arabia – be enforced by law.

There is also considerable debate and division among Muslim women about its significance. The Women's Action Forum (WAF) in Pakistan explicitly condemns all attempts to impose a dress code on women, arguing that it stigmatises women who are not veiled. The Revolutionary Association of the Women of Afghanistan (RAWA), while opposing the idea of a Muslim state and the imposition of dress codes, does not prioritise the 'unveiling' of women in its proposals for promoting women's rights, but rather education, health and issues of political participation. (See their web site at http://rawa.false.net/index.html.)

So far, veiling may appear to be inconsistent with visions of equality in general and feminism in particular. But a more recent trend challenges this assumption. By the 1990s, the term 'Islamic feminism' began to be used, first in Iran then in other countries, including by women who wore the *hijab*. It is defined as 'a feminist discourse and practice articulated within an Islamic paradigm' (Badran 2002). The exponents of Islamic feminism insist that the Qur'an actually authorises their struggle for equal rights for women, and they often engage in reinterpretations of key passages to campaign for legal reforms and changes. Their view is that women's advancement is quite compatible with the principles of Islam. Margot Badran, who identifies herself as an Islamic feminist, argues that it is now a global phenomenon, found in Islamic countries such as Iran, in countries where there is a Muslim minority such as Malaysia, in western countries such as the USA including among convert communities, and also in cyberspace. It is a feminism that transcends binaries, she insists, between East/West and religious/secular feminisms since it 'closes gaps and demonstrates common concerns and goals, starting with the basic affirmation of gender equality and social justice' (Badran 2002). Others suggest that this feminism is another, different one from western feminism, one that may be aware of western feminism but has developed in a very different social and religious context and may have a different conception of women and their rights (Moghadam n.d.). Fadwa El Guindi argues that a voluntary return to the *hijab* can even be interpreted as a kind of liberation, 'from imposed, imported identities, consumerist behaviors, and an increasingly materialist culture' (El Guindi 1999: 71).

Contrary to this, others claim that 'Islamic feminism' is an oxymoron, a contradiction in terms (Mojab 2001). Mojab, for example, insists that a separation between religion and politics is essential for the full realisation of women's rights, a separation that would entail dismantling, not simply reforming, Islamic states such as Iran. She also disputes Badran's suggestion that Islamic feminism affirms equality and social justice, arguing that it 'is not even ambitious enough to demand universal formal legal equality' (Mojab 2001: 139), but only openings for women too to become *ayatollahs*. Finally, Mojab points out that a relativist vision of Islamic feminism fits well with some current 'post' feminisms, that denies the universality of terms such as 'women' and 'rights' and which makes political organisation on a global basis problematic. This is a point also endorsed by Eid (2002) who, while recognising some validity in postcolonial feminist recognition of women's agency in their choice to wear *hijab*, also reminds us of the enormous social pressures, associated with the rise of fundamentalism, to adopt this dress. 'Post' feminists neglect such structural factors at their peril.

In conclusion, westerners must be ever aware that leaping to judgement about the veil can actually compromise non-western women's campaigns against the imposition of *hijab*, since they risk accusations of endorsing westernisation and betraying their culture. Feminists, western and non-western, have to deal with both 'the religious nationalist manoeuvre of equating veil wearing with pre-colonial cultural authenticity on the one hand, and feminist criticisms of the *hijab* with a Western-rooted form of neo-colonialism on the other' (Eid 2002: 48).

Summary

- Systems of colonialism and imperialism had very different consequences for men and for women, both in the colonies and at 'home'. They also played different parts in the relations of ruling and of subordination, and male and female colonial subjects were incorporated into them in different ways. Ethnicity and nationality played significant parts in the relations of ruling, as well as gender.

- The emerging international division of labour between countries was also a gendered division of labour that assigned different places to men and women. Western ideologies of appropriate roles and behaviour were often imposed on subject people, through missionary and educational activities, that often claimed to 'civilise' them.
- Postcolonial studies draw attention to persisting unequal relations between countries even when colonialism has ended. These relations also consist of the production of knowledge about those countries. This knowledge also reproduces gender stereotypes that serve Western fantasies.
- In the postwar world, a new gendered international division of labour has been established that incorporates men's and women's labour in different ways. This points to the significant feminisation of the labour force on a world scale. But this does not mean that women play the same role across the world, or even within a country.
- Third World feminists draw attention to certain tendencies
  in Western feminism either to assume a universal sisterhood (that ignores the different structural locations of women) or to assume that Third World women are all the same – victims of an extreme patriarchal oppression – in contrast to their enlightened sisters.
- In addition to criticising Western feminism in these terms, postcolonial feminism also criticises postcolonial studies' blindness to gender issues.

Further reading

Hoogvelt, A. (1997) *Globalisation and the Postcolonial World: The New Political Economy of Development*. London: Macmillan.

Kabbani, R. (1988) *Europe's Myths of Orient*. London: Pandora.

Loomba, A. (ed.) (1998) *Colonialism/Postcolonialism*. New York: Routledge.

McClintock, A. (1995) *Imperial Leather: Race, Gender and Sexuality in the Colonial Contest*. London: Routledge.

Chapter 8

Globalising feminisms

Chapter outline

Many social scientists suggest that the developments reviewed in the previous chapter as forms of postcolonialism are manifestations of the phenomenon they call 'globalisation'. Many see it primarily as an economic phenomenon, involving the increasing integration of national economies into the world market. New technologies make this integration possible so that distances across spaces become less significant barriers. The virtual collapse of the 'Second World' since the late 1980s that offered an alternative model of economic development has further hastened the process. Globalisation is undoubtedly a capitalist phenomenon, though it is not *only* a capitalist phenomenon.

The main focus of the chapter is on:

- Globalisation, and links with the previous analysis of postcolonialism.
- How globalisation, like colonialism and postcolonialism, is a process that has different implications for men and for women, across and within countries.
- Feminist coalition building. For feminists and other activists, globalisation has also meant intensified political activity across national boundaries. This has led to an interest in versions of international or **transnational** feminism, and of **transversal** politics.

'Globalisation' in social sciences

Economics and sociology are probably the two social science disciplines that have had the most to say about globalisation, what it is, whether it is a good or bad thing, and even whether it exists. Within economics, the term refers to the claim that there is (or is emerging) a global economy, not simply in the sense of international links between countries, but a global economy in which separate national economies and policies are increasingly irrelevant. Instead, national economies are subordinated to transnational corporations – or global capital – that owe no allegiance to any particular nation state, but locate and invest wherever the global market offers the best prospect for profit accumulation. In sociology, though there is reference to the emergence of a global economy, there is greater interest in political and cultural processes, which economists tend to skip over. Anthony Giddens has done as much as any sociologist to bring the term into popular use, not least with his Reith lectures in 1999. For Giddens, globalisation:

> is not primarily economic in and of itself. Globalisation refers to a set of changes, not a single dimensional change. Many of these changes are social, cultural and political, rather than purely economic, and one of the main drivers in addition to the global marketplace is something partly separable from it, which is the communications revolution.
>
> (Giddens 1999: 5)

Leslie Sklair (2002), on the other hand, sees globalisation as another phase of capitalist development.

'Globalisation' is also a significant term politically. Many people will be aware of it in relation to the various 'anti-globalisation' protests around the world that have accused it of intensifying global inequalities both between and within countries. I put the term 'anti-globalisation' in inverted commas since many of the demonstrators prefer to highlight the *constructive* aspects of their movement, as does the 'Globalise Resistance' movement.

But the globalisation thesis is not without critics. Paul Hirst and Grahame Thomson, for example, claim there are three main problems with the 'strong' globalisation thesis:

- There is no consensus on a model of the global economy.
- So there is nothing to measure trends against.

- There is a lack of historical depth and a tendency to portray current events as if they were unique and without precedent.

They do agree that there *are* trends to the internationalisation in financial markets, and in some manufacturing and service sectors, but they fall far short of a 'strong' globalisation thesis (Hirst and Thomson 1998).

Avtar Brah (2002) suggests it is also useful to distinguish between 'discourses of globalisation' (such as those above) and globalisation as a process. As Adam (2002) points out, the former:

> is a predominantly male discourse. Whether the emphasis is on economic and political processes, social relations, the role of technology or environmental impacts, gender is rarely the focus of attention. Yet it is clear that globalization impacts differently on men and women as workers, consumers, service providers, re/producers and loan/aid recipients . . . Only in the field of work has the gender blindness been largely transcended.
>
> (Adam 2002: 4)

Feminists have been concerned to remedy this gender blindness, and we will be examining some of their arguments in a later section of the chapter.

Globalisation and postcolonialism: condition and critique

Within sociology, one of the most developed accounts of globalisation that makes explicit links with postcolonialism as a condition is Ankie Hoogvelt's study *Globalisation and the Postcolonial World* (1997). Hoogvelt makes several claims about postcolonialism as a condition:

- Globalisation (by which she means flexible systems of production, the predominance of high tech industries, and the globalisation of markets and forms of regulation) has made it impossible for less developed countries (LDCs) ever to complete their own modernisation projects. Countries cannot seal themselves off from global capital.
- This means the 'end of the Third World' in two senses: after the end of the 'Second World', only the capitalist

course of development is open, and second, the 'Third World' no longer exists as a single category, with a single identity. Different countries have experienced change in different ways, and responded to them in different ways.

- The world is no longer structured along binary oppositions – First/Third Worlds, North/South, socialist/ capitalist, colonisers/colonised, West/the rest.
- The term postcolonialism tries to specify a movement going beyond not only colonialism but also neo-colonialism, in the sense of economic domination by a country after formal political independence.

Building on the second point, Hoogvelt goes on to argue that several different patterns or responses have emerged, which she calls postcolonial formations. She identifies four main types:

- The management of exclusion, typical of sub-Saharan African formations. This region is characterised by the debt crisis, and structural adjustment policies (SAPs) that have contributed to political anarchy and civil war. These crises have drawn in the international aid community, but to contain change and manage the symptoms, rather than remove the cause of conflict.
- The anti-developmentalism of militant Islam. Here, a failure of development, combined with Islamic renewal, in opposition to Western political, economic and cultural imperialism, produces a denial of globalisation and modernity. The radical Islam of the post-independence years mobilises the outcasts of a failed modernisation around the myth of a return to Islamic authenticity.
- The developmental states, especially of South and East Asia. These show the potential of regional alliances to cope with Western domination, though Hoogvelt is not optimistic about the long-term prospects of this strategy.
- Postdevelopmentalist strategy of liberation, found in parts of Latin America. Postdevelopment is different from anti-development, insofar as it does not reject globalisation or modernity, but tries to find some way of living with and/or transcending it.

Hoogvelt's model has both merits and flaws. It offers a broad, yet diverse, picture of the effects of and responses to globalisation that has a clear material base. As she explains, the diversity of formations depends on particular colonial and postcolonial regimes and experiences, and on religious and social factors. But the particulars of her account may be in need of qualification. Many Muslim women, for example, feel that Islamic revival is quite compatible with a feminism that is *not* against modernisation, only its Western variant.

Further, although Hoogvelt acknowledges feminist contributions to the field of development studies, and their focus on women's varying role in colonial and postcolonial formations, her own study is gender blind.

Globalisation and feminist development studies

Feminist approaches to globalisation take much of their inspiration from feminist development studies. Two perspectives on development, Women in Development (WID) and Women and Development (WAD) were mentioned in the previous chapter. Feminist approaches to development issues have continued to change since the 1970s, and feminist understandings of 'development' have also changed considerably, to become far more critical. 'Green' ideas have also influenced this more critical approach.

Typically, development of a country is measured by economic indicators, by the extent of industrialisation, by levels of growth in the economy, and its balance of trade. This tells us little about its development in a human sense, or how sustainable its development is. To measure development in this wider sense we may want to know not only how a country's wealth is distributed between people, but also whether it invests in arms or in education. Since the 1990s, the annual United Nations Development Programme's (UNDP) annual reports on how we are, or are not, developing has included not only these more social measures of development, but also broken them down by sex, in order to measure women's progress within and between countries.

Apart from WID and WAD, there is a third approach, GAD (gender and development) that focuses on gender relations *and* other forms of inequality such as class. It is also often associated with a grass roots, or 'bottom up', approach to development, that insists on women's (and some men's) role as agents of change rather than as passive beneficiaries of policies devised by outside experts.

The change from 'women' to 'gender', both as labels for feminist approaches and, increasingly, for particular development strategies and projects, is a controversial one. By those who prefer to highlight women's role, the preference for using 'gender' signals a marginalisation of feminism, and its accommodation and depoliticisation by funding agencies:

> The discourse of gender and development may once have been a radical and transformatory agenda for feminists, but the way it has been taken on by mainstream funding agencies and governments . . . pushes the radical politics of feminism to the margins.
>
> (Porter and Verghese 1999: 130)

On the other hand, GAD's proponents claim that 'gender' draws attention to and problematises relations between men and women, and the structures that continue to reproduce male domination:

> The use of gender as a category of analysis also shifts the focus away from the earlier one on women. A focus solely on women tended to imply that the problem – and hence the solution – could be confined to women. A focus on social relations extends the analysis . . . to the broader interconnecting relationships through which women are positioned as a subordinate group.
>
> (Kabeer 1994: 65)

The controversy over terms was especially evident at the UN Fourth World Conference on Women in Beijing in 1995. As Sally Baden and Anne Marie Goetz explain, the Conference 'reflected the extent to which gender issues have entered the "mainstream", at least at the level of rhetoric' (1997: 4). Indeed, 'mainstreaming' has itself become a buzzword in development discourse; it 'signifies a push towards systematic procedures and mechanisms within organisations . . . for explicitly taking account of gender issues at all stages. . . . It also represents a call for the diffusion of responsibility for gender issues beyond small and underfunded women's units' (Baden and Goetz 1997: 5).

Both the gender talk and mainstreaming were, however, criticised especially by women from the South. Mainstreaming was attacked as a scheme for professionalising and buying off once committed activists, while many women argued that the focus on gender was both premature and had allowed discussion to shift from women, to women and men, and finally back to men (Baden and Goetz 1997). As one development worker, quoted by Naila Kabeer, remarked, 'Do you think we are ready for gender in development in Bangladesh when we have not yet addressed the problems of women in development?' (Kabeer 1994: xii).

'The globalised woman'

This section takes its title from Christa Wichterich's book (2000) of the same name, a comprehensive and powerful review of globalisation, its effects on women, and woman's resistances to globalisation (Wichterich 2000). Before considering her arguments, some clarifications are necessary.

First we should note that some feminists find the term 'globalisation' unhelpful. Marianne Marchand and Sisson Runyan (2000), for example, prefer 'global restructuring' since the former term often contains so many assumptions about its inevitability and is associated with a pro free-market ideology. By global restructuring, they understand 'a set of multi-dimensional, multispeed and disjuncted processes. . . . it allows us to analyse how the market, state and civil society are embedded in and (re)constructed through these processes' (Marchand and Runyan 2000: 7). They also insist that developing a gender analysis means more than adding on or inserting 'gender' – for which we can often read 'women' – into already existing analyses.

It is now possible to identify some of the main features of the impact of globalisation (or global restructuring) which demonstrates that men and women are not caught up in it in the same way. It also demonstrates that not all women (or men) within sectors or countries are affected in the same way. We also need to take account of class and ethnic/'racial' differences between and across societies, and those societies' location in the different postcolonial formations. The effects of globalisation on women in Kenya are quite different from those affecting women in Bangladesh, in Brazil, in Taiwan or in the USA, and women in each of these countries are also affected differently. There are, however, some parallel trends: rising rates of employment, rising rates of migration, both forced and 'free', and rising rates of inequality, both within and between countries. Combined, these appear to have contradictory effects on women, making their lives and work at once more similar, and also sharpening differences between

them. We can examine these effects by a focus on migration, in
some of its various forms.

Employment and migration

We have already examined some aspects of the 'feminisation' of
the labour force, but it is worth emphasising that the increase in
women's employment is often in insecure, low-paid jobs wherever
they are located. A report from Income Data Services in 1999
pointed out that although the expansion of the knowledge industries, and of higher education, has created many well-paid jobs for
women in the professions in Britain, the fastest growth in new jobs
has been in the low-paid service sector. This accounts, the report
says, for the persisting gender pay gap between women and men
(Denny 1999).

Labour intensive production has commonly drawn in women
(and children) in the early stages of industrialisation, and this is
true whether we look at Britain in the early nineteenth century or
Mexico in the 1960s. In Bangladesh, 90 per cent of the 1.5 million
new jobs that have come there in the last twenty years, mainly in
textiles in Dhaka, have gone to women. Wichterich also points out
that there is a race to the bottom in wage costs, so that yesterday's
winners are today's losers. The average woman factory worker in
South Korea earned $60 a month in 1980, the same as her counter-
parts today in Vietnam, which is half that of women factory workers
in China (Wichterich 2000: 3). Little wonder that China increased
its exports by more than 25 per cent in 1997.

However, the picture changes if we look at capital intensive
production: in this sector men predominate, but their working
conditions and rights are also changing, to become more 'flexible',
less secure, more like the conditions that women experience.

This 'feminisation' of the global labour force is also associated
with increased rates of migration, within and between countries.
Sociological studies of labour migration have usually focused on
male migration, and men's employment in the less skilled sectors,
even when the migrants do possess skills and qualifications.
More recently, sociologists have been noting more complex and
diversified forms of migration, especially to what are called 'global
cities' (Sassen 1991). Migrants now include professionals and skilled
workers, and if men predominate in the financial and information
sectors, women make up a significant proportion of the middle
range health and welfare professional services (Kofman 2000a).

The UNDP Human Development Report for 2001 estimates that this 'brain drain' costs developing countries billions of dollars. India alone loses $2 billion dollars a year from the migration of professionals, primarily in the computing industries (UNDP 2002). Employment and the move to a city or EPZ is sometimes presented as the path to emancipation for women, a chance to escape the restrictions of village life, to have money in their hands for the first time, and even to develop a class and political consciousness. There is, indeed, evidence that wage earning does increase women's status; daughters are no longer seen as economic burdens but financial assets who can send money back to their families and contribute to their own dowries (Kabeer 2000). But often, one form of patriarchal control is replaced by or even added to another, capitalist exploitation. The jobs these women do are also highly precarious and short-lived, though intensive while they last, which makes worker organisation hard. It is not impossible though new forms of organisation may be needed (Rowbotham and Mitter 1994; Rowbotham and Linkogle 2001). Redundancies may be the cost of attempts to demand a better (or even the legal minimum) wage, and finally the threat that a company will simply pull out of that country or zone entirely is often enough to discourage worker organisation. Capital, as well as labour, migrates.

Migration and care work

The usual route for labour is migration from a poorer to a better-off region or country, and while much is legal, much is illegal. Many countries attempt to restrict labour migration by 'non-nationals', though exceptions are made for workers in essential services or for professionals. Their rights, once in a country, are often further restricted, tied to a particular job or employer. This migration is also increasingly feminised. In 1996, over half of those who legally migrated to the USA were women (Hochschild 2001). Many are now migrating not as dependants of male migrants but in their own right.

Some forms of official labour migration favour men, such as work in the construction and oil industries but 'the fastest growing form of work for immigrant women, as well as the principle means of legal employment, is domestic labour' (Kofman 2000a: 134). Many of these women have qualifications, especially in nursing and teaching, but find they can earn far more in Toronto, Hong Kong or Berlin than they can teaching or nursing in Manila. For these, migration is a form of de-skilling, although their remittances can be a major source of foreign earnings for their 'home' countries (Kofman 2000a).

Indeed, the gap between foreign and domestic wages can be so extreme that a woman who cares for the children of a family in Los Angeles can afford to employ *another* nanny for her own children in Manila (Hochschild 2001). These relations establish what Arlie Russell Hochschild calls 'global care chains', largely between women who, overwhelmingly, continue to be the ones responsible for the day-to-day care of others whether they are 'service providers' or 'service recipients'. Hochschild also points out that these care chains are racialised, and care work is passed down the 'race'/class/nation hierarchy, as each woman in turn takes up, then passes on this work.

Investigating these links offers a way of understanding the uneven impact of globalisation on women. The privatisation of care and increasing levels of female professional employment in the developed countries are the major reasons for this growing international demand for domestic labour. And the poverty and insecurity of the less developed countries provides the supply:

> Having access to a variety of jobs, and even a variety of national economies, can become an insurance policy against the very instabilities globalisation creates. . . . the more globalisation, the more insecurity, and the more people try to insure against insecurity by migrating.
>
> (Hochschild 2001: 133)

It is not, though, the very poorest who choose to migrate: they cannot afford it. Similarly, it is not *under*development that causes migration, but uneven development (Harvey 2000). As countries are increasingly incorporated into the global economy, insecurity at home leads people to look for alternative survival strategies away from home.

But, 'where are the men in this picture?' (Hochschild 2001: 138). For the most part, men, especially men at the top of the class/nation hierarchy, leave care work to women, whether their wives provide it or buy it in. Their jobs are often 'greedy' jobs, demanding of time and energy so that, however much they may regret it, men simply do not have time, or dare to take time, to care physically for their loved ones. Others, such as the husbands of the Filipina nannies in Los Angeles, are often away as well, timing their work contracts in the Gulf States to fit in with their wives' periodic returns home.

'From the critical modernist perspective [that Hochschild recommends] globalisation may be increasing inequities not simply in access to money, important as that is, but in access to care' (Hochschild 2001: 142). Much of the problem arises, Hochschild argues, from the low value attached to care work:

> The declining value of childcare anywhere in the world can be compared to the declining value of basic food crops, relative to manufactured goods on the international market . . . Just as the market price of primary produce keeps the Third World low in the community of nations, so the low market value of care keeps the status of women who do it – and by association, all women – low.
>
> (Hochschild 2001: 144)

In such a situation, a distinction between forced and free migration breaks down. But there are two other forms that women's migration takes that is more obviously, or at least legally, recognised as 'forced': sex **trafficking**, and migration due to armed conflict.

Sex trafficking and prostitution

Sex trafficking first came to public attention in the later part of the nineteenth century, when it was known as 'the White slave trade'. Such a label reflects certain racial imaginings, of European girls lured, by the promise of jobs or by the wiles of 'dark' men, to the brothels of foreign countries. Argentina, in particular, was thought to be the destination of many of the girls. While many of the girls working in the brothels were of European origin, one study argues that few ended up there because of trickery by procurers:

> Marginalised by the industrial revolution, driven out of their homelands by hunger . . . they saw emigration to a new land or even a new continent as the key to survival. Cheap steamship fares and imbalanced sex ratios in rapidly growing port cities made it easier and more attractive for them to emigrate . . . Fears of White slavery in Buenos Aires were directly linked to European disapproval of female migration. Racism, nationalism, and religious bigotry fuelled anxieties.
>
> (Guy 1995: 7)

When procurers could be identified, the considerable numbers of European Jews among them inflamed anti-Jewish sentiments, although Jewish groups were among the first to identify and try to control trafficking. Donna Guy argues that Jewish men and women became involved in prostitution rings following pogroms in Germany, Austria, Russia and Poland, which broke down normal family structures and plunged them into economic desperation (Guy 1995).

Similar conditions lie behind many of the current accounts of sex trafficking, though the scale and the numbers of countries involved has increased. Some experts speak now of an international trade in women's bodies, drawing parallels between this market and those for domestic workers, mail-order brides and sweatshop workers (Coomeraswamy 1997). Two relatively new factors, however, appear to be implicated in the expansion in sex trafficking: armed conflict and its aftermath, and tourism. In addition, ironically perhaps, demand for prostitutes escalates when UN peace missions and aid workers arrive in a country (Wichterich 2000: 61).

Racialisation, and its fantasies, still operates as well. If 'White' women are highly valued in the 'East' (the Thai embassy in Moscow receives nearly 1000 visa applications a day from Ukrainian women (Wichterich 2000: 62), then 'dark, exotic beauties' are prized in Amsterdam.

Thailand is one of the major centres of sex tourism where, since the 1980s, NGOs have been working to highlight issues of trafficking, to establish support groups, and to change laws (Jeffrey 2002). More recently, however, women's groups have found that 'Thai women were not simply victims of evil traffickers and foreigners but that there was a certain amount of agency involved in becoming/ remaining a prostitute' (Jeffrey 2002: 10). Even though most of the money that women earn goes to pimps, middle men and officials who have to be paid off, 'prostitution can provide a better income than factory or domestic work' (Jeffrey 2002: 11). The women are often dutiful daughters who have not abandoned or been abandoned by their families, but send money back to them in the countryside. Leslie Jeffrey also argues that a focus on their victimisation detracts attention from the 'poor economic conditions in the countryside which are the result of government policies emphasising production for export' (Jeffrey 2002: 11).

Significantly, for many of these sex workers, stopping this trade is not their preferred option – even if it were possible. What many of these women want are simply better working conditions for the 'choices' they have been forced to make. This is not to say that abduction, deception, force, the sale of women, and the use of children should not be criminalised, but that campaigns and legislation should take account of the fact that for many women, 'prostitution is the choice made by those who have no choice' (Wichterich 2000: 63).

Anti-trafficking groups have been divided over the issues. Some, such as the Coalition Against Trafficking in Women (CATW), says it works to combat sexual exploitation in all its forms, which does not only mean sex trafficking but all prostitution, pornography and mail-order brides. Others such as the Global Alliance Against Traffic in Women, a Thai-based international NGO formed in 1994 distinguishes between prostitution as a legitimate form of work for women and the forced prostitution resulting from deceit and violence. They are particularly concerned to see that anti-trafficking conventions are not used to criminalise the women: 'This includes both moving away from those formulations that rationalise the social control and criminalisation of migrant women, and fostering the development of a human rights, immigrant workers' and workers' rights approach to combating abusive and exploitative travel, living and working conditions' (www.inet.co.th/org/gaatw/). They have supported, for example, the formation of a prostitute's union in Cambodia, and women's savings groups in Vietnam.

Migration and conflict

Migration is often seen primarily as an economic phenomenon, the outcome of people's choices, to seek a better standard of living elsewhere. Political factors too generate migration, from government resettlement programmes, to slavery, trafficking, conflicts and human rights violations.

In theory, international refugees have the most protection in international law, under the UN Convention on refugees and stateless persons, enacted in 1954. A refugee is defined as someone who:

> owing to a well-founded fear of being persecuted for reasons of race, religion, nationality, membership of a particular social group, or political opinion, is outside the country of his nationality, and is unable to or, owing to such fear, is unwilling to avail himself of the protection of that country.
>
> (The 1951 Convention relating to the Status of Refugees)

In practice, different countries interpret their obligation towards refugees in varying ways, and recognise (or not) their rights to refuge in another country. Some European countries, for example, do not recognise people who are fleeing war or persecution by militias, as refugees. Internally displaced people, whatever the reason for their flight, are also not covered, although in practice the United Nations High Commission for Refugees sometimes lends them assistance.

It was, however, a Convention drawn up with a male norm in mind. The Convention, drafted by an all-male panel, 'did not deliberately omit persecution based on gender – it was not even considered' (Wilkinson 2002). After years of intensive lobbying by NGOs, the situation began to change in the 1980s with the inclusion of various forms of gender and sexuality related persecution. Women now may have rights to asylum on the basis of gender-related persecution, including restrictive social codes and the threat of rape in wartime. Homosexuals too may be considered as refugees if, in their countries of origin, they face serious discrimination or attack because of their sexual orientation. Again, in practice, asylum applicants may face an uphill struggle to have their cases recognised, as those reviewing their cases may have little understanding of the particular persecution they have faced.

Since the Convention was drafted, the numbers and proportions of refugees who are fleeing conflict have increased, as has the proportion of civilians who are casualties of wars. According to UNHCR, they now make up 90 per cent of all war casualties, and 80 per cent of the small arm casualties are women and children. Around half of the 21.8 million refugees for whom the UNHCR provides assistance are women and girls. More than 300,000 young people, many of them female refugees, are currently serving as child soldiers and the girls are often forced into various forms of sexual slavery. Since 1998, the International Criminal Court has recognised these and similar gender related offences as war crimes, and in 2001 the first conviction for rape was handed down for three Bosnian Serb officers (Wilkinson 2002).

For many refugees, flight does not end their vulnerability: the elderly, women and children are particularly at risk of further violence during their flight, in refugee camps, from officials, locals and other refugees. Increasingly, as civilians become targets of sectarian conflicts, rape is a common element in the pattern of persecution that drives people from their homes.

Case study 8.1 The lost children of the Sudan

In the late 1980s, thousands of children were driven from their homes in the Sudan by fighting between rebels and government troops. Many became separated from their families and wandered through the East African savannah for years. Some eventually reached refugee camps in Kenya, where they remained for yet more years. In 2000, the USA agreed to settle around 4,000 boys whose parents had died or could not be traced. Any with HIV infections were, however, turned down for resettlement. Once in the USA, they became instant media celebrities, interviewed about their ordeals and their reactions to seeing snow and television sets for the first time in their lives.

But 'forgotten in all this hoopla about Sudan's Lost Boys were the fates of several thousand girls aged between 8–10 who had undergone similar ordeals' (Nyabera 2002: 8). Many had been absorbed into foster homes near the camps or back in the Sudan, and so disappeared from official attention. Aid workers assumed that the girls would be safe and well cared for in their new families.

But as the girls grew up, they did come to the attention of adult men. Emmanuel Nyabera recounts the stories of two girls. Achol Kuol (not her real name), now 17, has already survived one attempt to kidnap her into a forced marriage back in Sudan. The dowry of 50 cattle, which her 'suitor' offered her foster parents, represents a huge sum locally, and she fears it is only a matter of time before they accept. Another 'Lost Girl', Yar Jok (also a pseudonym), now has a baby daughter, Monday-riak, meaning 'war' in her Dinka language:

> One night a man entered her hut and raped her. Initially she kept the assault secret, worried that 'if people got to know I was raped, no man would want to marry me' . . . She was rejected by both her foster parents and the refugee community, but eventually moved in with a woman from her mother's clan.
>
> (Nyabera 2002: 9)

Consequently, few girls now qualify for resettlement, for which they need to be single, healthy, unaccompanied minors. Kofi Mable, head of the refugee agency in the main camp in Kenya feared there is nothing that can now be done for the girls: 'We have lost them . . . they are completely lost. They have lost that status of lost girls' (Matheson 2002).

Post-conflict situations

More recently, women's groups, NGOs and UNHCR have been emphasising women's role in peace building. Women, just as much as men, have been affected by conflicts, although often in different ways. They may have been particularly targeted for gender related violence and may, in consequence, have been abandoned by their family. Still in their 'teens, they may have become providers and physical protectors of other family members. Their educational and health needs may have been neglected in refugee camps, where they may still be subject to violence, intimidation and sexual assault. Pregnancy and sexually transmitted disease rates may also rise among refugee women.

In February 2002, UNHCR and Save the Children published a report detailing the sexual exploitation of children by both local and international aid workers in camps in West Africa. The victims were mostly girls aged 13–18, and the most vulnerable were orphans and children separated from their parents. Reportedly, workers demanded sexual favours in exchange for food, and the refugees felt unable to report them since they were dependent on them for food and services. The inadequacy of food rations, and local prohibitions on refugees finding employment, exacerbated their situation (www.alicubi.com/news/irin_21.html).

Women may also have special needs after the end of conflict when they return home, due to a combination of the gender based impact of conflict and of existing laws and practices. Around 70 per cent of the population in post-conflict Rwanda are female, and around a third of them are widows (Byrne et al. 1995). Women did and still do not have independent access to land but only through their husbands. Many returned home to find that their husbands' relatives had claimed 'his' land, leaving widows with no homes or means of survival. Widows' support and advocacy groups are springing up around Rwanda, but for reconstruction to succeed, not only must the desperate situation of these women be addressed, but also women's and widows' rights to land more generally. But women are not helpless victims: one UNHCR report points out that although aid programmes may meet their basic needs for shelter and food, they may operate at a cost of the 'empowerment' projects that could provide them with better skills that they may need when they return home or are resettled (Hunt 2002).

Empowerment also consists of offering women leadership and advocacy skills they could utilise both in peace negotiations and reconstruction work. Swanee Hunt identifies several reasons why women are crucial to peace building, though their official inclusion is still rare. Official negotiators rarely want women on their teams because they are afraid they will compromise: 'Isn't that the point? For lasting stability, we need peace promoters, not just warriors, at the negotiating table' (Hunt 2002: 10).

A final point to make in this section is that although it may be possible to identify winners and losers globally, there are 'losers' within 'winning' countries, and 'winners' within 'losing' countries. Arguably, globalisation has increased national and international disparities. The UNDP annual human development reports provide one of the most reliable measures of development in and between countries on the basis of factors such as average income, life expectancy and literacy.

In 2001, Norway ranked first in the composite measures, with Australia second. The USA dropped from third to sixth place, losing out to countries such as Japan and Spain on educational enrolment and life expectancy. All the bottom 28 countries are in Africa, with Sierra Leone last. Although the human development indicators (HDIs) have been rising for most countries in recent years, there is a group of countries in Africa, Eastern Europe and the former Soviet Union where the HDI is falling. The report also notes that income disparities between regions are increasing: although income levels have been rising in East and South Asia, the rate of increase in the developed countries is far outstripping them. Within countries, disparities remain and even increase between urban and rural areas in relation to indicators such as income, and access to clean water. The effect of health and education policies can also affect a country's place in the rankings: Pakistan and Vietnam have similar average incomes, but Vietnam has translated this more effectively into human development.

While development economists have largely been concerned about income inequalities *between* countries, inequalities *within* countries matter too. These appear to have been increasing in every developed country since the early 1970s. Only in Denmark have they been declining.

Since 1995, the reports also measure gender disparities and demonstrate that in every country in the world the Gender-related Development Index is lower than the HDI. Though most countries are improving, in 27 countries girls' enrolment in secondary education, for example, has been dropping since 1987. Again, they are mainly in the former Soviet Union and Africa, and also some

Arab States. (All data taken from UNDP Human Development Report for 2001: www.undp.org/hdr2001/.)

Globalising politics

We have seen that globalisation affects men and women differently, but apart from changing employment patterns this has received relatively little attention in the mainstream globalisation debates.

Globalisation has also affected national politics as well as national economies, and Marianne Marchand and Sisson Runyan (2000) argue that the role of the state has changed considerably. Typically, the state's room for developing national policies, not only economic but also welfare policies, is held to have declined as globalisation increases. There is also a gendering of these processes. Global restructuring, they argue, has operated:

> to privilege particular agents and sectors over others, such as finance capital over manufacturing, the market over the state, the global over the local, and consumers over citizens. In each of these cases, the latter is constructed as 'feminized' in relation to the former.
>
> (Marchand and Runyan 2000: 13)

They emphasise that 'the state' is not, however, a monolithic bloc: in the process of restructuring, parts of it, such as ministries of finance, through their relation to the global economy are becoming 'internationalised' and thus invested with 'masculine' authority. By contrast, ministries of education, welfare and health (which is often where the few women who are in government are to be found) are becoming increasingly at a disadvantage, simply responsive to forces and policies outside their control:

> As the public arena itself is being redefined and subordinated to private capital, women are even further distanced from power even as they become workers and elected officials because the nature of work is being degraded and the powers of the legislature are being diminished. The locus of power is shifting from the public world of politics to the privatizing, and thus, depoliticizing, world of economics.
>
> (Marchand and Runyan 2000: 15)

However, the picture is not all gloomy: 'the latter is, in turn, repoliticized by labor, environmental and women's activists (among others) who are increasingly demanding more accountability and transparency from firms and international institutions' (Marchand and Runyan 2000: 15).

As other critics, such as Klein (2000) and Wichterich (2000), emphasise, consumers are also repoliticising the economic sphere, by campaigns and boycotts that are forcing TNCs to respect environmental, child and minimum wage laws in countries where they operate, subcontract or buy their goods. Much of the information exchange and campaigning for these boycotts is transmitted via the web (an upside to the globalisation of new technologies?), at sites such as No Logo (www.nologo.org/), Corpwatch (www.corpwatch.org/) and Urban 75 that updates a weekly list of 'corporate villains'. Currently (September 2003), Number 1 is Esso who, they explain, made record profits in 2000 but spent not a cent on renewable energy (www.urban75.com/Action/boycott.html).

Feminist politics and globalisation

As Wichterich (2000) explains, feminist organisations have overwhelmingly seen globalisation as a threat to women the world over. It is a process that has been 'generating growth without jobs in the North, structural adjustment in the South, privatization in the East, and spending cuts everywhere' (Wichterich 2000: 158).

She goes on to identify a number of women's political responses to globalisation that have been both positive and critical. On the positive side, globalisation is seen to offer women new opportunities in employment, and for communication through new technologies – at least, for those with access to them. For those more critical of globalisation, new means of organising to reshape its agenda and to build up countervailing forces have to be sought.

Two of the strategies Wichterich identifies are:

- transformation through participation;
- use of human rights legislation.

Transformation through participation has become integrated into alternative development models and places empowerment at the centre of transformation, in markets, the state and civil society. Various instruments, such as quotas, have been used to effect such a transformation at every level from the local to the global:

As an aid to empowerment in institutions at every level, women's movements demand a quota system of positive discrimination. These were supposed to ensure that . . . women formed a 'critical mass' of at least a third. For there is simply no way individual campaigners can set structural changes in motion, and it is extraordinarily difficult for them to avoid being coopted and instrumentalized.

(Wichterich 2000: 159)

Although quotas are controversial, they have been instrumental for women in breaking through barriers to political representation in countries such as South Africa and India. Activists have been helped by the passage in 1979 of the UN Convention on the Elimination of All Forms of Discrimination Against Women (CEDAW). This allows the 174 states that have ratified it to enact temporary legislation, such as quotas, that is aimed at counteracting previous discrimination, both direct and indirect. Signatories range from Afghanistan in 1980, though it has never reported on its programme, to Zimbabwe in 1991, which has also never submitted a report. In 2003, the most recent new signatories were Sao Tome and Principe, and Timor.

Other feminists have put the emphasis on participation, from the most local to the global level. For years, feminists have been 'watching' and commenting on institutions such as the World Bank, but more recently have also been lobbying for their voices and their organisations to be heard *in* them. Many feminists now work as consultants to them, but continue to operate with grass roots organisations 'outside'. As Wichterich comments, 'Only through such a functioning alliance can women's movements become a force to shape and change society' (2000: 162).

A second response Wichterich identifies is women's use of universal human rights principles that are enshrined in the various UN charters and conventions. Feminists have also been instrumental in shifting the interpretation of rights from individual ones to social, economic and political ones. This raises issues about social structures and practices that deprive women (and men) of their rights or their capacities to exercise their rights. One example of this is the priority that UNIFEM now gives to strengthening women's economic capacity. Although this may not seem like a 'rights' issue, 'strengthening women's business associations and coalitions, UNIFEM is helping them to advocate for their economic rights and for trade and other economic policies that benefit them' (www.unifem.undp.org/ec_pov.htm). This relates, therefore, to another of UNIFEM's priorities, 'Engendering Governance and Leadership'.

Women's groups have both used existing charters and also lobbied to extend their interpretation and application. The Cairo conference on population and development in 1994, for example, recognised that women's reproductive rights were an integral part of human rights, and also shifted the focus from meeting demographic targets to meeting women's needs.

The emphasis that has been placed on eliminating violence against women has also been phrased in terms of a violation of their human rights. Violence is understood to include 'private' violence, and also certain 'traditional' practices such as female genital mutilation, that states where they are practised have been called on to eliminate. Another recent focus has been on the effects of violent conflict on women, with special missions to Sierra Leone and Colombia that address the widespread violence committed against women and to ensure that post-conflict programmes safeguard women's rights.

Case study 8.2 Women's rights and HIV/AIDS

The issue of HIV/AIDS also exemplifies another way in which human rights principles can be applied. As a recent report argues, 'women are not increasingly represented among the vulnerable, the affected and the infected simply because they are women, but because of the discrimination and inequality that distorts and impairs virtually every aspect of their lives' (Waldorf 2001: 2). By 2000, an estimated 9 million adult women had died compared with 8.5 million adult men and 4.3 million children (Waldorf 2001: 2). As Lee Waldorf points out, the AIDS pandemic is not only a matter of women's rights to health, but it has spread to such devastating effect because of the denial of women's rights in many areas.

> Women face greater danger of HIV infection for biological reasons, but also socially. Cultural norms of sexual ignorance and purity for women block their access to prevention information. Gendered power imbalances make it difficult for women to negotiate safer sexual practices with their partners, and economic dependence and the fear of violence can effectively force women to consent to unprotected sex.
> (Waldorf 2001: 2)

A gender perspective also helps to explain why certain groups of women are especially vulnerable, both to exposure to HIV and are also less able to access appropriate health services. Two of the groups that the report identifies are sex workers, and refugee and internally displaced women.

Many sex workers are in highly coerced situations, especially if they are minors or have been trafficked for prostitution. They have little power to insist on safer sex practices, and risk forcible detention, testing and deportation in countries where prostitution is criminalised.

It is widely recognised that armed conflicts threaten civilians more than ever before. Modern wars have also revealed that women and girls are often targeted for rape and other forms of sexual violence, and are at risk whether they are at home or in camps for displaced people. Around 80 per cent of displaced people are women and children (www.unifem.undp.org/gov_paxissues.html), and unable to access the normal health and support services.

Sometimes these universal declarations clash with national and religious practices, which has led to considerable argument over whether human rights are universal or culturally specific. In sociology too, the concept of rights is controversial. There is the Marxist critique of the liberal concept of rights that, although claiming to be universal, actually enshrines and promotes a bourgeois and individualist conception of them. The 'right' to own property, for example, is completely meaningless to the mass of the non-propertied proletariat who only have the 'right' to sell their labour. As Engels argued in *The Anti-Duhring* (1878), a universal set of human rights would only make sense in a classless society that would involve the abolition of established bourgeois rights such as the right of heirs to inherit property. From this point of view, although capitalist societies might appear to guarantee individual rights – economic, political and legal – they did so to abstract individuals in a way that neglects the actual differences in wealth, property and privilege between people.

Postmodernists too are sceptical of the concept of universal human rights, as they are about any universalising concept or claim. Certainly, many feminists too take a similar line, pointing out that definitions of rights have been centred on notions of a male person, masquerading as human under the facade of the 'rights of *man*'. This indeed was the line of criticism advanced by Mary

Wollstonecraft in her *Vindication of the Rights of Woman*, a reply to Tom Paine's *The Rights of Man*. But this, at least, was not identical to the postmodernists' criticisms; Mary Wollstonecraft was arguing for women's inclusion in these rights, not for the deconstruction of 'rights'.

Closely associated with a postmodern scepticism about universal rights, is a cultural relativism, a claim that each culture, its knowledges and its truths are specific and cannot be generalised. There are no core values, each culture, each identity within a society, has its own world view, and each is as valid as every other. While this may once have been an important tool for anthropologists to argue that 'we' are in no position to judge 'other' cultures as primitive, barbaric, superstitious and backward, it now constitutes a very thorny problem for international organisations such as the UN and the International Criminal Court.

Stan Cohen (2001) provides one of the most powerful sociological attacks on postmodern cultural relativism. His *States of Denial* is a study of 'knowing about atrocities and suffering', as the subtitle suggests, knowing about them at one level, but denying them at another. Denial can be individual and/or social, it can be practised by individuals or by nation states, it can be about the woman next door being abused (because it's a private matter), or about the genocide in Rwanda (it's a thousand miles away; Tutsis are cockroaches).

Cohen is particularly interested in the various tribunals and commissions that have investigated atrocities on a social scale, such as the South African Truth and Reconciliation Commission in 1997. In his study of cultures of denial, denial of atrocities and suffering, he argues that cultural relativism (we are different, this is our tradition) provides a vocabulary of motives or alibis for the denial of atrocities or human rights violations by governments: 'Avant-garde theories of cultural specificity are explicitly co-opted. The powerful go on doing what they have always done . . . Their denials now look respectable, even intellectually dignified' (Cohen 2001: 285–6). Although Cohen concedes that postmodern theories are interesting:

> It's just that as a citizen of South Africa, Ethiopia, Cambodia or Zaire, I would prefer not to have a deconstructionist appointed to be chairperson of our Truth and Justice Commission. The resulting text would be interesting, but not in my interests.
>
> (Cohen 2001: 286–7)

Wichterich concludes that women's use of a rights-based framework has proved very effective: 'Women's understandings of themselves as subjects of rights [has] altered the ways in which political action was conceived: that is, not mainly as calls for help as victims, but as ringing demands for the respect of human rights' (2000: 163).

Global feminisms

International arenas have provided a very effective opportunity for feminist organising. International conventions have also offered women a lever to lobby national governments. This is not to say, though, that feminist politics are easy, still less that there is a global 'sisterhood' that encompasses all women. Although the multitude of women's groups that meet at the various UN and international conferences often find common cause and much to learn from one another's problems and practices, the idea of a 'global feminism' that unites them has also been criticised (Briskin 2002). It implies a single, unitary (and usually Western) model and movement for emancipation that 'assumes alliances among women rather than pro-actively building links cognisant of differences' (Briskin 2002: 85).

Women both do and do not share experiences, they are all affected by globalisation but have different places within various postcolonial formations. Major differences and gaps remain between more and less 'developed' countries, and between women within and across these countries that seriously affect their life chances, from birth to death. The term 'transnational feminism' is sometimes used to name a feminism arising in the context of globalisation and influenced both by postcolonial studies and by developments in feminist politics. The preference for 'transnational' rather than 'international' works to question and destabilise boundaries of national identity. Those who adopt the term insist that transnational feminism does not represent a new, cleaned up international feminism, for no feminism can ever be free of unequal power relations. The term also draws attention to one factor that has connected women and men, over generations: colonialism. De-colonisation is thus a central motif in transnational feminism, including de-colonisation of our minds.

The politics that works across differences is sometimes called transversal politics. It aims not to ignore or suppress differences, but to work through them, looking for what can unite women, at least here and now, on this issue, rather than looking for a one size fits all feminism.

Another feature relates to connections between local and global levels, of analysis and of politics. The anti-violence campaigns discussed previously are a good example. Women's struggles against violence emerged first as small community based movements and were then able to link up with others, through national and eventually 'transnational' networks and also to frame the question as one of universal human rights.

But if transnational feminism is a product of globalisation, then the same inequalities that globalisation reproduces and even intensifies will also be present in the feminism it engenders. Sonia Alvarez, for example, has pointed to what she calls the 'NGO-ization' of social movements (Alvarez 1999), the creation of a group of professional experts. Although networks are formed across North–South lines, they coalesce around those groups who possess resources and skills that enable them to attend international conferences, access new technologies, and participate in what may be a 'virtual' feminist community. Gaps can open up between the global (professional, experts) and the local (volunteers), though not all the professionals are Northern feminists, nor the local activists Southern feminists.

Not all the activists would call themselves 'feminist' either, or they would prefer to talk of 'feminisms'. An essay by Ien Ang (2001) summarises some of these dilemmas, and the problems of building alliances across differences: 'To me, non-White, non-Western women . . . can only begin to speak with a hesitating "I'm a feminist, but . . .", in which the meaning and substance of feminism itself become problematized' (Ang 2001: 394). She questions feminists' attempts to cope with the problem of 'difference' by formulating a politics of inclusion, 'born of a liberal pluralism which can only be entertained by those who have the *power* to include' (Ang 2001: 407). Instead, she recommends a politics of partiality, that: 'accepts the principle that feminism can never be an encompassing political home for all women . . . because for many groups of "other" women other interests, other identifications are sometimes more important and politically pressing' (Ang 2001: 408).

Sedef Arat-Koc (2002) reinforces Ang's point and points out that there is a special urgency in rethinking feminism after 11 September 2001:

Recently, Third World countries are being left with very few choices in the new world order being defined. Ultimatums such as 'you're either with us or you are the enemy' means that Third World countries can either embrace 'their difference' of not just exotic, but dangerous 'other' to Western civilization; or, they can remain passive and silent partners to the 'self' defined by one world power. Neither of the options is acceptable to Third World peoples who have any commitment to self-determination, democracy and equality. Neither of the options promise to provide a fertile environment to define and practice 'women's rights' as acceptable to Third World women.

(Arat-Koc 2002: 63)

Instead, she argues that feminism has to move beyond:

what is typically conceived as feminism, namely a concern and activism with women ... [to include] civil liberties, human rights, 'terrorism', imperialism, internationalism and national sovereignty ... If critical thinking about these issues is ignored, we face the possibilities of remaining complacent, or at least indifferent or acquiescent to changes towards a totalitarian world (and national) order being created not just in front of our eyes, but also (partly) in our name.

(Arat-Koc 2002: 63)

This chapter has, I hope, demonstrated that feminism is facing up to this challenge.

Summary

- Global changes in forms of production and in the international division of labour have had diverse impacts on the lives of women and men. They have led to changes in the location of production, and in the composition of the labour force.
- Increased employment opportunities for young women in developing societies have not, however, all been beneficial. The jobs women fill resemble the roles expected of women, often also 'racially' and ethnically different women. Increasingly, the conditions under which men are employed are coming to resemble those that women have traditionally experienced.

- These changes have also led to increasing levels of migration – both forced and free – in which women play a major part, although this 'gendering' of migration has not been fully recognised by policy and law makers. Although nation states are lowering barriers to the movement of goods in international trade, they are raising the barriers to the movement of people.
- Feminists working in the field of development studies are transforming our understandings of 'development' and advocating grass roots, participatory projects.
- Increasingly, feminists and others are organising across borders. Various networks of activists and analysts are combining efforts to lobby organisations and governments, with some success. Transversal politics does not imply there is a universal sisterhood, but that it is possible to organise effectively across differences, and to respect those differences.

Further reading

Eschle, C. (2001) *Global Democracy, Social Movements, and Feminism.* Oxford: Westview Press.

Grewal, I. and Kaplan, C. (eds) (1994) *Scattered Hegemonies: Postmodernity and Transnational Feminist Practices.* Minneapolis: University of Minnesota Press.

Mohanty, C.T. (2003) *Feminism Without Borders: Decolonising Theory, Practising Solidarity.* North Carolina: Duke University Press.

Rowbotham, S. and Linkogle, S. (2001) *Women Resist Globalization: Mobilizing for Livelihoods and Rights.* London: Zed Books.

Rowbotham, S. and Mitter, S. (eds) (1994) *Dignity and Daily Bread: New Forms of Economic Organising Among Poor Women in the Third World and the First.* London: Zed Books.

Glossary

The terms defined and discussed here include both sociological and feminist ones. The explanations concentrate on the way the terms have been used in this book. The term is printed in bold the first time it is used in the book.

binary: made up of two parts. The term signifies labelling things as only one of a two category system into which everything must fit; night *or* day (no 'evening'). Our sex and gender systems are often described as binary systems, in spite of evidence that many people are born as intersexed people (once called hermaphrodites), displaying features of both sexes. This last phrasing, 'both', demonstrates just how hard it is to rid ourselves of binary thinking (there really are just two sexes though some people may fail to fall clearly into one or the other). Another way of thinking would be to recognise three (or more) sexes from the start, though relatively few will fall into the third. Other cultures also recognise more than two genders.

Black: originally a pejorative term used by slavers and traders by which to describe the varied peoples of Africa, to distinguish them *en masse* from 'White' Europeans (also an invented and homogenising category). More recently, 'Black' has been reclaimed not as a 'racial' label but as a positive political identity. Who counts as 'Black' is variable and sometimes contentious. Where do 'Asians' stand? A focus on 'Black/White' racism can, misleadingly, contribute to a lack of attention to forms of racism that are not based on skin colour, such as anti-Semitism.

capitalism: an economic system depending on the private ownership of the means of production. Capitalist systems need have only two classes: the bourgeoisie who own the means of production, and the proletariat who have to sell their labour. In practice, they have other classes, such as a peasantry. Sociology could be said to originate with Marx and Weber's accounts of the development of capitalism in Europe. Capitalist production has undergone various changes since then, to become a global phenomenon.

class: a group of people who have the same economic and social standing. In sociology 'class' is most often defined in terms of occupation and income. Sociologists distinguish between subjective and objective class positions. The former refers to one's consciousness, the likelihood that one will identify oneself or society more generally in class terms. The second refers to class structures in which we are all placed, *whether we recognise it or not.*

colonial and colonialism: the process whereby nations establish their political and economic rule over less powerful nations in order to exploit their natural and human resources.

construction: generally meaning 'to build' or 'to make', in sociology it refers to a fundamental claim that many of our concepts and categories are social constructions. The perspective offers sociologists a tool with which to criticise **essentialist** or naturalistic explanations, not only of our gender and sexuality systems but also terms such as 'crime', 'intelligence' and 'disability'. Sociologists also find it useful to analyse how certain issues may come to be constructed as 'problems' (for example, 'failing boys'), what kind of problems they are, for whom, and the role that the media might play in their construction. (See also **deconstruction**.)

deconstruction: often described as a postmodern method of analysis that unpacks concepts and ideas to reveal how they have been made up, and the unexamined or suppressed assumptions in them. We could deconstruct the idea of 'Mr Right' by examining his features – tall, dark, handsome, solvent, sober – by contrasting him with 'Mr Wrong' and his features, and by examining suppressed assumptions such as 'why marry?' or 'why not *Miss* Right?' Originally applied to literary texts, deconstruction can also be used to unpack how meanings are created in many systems of thought – including sociology. As such, it is the exercise of a basic and self-critical sociological imagination. (See also **construction**.)

development: a process of growth and improvement. Economic development is no longer the main criterion for assessing this, and feminist and other critics have further argued that economic growth is an impediment to development in the sense of improving social and ecological justice. Development in the conventional sense is presented as something that can be achieved by all, rather than seen dialectically. From this point of view, the status of 'developed' society can only be achieved at the cost of exploiting others, turning them into *under*developed societies. Hence: 'underdeveloped' = 'overexploited'.

difference: the term has acquired a variety of more or less technical meanings within feminism and sociology. Most commonly in sociology, the term signifies: (a) the construction of difference (not only between men and women but also between women), and (b) the significance of that difference. Certain differences are made to be more socially significant than others, and may only acquire their significance by contrasting them with their 'opposite'. The term 'feminist' in some popular discourses has been given a certain meaning by contrasting it with 'ordinary women' who, it is assumed, have no interest in feminism. 'Difference' does not simply imply a multitude of various unmarked variations, but a hierarchy of differences where some are taken as the norm against which others are judged. The politics of difference, also called identity politics, refers to movements who use their different identities as the basis for social and political action. (See also **Other**.)

discourse: sets of related ideas and concepts that are taken as well-founded knowledge, elaborated by experts, and often found in material practices. Discourses about sexuality, for example, have been produced by religion and the church(es), medicine and doctors, and the law and lawyers to name a few. Discourses do not only 'say' things, they also 'do' things, treat us as sinners, as sick, or as criminals, hence the link between knowledge and power. However, subjects of a discourse, homosexuals and lesbians, may challenge it and 'do' different things with it – proclaim they are 'glad to be gay'. This is a 'reverse discourse'. Also in sociology, 'dominant discourse' refers to taken-for-granted ways of thinking that invariably represents the logic of the dominant group. One of the tasks of sociology and of feminism is to uncover this and to include the perspective of the **Other**.

division of labour: the specialisation of work tasks or occupations. All societies have some division of labour based on gender and age, and often class and 'race'. Tasks become **gendered** both in and outwith households, in ways that vary between societies but in a patterned and non-random way. The domestic division of labour refers to the allocation of household tasks between men and women, adults and children.

essentialism, essentialist: a type of explanation that claims to identify the fixed and unchanging essence of a thing or person. References to 'human nature' or instinct are essentialist when they insist that these innate features adequately explain *social* behaviour. In the past, women's roles were often explained by reference to their nature, or biology and so not capable of change. Essentialism can be an **ideology**. Feminism challenges this, claiming that it is patriarchy rather then nature that explains women's roles. Some feminisms have been accused of essentialist tendencies when they attribute universal characteristics to women as a group, such as being peace loving. Such thinking also often takes a **binary** form (men are warmongers).

ethnicity, ethnic: membership of a group sharing a common cultural **identity**, distinguishing them from other groups around them. The identity may rest on linguistic, religious and/or historical markers. Although it may seem a more acceptable term than 'race', the term can also be used in a way that signifies **essentialist** imaginings, of irreconcilable and fixed divisions between groups, who 'naturally' only want to mix with their own ethnic group. Ethnic mobilisation can also be used in extremely dangerous ways to create hatred and persecution between groups, and to cleanse a country or region of ethnic '**others**'. Ethnicity is most usefully seen as a dynamic and constructed category, one that is made and re-made.

ethnocentrism: the tendency to judge other cultures by the standards of one's own culture. The belief that the values, practices, and general social set-up of one's own native culture are superior to all others. Such a view tends to justify exploitation by more militant societies.

feminisms: it is more accurate to think of a variety of feminisms, rather than attempt a definition of feminism (singular), since there is no single agreed upon definition. The plural term also captures the multiplicity of visions that have inspired (some) women and (some) men. Nevertheless, I have some sympathy with the comment of the journalist and novelist Rebecca West who is reputed to have said 'People call me "feminist" whenever I express sentiments that differentiate me from a doormat'.

gender: the division of people into (usually) two **binary** groups, either 'masculine' or 'feminine'. Common sense supposes that this naturally follows from the biological division into two sexes, male or female. Sociologists have found it necessary not only to differentiate between biological '**sex**' and 'social' gender, but also to point out that there is no necessary link between the two. The features that different societies imagine are 'masculine' and 'feminine' vary considerably, and have also changed over time in any one society. A century ago, I would have been considered masculine if I wore trousers and worked in a university. This example also shows that things (clothes, places) as well as people can have gender attributes, can be **gendered**.

gendered: a process of attributing masculine or feminine characteristics to a person, place, institution or thing – animals included. Dogs are boys and cats are girls, as many toy manufacturers know, in spite of Tom and his Jerry.

genocide: the systematic, planned annihilation of an ethnic, 'racial' or political group. Since 1998 when the International Criminal Tribunal for Rwanda handed down the first conviction for genocide that included rape, rape in war may be considered an act of genocide when women are specifically assaulted as members of a targeted **ethnic** group.

global city: a type of city, such as London, New York and Tokyo, that is significantly oriented to international rather than national business and trade.

globalisation: the development of extensive worldwide patterns of integrated economic and political relationships that supersede nation states. Also, the tendency for these relations to be organised along capitalist lines. The global arena provides an increasingly important ground for **transnational** feminist politics.

hybrid, hybridity: a recognition that our identities are not simple, but composed of a changing mix of features that may often seem contradictory, as 'Black' and 'British' once were.

identity: the label we choose for ourselves, or are given by others. We do not have just one, nor does it remain the same. Many sociologists emphasise the possibilities of choosing or making our identity (which can produce a **postmodern** anxiety) rather than inheriting it from an ascribed position as a member of a class, or family or gender. This may fit our experiences to some extent, and even be a political project (to reclaim, to redefine, to **deconstruct** what it means to be a woman, or Black, or gay, once these are all seen as **constructions**). Feminists have often found it empowering to name their identities, especially when they have been constructed as **Other**. But there are dangers when a politics is based on identity, seen as a hard and fast thing that *divides*.

ideology: shared ideas or beliefs that serve to justify and support the interests of a particular group, although an ideology may be passed off as a truth. Marx argued that the ruling class was able to dominate the **production** of ideas as well as the production of goods. Feminists have added that there are patriarchal as well as bourgeois ideologies that legitimise male domination.

international division of labour: a division of labour between countries in relation to production and trade. The 'old' division was between producers of basic raw commodities, and manufacturers and consumers of finished goods. Feminists point out that both the old and new divisions are gendered; they assign different roles to men and to women, and have different implications for men and women. Gender is not the only differentiation, though; the international divisions of labour are also racialised.

mainstreaming: bringing into the mainstream. It is used to refer to a strategy within feminist approaches to the development of incorporating a gender analysis into all policies. It represents a move beyond establishing separate women's projects as additions to the normal business of development that remains unchanged. But see also **malestream**.

malestream: analysis, practice and thought judged by men to constitute the mainstream.

Marxism/Marxist: contemporary social theory deriving its main elements from Marx's ideas. This perspective strongly emphasises conflict, class struggle and material causation.

materialism/materialist: the claim that 'material conditions' (usually economic and technological factors) have the central role in determining social change.

modernism, modernist, modernity: everything that seems new at the time someone is experiencing or describing it. More specifically, a movement in the arts evident between the second half of the nineteenth and first half of the twentieth centuries. The discipline of sociology begins as an analysis of modernity, an analysis of how it differed from what had gone before. 'Modernity' largely coincides with the development of **capitalism**, but is preferred as a term by some sociologists since it seems less oriented to a central focus on production.

oppression: discrimination against people, on an individual or collective basis, through action and/or negative stereotyping. Only those who have institutional power are able to discriminate against groups on a systematic basis.

Orientalism, Orientalist: originally the study of Oriental culture, and a style of art depicting Oriental scenes. In sociology it refers to Edward Said's (1978) thesis that Orientalism is a **discourse** produced by Europeans about a place and a people with characteristics quite different from those supposed to characterise 'the West'. Feminist critics have added that these and other **colonial** discourses are also **gendered**.

'Other', othering: the term 'other' was first associated with French existentialist thought, and taken up by Simone de Beauvoir in *The Second Sex* (1963). She used it to refer to the way women as a category were defined as men's 'other', always different from the (male) norm. More recently, those categorised as 'other' on the basis of their sexuality, 'race', ethnicity, as well as gender, argue that their difference should be celebrated as a way they can empower themselves. (See also **difference**.)

patriarchy: originally meaning 'rule of the father' over women and younger males in a household, it has come to mean male domination more generally. Although the term has proved very useful for feminists examining male domination as a system of power and privilege that extends beyond the household, it has proved difficult to give it a clear and agreed definition. Many feminists now prefer to use the adjective 'patriarchal', to describe relations, practices and institutions that may reproduce male domination *as well as* other forms of oppression.

postcolonial: literally 'after colonialism' it can signify both a critique and a condition. A critique of cultures, especially literatures, produced by and about (ex)colonies that foregrounds the experience of colonisation. As a condition it refers to the various social and economic formations that post-date formal independence. It has also been an important influence as a critique of Western feminism.

postfeminism: originally, this refers to a claim either that feminism has 'won' and is therefore redundant, or has even gone 'too far'. A postfeminist might either be a woman who was sure of her rights and her equality with men and so did not need to be strident and aggressive, or she might be a woman worn down with trying to 'have it all', with no lover, and an empty womb. Some academics have tried to reclaim the term to mark their difference from the perspectives and aims of Second Wave Feminism, and register their cognisance of the various post positions.

postmodernism, postmodernist: originally a style within the arts that rejected modernism. More generally, a movement within the social sciences and humanities that claims we have moved beyond modernity, but not arrived at another type of society that deserves a new name. In its most radical version, it offers a critique of some of modernity's promises, for progress, for enlightenment, and the rule of reason, that have not been met or have even lead to disastrous political consequences. If you feel that you cannot trust anything – God, the government, the media, science, your tutors – if life (and art) appear to have no meaning, if you can't tell the difference between virtual and real realities or wonder if the former are actually all there is, then you are suffering from the postmodern condition. The term also refers to a type of analysis that questions previous certainties about science, truth, history – 'big' theories and 'big' claims ('grand narratives' or 'meta-narratives'). There is some dispute whether feminism is one of those grand narratives that postmodernists should reject, or whether it is on the side of postmodernism, as part of an attack on another grand narrative – about 'man'.

production: the making of goods for use, for exchange, for sale. Marxists identify various modes of production, including a capitalist mode. In different societies particular property relations and divisions of labour organise tools and people into a distinctive mode of production.

'race': sometimes taken to be a real genetically based category of people who share the same physical characteristics, scientists and sociologists insist that it is a socially constructed category. Its development in the West has been closely associated with the justification of unequal treatment, even murder, of those imagined to be racially inferior. Because of this association, and to emphasise that it is not a real category but a **construction**, many sociologists prefer to put it in inverted commas. **Racism**, however, is real.

racism/racist: most commonly defined as prejudice against people imagined to be of a different 'racial' group; someone who holds such beliefs. More recently, the term has been expanded to include 'institutional racism'. This has proved important in recognising that racism can pervade whole institutions, such as the police, but on the other it can lead to making the individuals and practices that enact it invisible, reducing racism to an effect of the unintended 'culture' of an institution. It is important, however, to recognise that certain practices and laws can have racist consequences regardless of the beliefs of individuals who exercise them. The UK's laws on immigration are racist whether or not immigration officials hold racist beliefs. The most committed White antiracists are still in a position of structural advantage.

reproduction: in sociology, this has little connection with reproduction in the biological sense. Engels originally used the term to signify the social organisation of family/household/kinship relationships. The mode of reproduction ensures, crucially, the reproduction of labour on a day-to-day and generational basis. It is also part of the way in which women's oppression is reproduced. But using the same term in a biological and in a social sense has been confusing, and has contributed to an **essentialist** assumption that women's oppression is explained by their role in biological reproduction. 'Reproduction' has also been used, following the French Marxist Louis Althusser, to signify the reproduction of relations, especially relations of production. Class relations can be said to be reproduced when institutions operate to perpetuate the existing class structure and patterns of relative advantage and disadvantage. He analysed the role of institutions such as the church, schools and the media in this. Feminists added that oppressive gender relations were also being reproduced in these institutions.

sex: the biological categories of females and males based on reproductive (in a biological sense) characteristics of males and females. (See also **binary**.)

sexuality: often supposed to derive directly from our **sex**, sexuality refers to a number of features including behaviour, orientation, fantasy and identity. These need not all point the same way. In a massive survey of American males in the 1940s, researcher Alfred Kinsey discovered that 37 per cent reported having had at least one same-sex experience to the point of orgasm (behaviour) while far fewer would label themselves as 'homosexual' (identity). Our ideas about sexuality are typically **binary**, labelling us as homosexual *or* heterosexual with some awkwardness relating to a both/and category of bisexuality. Kinsey, on the other hand, advised us to think of a seven point continuum between exclusively homosexual and exclusively heterosexual.

Third World: the term 'Third World' came into use in the 1950s as a label for those newly independent states who were seeking to find their own path of development outwith the models offered by the First (capitalist) and Second (socialist) worlds. The term is used less now, as differences *within* these blocs have grown, and the Second World has virtually disappeared. Other terms now used include Newly Industrialising Countries (NICs), and North and South. North and South stem from the Brandt Report of 1980 on international development, and its terminology was a deliberate attempt to circumvent older notions of a world divided along political lines. Made up of former leaders from both the developing and the developed world, the Commission argued that the stark economic disparities between North and South would lead to chronic instability in *both* worlds. Nevertheless, First and Third remain convenient shorthand labels, and 'Third World' in particular reminds us that these countries have been at the forefront of formulating a critique of an unequal world.

trafficking: illegal transportation across national borders. Originally used to refer to the trafficking of drugs and arms, since 2000 the UN Protocol to Prevent, Suppress and Punish Trafficking in Persons defines it is as the transport of persons for the purpose of exploitation through force, coercion and deception. Although much attention is focused on sex trafficking, it can also include other forms of labour trafficking, and trafficking for human organs. The Protocol was the result of years of feminist lobbying, although other feminists and some sex workers fear it will be used to criminalise and deport women without tackling those who exploit them.

transnational: a term that attempts to destabilise conventional boundaries of the 'nation'. While 'international' signifies links between and across distinct nations, 'transnational' feminism or practices involves not only alliances between and across national boundaries but deliberately attempts to break these boundaries down. Capital and business corporations were probably the pioneers of transnational practices.

transversal: a democratic practice of talking and organising across **difference**. The term represents a way of trying to practise feminism without imposing a single agenda or analysis (usually that of a dominant group), or giving up and retreating into differences that are seen as unbridgeable.

White: not only the inverse of **Black**. 'White' too is a constructed but relatively unmarked racial, or political, category since it is often simply seen as the norm, at least in the West. Both White supremacists and sociologists have ensured it cannot remain unexamined. In the way that there has been some argument about who qualifies as Black, historians have demonstrated that not all Europeans have always qualified *as* white. 'White' women have often been constructed as guardians of 'racial' purity and relations between them and 'non-White men' were seen as far more polluting of racial purity than those between White men and 'non-White' women. Further, their mythical purity has only been made possible in contrast to the mythical hyper-sexuality of Black women.

Bibliography

Abbot, S. and Love, B. (1972) *Sappho Was a Right-On Woman: A Liberated View of Feminism*. New York: Stein and Day.

Abbott, P. and Wallace, C. (1997) *An Introduction to Sociology: Feminist Perspectives*. London: Routledge.

Abou-Lughod, L. (2002) 'Interview with Lila Abou-Lughod'. *Asia Source*, August.

Abrar, S. (1996) 'Feminist Intervention and Local Domestic Violence Policy', in J. Lovenduski and P. Norris (eds) *Women In Politics*. Oxford: Oxford University Press.

Adam, B. (2002) 'The Gendered Time Politics of Globalisation'. *Feminist Review*, 70: 3–29.

Adkins, L. (1995) *Gendered Work: Sexuality, Family and the Labour Market*. Buckingham: Open University Press.

Agarwal, B. (1992) 'The Gender and Environment Debate: Lessons from India'. *Feminist Studies*, 18 (1).

Alvarez, S. (1999) 'Advocating Feminism: The Latin American Feminist NGO "boom"'. *International Journal of Feminist Politics*, 1: 2.

Amos, V. and Parmar, P. (1984) 'Challenging Imperial Feminism'. *Feminist Review*, (17): 3–20.

Ang, I. (2001) 'I'm a Feminist but . . .', in K. Bhavnani (ed.) *Feminism and 'Race'*. Oxford: Oxford University Press.

Arat-Koc, S. (1992) 'Immigration Policies, Migrant Domestic Workers and the Definition of Citizenship in Canada', in V. Satzewich (ed.) *Deconstructing a Nation: Immigration, Multiculturalism and Racism in '90s Canada*. Nova Scotia: Fernwood Publishing. pp. 229–42.

Arat-Koc, S. (2002) 'Imperial Wars or Benevolent Interventions? Reflections on "Global feminism" Post September 11'. *Atlantis*, 26(2): 53–65.

Arneil, B. (1999) *Politics and Feminism*. Oxford: Blackwell.

Ashcroft, B., Griffiths, G. and Tiffin, H. (eds) (1995) *The Post-Colonial Studies Reader.* London: Routledge.

Aslanbegui, N., Pressman, S. and Summerfield, P. (eds) (1994) *Women in the Age of Economic Transformation.* London: Routledge.

Assiter, A. (1996) *Enlightened Women: Modernist Feminism in a Postmodern Age.* London: Routledge.

Baden, S. and Goetz, A. (1997) 'Who Needs (Sex) When you can Have (Gender)?'. *Feminist Review,* 56: 3–18.

Badran, M. (2002) 'Islamic Feminism: What's in a Name?'. *Al-Ahram Weekly Online,* 569.

Bairoch, P. (1981) 'The Main Trends in Economic Disparities Since the Industrial Revolution', in P. Bairoch and M. Levy-Loboyer (eds) *Disparities in Economic Development Since the Industrial Revolution.* London: Macmillan.

Bairoch, P. (1982) 'International Industrialisation Levels from 1750–1980'. *Journal of European Economic History,* 11.

Balibar, E. (1994) *Masses, Classes, Ideas: Studies on Politics and Philosophy Before and After Marx.* London: Routledge.

Barrett, M. (1980) *Women's Oppression Today.* London: Verso.

Barrett, M. (1982) 'Feminism and the Definition of Cultural Politics', in R. Brunt and C. Rowan (eds) *Feminism Culture and Politics.* London: Lawrence and Wishart.

Barrett, M. (1992) 'Words and Things: Materialism and Method in Contemporary Feminist Analysis', in M. Barrett and A. Phillips (eds) *Destabilising Theory: Contemporary Feminist Debates.* London: Verso.

Barrett, M. and McIntosh, M. (1982) *The Anti-Social Family.* London: Verso.

Barrett, M. and McIntosh, M. (1985) 'Ethnocentrism and Socialist Feminism'. *Feminist Review,* 20.

Barrett, M. and Phillips A. (eds) (1992) *Destabilising Theory: Contemporary Feminist Debates.* London: Verso.

Baudrillard, J. (1988) *America.* London: Verso.

Bauman, Z. (1990) *Thinking Sociologically.* Oxford: Blackwell.

Beauvoir, S. de (1963) *The Second Sex.* London: Jonathon Cape.

Becker, H. (1963) *Outsiders.* New York: Free Press.

Beechey, V. (1979) 'On Patriarchy'. *Feminist Review,* 3: 66–82.

Beechey, V. and Perkins, T. (1987) *A Matter of Hours: Women, Part-Time Work and the Labour Market.* Cambridge: Polity Press.

Beller, A. (1982) 'Occupational Segregation by Sex: Determinants and Changes'. *Journal of Human Resources,* 17.

Berger, J. (1972) *Ways of Seeing.* London: BBC in association with Penguin Books.

Bernal, M. (1987) *Black Athena: The Afroasiatic Roots of Classical Civilisation.* London: Free Association Books.

Beynon, H. (1973) *Working for Ford.* London: Allen Lane.

Bhavnani, K.-K. and Coulson, M. (1986) 'Transforming Socialist-Feminism: The Challenge of Racism'. *Feminist Review,* 23: 30–45.

Bilton, T., Bonnett, K., Jones, P., Lawson, T., Skinner, D., Stanworth, M. and Webster, A. (eds) (1996) *Introductory Sociology.* Basingstoke: Macmillan.

Birke, L. (1985) *Women, Feminism and Biology.* Brighton: Wheatsheaf.

Birke, L. (1999) *Feminism and the Biological Body.* Edinburgh: Edinburgh University Press.

Bonnett, A. (2000) *White Identities: Historical and International Perspectives.* Harlow: Pearson Education.

Bordo, S. (1993) *Unbearable Weight: Feminism, Western Culture and the Body.* Berkeley: University of California Press.

Boserup, E. (1970) *Women's Role in Economic Development.* London: Allen and Unwin.

Boston Women's Health Collective (1976) *Our Bodies, Ourselves.* New York: Simon and Schuster.

Bradley, H. (1989) *Men's Work, Women's Work: A Sociological History of the Sexual Division of Labour in Employment.* Cambridge: Polity Press.

Bradley, H. (1996) *Fractured Identities: Changing Patterns of Inequality.* Cambridge: Polity Press.

Bradley, H. (1999) *Gender and Power in the Workplace: Analysing the Impact of Economic Change.* Basingstoke: Macmillan.

Brah, A. (2002) 'Global Mobilisation, Local Predicaments'. *Feminist Review,* 70: 30–45.

Braidotti, R., Charkiewicz, E., Hausler, S. and Wieringa, S. (eds) (1994) *Women, the Environment and Sustainable Development: Towards a Theoretical Synthesis.* London: Zed Books.

Briskin, L. (2002) 'Women's Organising: A Gateway to a New Approach to Women's Studies'. *Atlantis,* 26(2): 78–91.

Brodribb, S. (1992) *Nothing Mat(t)ers: A Feminist Critique of Postmodernism.* Melbourne: Spinifex. (Extract in D. Bell and R. Klein (eds) (1996) *Radically Speaking: Feminism Reclaimed.* London: Zed Books.)

Brook, B. (1999) *Feminist Perspectives on the Body.* London: Longman.

Brooks, A. (1997) *Postfeminisms: Feminism, Cultural Theory and Cultural Forms.* London: Routledge.

Brown, R. (1976) 'Women as Employees: Some Comments on Research in Industrial Sociology', in D. Leonard Barker and S. Allen (eds) *Dependence and Exploitation in Work and Marriage.* London: Tavistock.

Bryan, B., Dadzie, S. and Scafe, S. (1985) *The Heart of the Race: Black Women's Lives in Britain.* London: Virago.

Burman, S. (ed.) (1979) *Fit Work for Women.* London: Croom Helm.

Burton, A. (ed.) (1999) *Gender, Sexuality and Colonial Modernities.* London: Routledge.

Butler, J. (1993) *Bodies That Matter.* London: Routledge.

Butler, J. (1995) 'For a Careful Reading', in S. Benhabib, J. Butler, D. Cornell and N. Fraser (eds) *Feminist Contentions: A Philosophical Exchange.* London: Routledge.

Byrne, B., Marcus, R. and Power-Stevens, T. (1995) 'Land Rights in Post-conflict Rwanda', *Gender, Conflict and Development* (BRIDGE Report 25). Sussex: Income Data Services.

Callinicos, A. (1989) *Against Postmodernism: A Marxist Critique.* Cambridge. Polity Press.

Carvel, J. (2001) 'Old Habits Die Hard for New Man', *The Guardian,* 12 July.

Cavendish, R. [Glucksmann, M.] (1982) *Women on the Line.* London: Routledge and Kegan Paul.

Chicago, J. (1980) *Embroidering Our Heritage: The Dinner Party Needlework.* New York: Anchor/Doubleday.

Chodorow, N. (1978) *The Reproduction of Mothering.* London: University of California Press.

Christian, B. (1989) 'The Race for Theory', in L. Kauffman (ed.) *Gender and Theory: Dialogues on Feminist Criticism.* Oxford: Basil Blackwell.

Cockburn, C. (1981) 'The Material of Male Power'. *Feminist Review,* 9: 41–59.

Cockburn, C. (1983) *Brothers: Male Dominance and Technological Change.* London: Pluto Press.

Cockburn, C. (1986) 'The Relations of Technology', in R. Crompton and M. Mann (eds) *Gender and Stratification.* Cambridge: Polity Press.

Cockburn, C. (1991) *In the Way of Women: Men's Resistance to Sex Equality in Organisations.* London: Macmillan.

Codell, J. and Sachko Macleod, D. (eds) (1998) *Orientalism Transposed: The Influence of the Colonies on British Culture.* Aldershot: Ashgate.

Cohen, S. (2001) *States of Denial: Knowing About Atrocities and Suffering.* Cambridge: Polity.

Coles, F. (1999) 'Feminine Charms and Outrageous Arms', in J. Price and M. Shildrick (eds) *Feminist Theory and the Body.* Edinburgh: Edinburgh University Press.

Collins, P.H. (2000) *Black Feminist Thought: Knowledge, Consciousness and the Politics of Empowerment.* New York and London: Routledge.

Connell, R. (1987) *Gender and Power*. Cambridge: Polity Press.

Coomareswamy, R. (1997) *Report of the Special Rapporteur on Violence Against Women, its Causes and Consequences*. NY: UN ECOSOC Commission on Human Rights.

Coomareswamy, R. (2000) 'Integration of the Human Rights of Women With a Gender Pespective: Violence Against Women', United Nations Economic and Social Council (E/CN.4/2000/68).

Coote, A. and Campbell, B. (1987) *Sweet Freedom: The Struggle for Women's Liberation*. Oxford: Blackwell.

Corea, G. (1987) *Man-made Women: How New Reproductive Technologies Affect Women*. Bloomington: Indiana University Press.

Cott, N. (1987) *The Grounding of Modern Feminism*. London: Yale University Press.

Coward, R. (1984) *Female Desire*. London: Paladin.

Crompton, R. (1986) 'Women and the Service Class', in R. Crompton and M. Mann. *Gender and Stratification*. Cambridge: Polity Press.

Crompton, R. (ed.) (1999) *Restructuring Gender Relations and Employment: The Decline of the Male Breadwinner*. Oxford: Oxford University Press.

Crompton, R. and Mann, M. (eds) (1986) *Gender and Stratification*. Cambridge: Polity Press.

Crompton, R. and Sanderson, K. (1990) *Gendered Jobs and Social Change*. London: Unwin Hyman.

Dalsimer, M. and Nisonoff, L. (1997) 'Abuses Against Women and Girls Under the One-Child Family Plan in the People's Republic of China', in N. Visvanathan, L. Duggan, N. Nisonoff and F. Wiegersma (eds) *The Women, Gender and Development Reader*. London: Zed Books.

Daly, M. (1978) *Gyn/Ecology: The Metaethics of Radical Feminism*. Boston, MA: Beacon Press.

Davin, A. (1979) '"Mind That You Do As You Are Told": Reading Books for Board School Girls'. *Feminist Review*, 3: 89–98.

Davis, A. (1982) *Women, Race and Class*. London: The Women's Press.

Davis, A. (1985) 'Women and Sex: Egypt'. New Internationalist (ed.): *Women, a World Report*. London: Methuen.

Davis, M. (1988) 'Urban Renaissance and the Spirit of Postmodernism', in E.A. Kaplan (ed.) *Postmodernism and its Discontents*. London: Verso Press.

Davis, M. (2001) *Late Victorian Holocausts: El Nino Famines and the Making of the Third World*. London: Verso.

Davis, T. (1991) *Actresses as Working Women*. London: Routledge.

Delamont, S. (2001) *Changing Women, Unchanged Men?: Sociological Perspectives on Gender in a Post-industrial Society*. Buckingham: Open University Press.

Delmar, R. (1976) 'Looking again at Engels' "Origins of the Family"', in J. Mitchell and A. Oakley (eds) *The Rights and Wrongs of Women.* Harmondsworth, Middlesex: Penguin Books.

Delphy, C. (1976) 'Continuities and Discontinuities in Marriage and Divorce', in D. Leonard Barker and S. Allen (eds) *Sexual Divisions and Society: Process and Change.* London: Tavistock.

Delphy, C. (1984) *Close to Home.* London: Hutchinson Education.

Delphy, C. (1996) 'Rethinking Sex and Gender', in D. Leonard and L. Adkins (eds) *Sex in Question: French Materialist Feminism.* London: Taylor and Francis.

Denny, C. (1999) 'Women Still Bottom of the Earnings Pile', *The Guardian,* 13 December.

Dobash, R. and Dobash, R. (1980) *Violence Against Wives.* London: Open Books.

Doezema, J. (2000) 'Loose Women or Lost Women?' *Gender Issues,* 18 (1).

Douglas, S.J. (2002) 'Manufacturing Postfeminism', *In These Times,* 26 April.

Dworkin, A. (1983) *Right-Wing Women: The Politics of Domesticated Females.* London: Women's Press.

Dworkin, A. (1996 [1990]) 'Dworkin on Dworkin', in D. Bell and R. Klein (eds) *Radically Speaking: Feminism Reclaimed.* London: Zed Books.

Dworkin, S. and Messner, M. (1999) 'Just Do . . . What? Sport, Bodies and Gender', in M. Feree, B. Hess and J. Lorber (eds) *Revisioning Gender.* London: Sage.

Ehrenreich, B. (1983) *The Hearts of Men: The American Dream and the Flight from Commitment.* London: Pluto Press.

Ehrenreich, B. and English, D. (1979) *For Her Own Good: 150 Years of the Experts' Advice to Women.* London: Pluto Press.

Eid, P. (2002) 'Post-colonial Identity and Gender in the Arab World: The Case of the Hijab'. *Atlantis,* 26 (2): 39–51.

El Guindi, F. (1999) 'Veiling Resistance'. *Fashion Theory,* 3 (1).

Elson, D. (1983) 'Nimble Fingers and Other Fables', in W. Chapkis and C. Enloe (eds) *Of Common Cloth: Women in the Global Textile Industry.* Amsterdam and Washington: Transnational Institute.

Elson, D. (1989) 'The Impact of Structural Adjustment on Women', in B. Onimode (ed.) *The IMF, the World Bank and the African Debt: Vol. 2.* London: Zed Books.

Elson, D. and Pearson, R. (1981) 'Nimble Fingers Make Cheap Workers'. *Feminist Review,* (7): 87–107.

Engels, F. (n.d.) *The Origin of the Family, Private Property and the State.* London: Lawrence and Wishart.

Engels, F. (1972) *The Condition of the Working Class in England.* London: Granada Publishing.

England, P. (1982) 'The Failure of Human Capital Theory to Explain Occupational Sex Segregation'. *Journal of Human Resources*, 17.

Equal Opportunities Commission (2001) *Women and Men in Britain: The Lifecycle of Inequality*. London: EOC.

Eschle, C. (2001) *Global Democracy, Social Movements, and Feminism*. Oxford: Westview Press.

Etienne, M. and Leacock, E. (eds) (1980) *Women and Colonization: Anthropological Perspectives*. New York: Praeger.

Evans, M. (1981) 'The Case for Women's Studies'. *Feminist Review*, 10: 61–74.

Evans, M. (ed.) (1982) *The Woman Question: Readings on the Subordination of Women*. London: Fontana.

Evans, M. (1997) *Introducing Contemporary Feminist Thought*. Cambridge: Polity Press.

Faludi, S. (1992) *Backlash: The Undeclared War Against Women*. London: Chatto and Windus.

Faludi, S. (1999) *Stiffed*. London: Chatto and Windus.

Felski, R. (1995) *The Gender of Modernity*. London: Harvard University Press.

Ferguson, M. (1983) *Forever Feminine*. London: Heinemann Books.

Finch, J. (1984) '"It's Great to Have Someone to Talk To": The Ethics and Politics of Interviewing Women', in C. Bell and H. Roberts (eds) *Social Researching: Politics, Problems and Practices*. London: Routledge and Kegan Paul.

Firestone, S. (1972) *The Dialectic of Sex: The Case for Feminist Revolution*. London: Paladin.

Flax, J. (1987) 'Postmodernism and Gender Relations in Feminist Theory'. *Signs: Journal of Women in Culture and Society*, 12 (4): 621–43.

Foucault, M. (1977) *Discipline and Punish*. London: Penguin Books.

Foucault, M. (1984) *Introduction to the History of Sexuality*. London: Penguin Books.

Fox-Genovese, E. (1988) *Within the Plantation Household: Black and White Women of the Old South*. Chapel Hill and London: University of North Carolina Press.

Frankenberg, R. (1976) 'In the Production of Their Lives, Men (?) . . . Sex and Gender in British Community Studies', in D. Leonard Barker and S. Allen (eds) *Sexual Divisions and Society: Process and Change*. London: Tavistock.

Frankenberg, R. (1993) *White Women, Race Matters: The Social Construction of Whiteness*. Minneapolis: University of Minnesota Press.

Fraser, N. (ed.) (1990) *Feminism/postmodernism*. London: Routledge.

Gewertz, D. and Errington, F. (1991) 'We Think, Therefore They Are? On Occidentalizing the World'. *Anthroplogical Quarterly*, 64 (2): 80.

Giddens, A. (1990) *The Consequences of Modernity*. Cambridge: Polity Press.

Giddens, A. (1999) *Runaway World: The Reith Lectures Revisited*. London: Polity Press.

Gilman, S. (1985) *Difference and Pathology: Stereotypes of Sexuality, Race and Madness*. Ithaca, NY: Cornell University Press.

Gilman, S. (1992) 'Black Bodies, White Bodies: Toward an Iconography of Female Sexualities in Late Nineteenth Century Art, Medicine and Literature', in J. Donald and A. Rattansi (eds) '*Race*', *Culture and Difference*. London: Sage.

Gittins, D. (1982) *Fair Sex: Family Size and Structure 1900–1932*. London: Hutchinson.

Glucksmann, M. (1994) 'The Work of Knowledge and the Knowledge of Women's Work', in M. Maynard and J. Purvis (eds) *Researching Women's Lives From a Feminist Perspective*. London: Taylor and Francis.

Gordon, L. (1976) *Women's Body, Woman's Right: A Social History of Birth Control in America*. New York: Grossman.

Gordon, L. (1989) *Heroes of Their Own Lives*. London: London.

Grewal, I. and Kaplan, C. (eds) (1994) *Scattered Hegemonies: Postmodernity and Transnational Feminist Practices*. Minneapolis: University of Minnesota Press.

Griffin, S. (1978) *Woman and Nature: The Roaring Inside Her*. New York: Harper Row.

Grosz, E. (1994) *Volatile Bodies*. St Leonards: Allen and Unwin.

Guy, D. (1995) *Sex and Danger: Prostitution, Family and Nation in Argentina*. Lincoln and London: University of Nebraska Press.

Hakim, C. (1979) *Occupational Segregation: A Comparative Study of the Degree and Pattern of Differentiation Between Men and Women's work in Britain, the United States and Other Countries*. London: Department of Employment.

Hakim, C. (1996) *Key Issues in Women's Work*. London: Athlone Press.

Hall, C. (1992) *White, Male, Middle Class*. Cambridge: Polity Press.

Hall, C. (1997) *Daughters of the Dragon: Women's Lives in Contemporary China*. London: Scarlet Press.

Hall, J.D. (1984) '"The Mind That Burns in Each Body": Women, Rape, and Racial Violence', in A. Snitow, C. Stansell and S. Thompson (eds) *Desire: The Politics of Sexuality*. London: Virago.

Hall, L. (2000) *Sex, Gender and Social Change in Britain Since 1880*. London: Macmillan.

Hall, S. and Jefferson, T. (eds) (1976) *Resistance Through Rituals*. London: Hutchinson.

Hammonds, E. (1997) 'Towards a Genealogy of Black Female Sexuality', in J. Alexander and C.T. Mohanty (eds) *Feminist Genealogies, Colonial Legacies, Democratic Futures.* London: Routledge.

Hancock, M. (1999) 'Gendering the Modern', in A. Burton (ed.) *Gender, Sexuality and Colonial Modernities.* London: Routledge.

Harding, S. (1984) 'Is Gender a Variable in Conceptions of Rationality? A Survey of Issues', in C. Gould (ed.) *Beyond Domination.* New Jersey: Rowman and Allenheld.

Harding, S. (1986) *The Science Question in Feminism.* Milton Keynes: Open University Press.

Harding, S. (ed.) (1987) *Feminism and Methodology: Social Science Issues.* Bloomington: Indiana University Press and Milton Keynes: Open University Press.

Hartmann, H. (1979) 'Capitalism, Patriarchy and Job Segregation by Sex', in Z. Eisenstein (ed.) *Capitalist Patriarchy and the Case for Socialist Feminism.* London: Monthly Review Press.

Hartmann, H. (1981) 'The Unhappy Marriage of Marxism and Feminism: Towards a More Progressive Union', in L. Sargent (ed.) *Women and Revolution.* London: Pluto Press.

Hartsock, N. (1990) 'Foucault on Power: A Theory for Women?', in L. Nicholson (ed.) *Feminism/Postmodernism.* London: Routledge.

Hartsock, N. (1998) 'The Feminist Standpoint: Developing the Ground for a Specifically Feminist Historical Materialism', in N. Hartsock, *The Feminist Standpoint Revisited and Other Essays.* London: Westview Press.

Harvey, D. (2000) *Spaces of Hope.* Edinburgh: Edinburgh University Press.

Heidensohn, F. (1985) *Women and Crime.* Basingstoke: Macmillan.

Hekman, S. (1990) *Gender and Knowledge: Elements of a Postmodern Feminism.* Cambridge: Polity Press.

Hester, M., Kelly, L. and Radford, J. (eds) (1996) *Women, Violence and Male Power: Feminist Activism, Research and Practice.* Buckingham, Philadelphia: Open University Press.

Hillier, S. (1988) 'Women and Population Control in China: Issues of Sexuality, Power, and Control'. *Feminist Review,* 29: 101–13.

Hirst, P. and Thomson, G. (1998) *Globalization in Question: The International Economy and the Possibilities of Governance.* Cambridge: Polity Press.

Hochschild, A.R. (2001) 'Global Care Chains and Emotional Surplus Value', in A. Giddens and W. Hutton (eds) *On the Edge: Living with Global Capitalism.* London: Vintage.

Holland, J., Ramazanoglu, C., Sharpe, S. and Thomson, R. (eds) (1998) *The Male in the Head.* London: Tufnell Press.

Hoogvelt, A. (1997) *Globalisation and the Postcolonial World: The New Political Economy of Development.* London: Macmillan.

hooks, b. (1982a) *Ain't I a Woman? Black Women and Feminism*. London: Pluto Press.

hooks, b. (1984) *Feminist Theory from Margin to Center*. Boston, MA: South End Press.

hooks, b. (1991) *Yearning: Race, Gender and Cultural Politics*. London: Turnaround.

hooks, b. (1992) *Black Looks, Race and Representation*. London: Turnaround Press.

Hunt, S. (2002) 'Women in Peacemaking'. *Refugees Magazine*, 126 (April).

Huyssen, A. (1986) 'Mass Culture as Woman: Modernism's Other', in T. Modleski (ed.) *Studies in Entertainment: Critical Approaches to Mass Culture*. Bloomington: Indiana University Press.

Ignatiev, N. (1995) *How the Irish Became White*. New York: Routledge.

Jameson, F. (1988) 'Postmodernism and Consumer Society', in E.A Kaplan (ed.) *Postmodernism and its Discontents*. London: Verso Press.

Jameson, F. (1991) *Postmodernism, or the Cultural Logic of Late Capitalism*. London: Verso Press.

Jeffrey, L. (2002) '"Because they want nice things": Prostitution, Consumerism and Culture in Thailand'. *Atlantis*, 26: 2.

Jones, A. (1994) 'Postfeminism, Feminist Pleasures, and Embodied Theories of Art', in J. Frueh, C.L. Langer and A. Raven (eds) *New Feminist Criticism: Art, Identity, Action*. New York: HarperCollins Publishers.

Kabbani, R. (1988) *Europe's Myths of Orient*. London: Pandora.

Kabeer, N. (1994) *Reversed Realities: Gender Hierarchies in Development Thought*. London: Verso Press.

Kabeer, N. (2000) *Power to Choose: Bangladeshi Women and Labor Market Decisions in London and Dhaka*. London: Verso Press.

Kaplan, E.A. (ed.) (1988) *Postmodernism and its Discontents*. London: Verso Press.

Keita, S. (2001) *Moffou*. South Africa: Universal Music.

Keller-Hertzog, A. (1996) *Globalisation and Gender: Development Perspectives and Interventions*. Quebec: Canadian International Development Agency, Women in Development and Gender Equity Division.

Kelly, L., Burton, S. and Regan, L. (1994) 'Researching Women's Lives or Studying Women's Oppression?', in M. Maynard and J. Purvis (eds) *Researching Women's Lives From a Feminist Perspective*. London: Taylor and Francis.

Kerr, J. (1999) 'Responding to Globalization: Can Feminists Transform Development?', in M. Porter and E. Judd (eds) *Feminists Doing Development: A Practical Critique*. London: Zed Books.

Klein, N. (2000) *No Logo: No Space, No Choice, No Jobs*. London: Flamingo.

Kofman, E. (2000a) 'Beyond a Reductionist Analysis of Female Migrants in Global European Cities', in M. Marchand and A.S. Runyan (eds) *Gender and Global Restructuring: Sightings, Sites and Resistance.* London: Routledge.

Kofman, E. (ed.) (2000b) *Gender and International Migration in Europe: Employment, Welfare and Politics.* London: Routledge.

Kristof, N. and Wuduun, S. (1994) *China Wakes.* New York: Random House.

Kuhn, A. (1982) *Women's Pictures: Feminism and Cinema.* London: Routledge and Kegan Paul.

Kuhn, A. (1985) *The Power of the Image.* London: Routledge and Kegan Paul.

Kulkarni, S. (1986) 'Sex Determination Tests in India'. *Radical Journal of Health,* 1 (3).

Laqueur, T. (1992) *Making Sex: Body and Gender from the Greeks to Freud.* Cambridge, MA: Harvard University Press.

Laws, S. (1990) *Issues of Blood: The Politics of Menstruation.* Houndmills: Macmillan.

Leeds Revolutionary Feminist Group (1982) 'Political Lesbianism: The Case Against Heterosexuality', in M. Evans (ed.) *The Woman Question.* London: Fontana.

Leonard, D. and Adkins, L. (eds) (1996) *Sex in Question: French Materialist Feminism.* London: Taylor and Francis.

Lewis, J. (1984) *Women in England 1870–1950.* Sussex: Wheatsheaf Books.

Lim, L. (1983) 'Capitalism, Imperialism and Patriarchy: The Dilemma of Third-World Women Workers in Multinational Factories', in J. Nash and M.P. Fernandez-Kelly (eds) *Women, Men and the International Division of Labour.* Albany, NY: SUNY Press.

Lim, L. (1990) 'Women's Work in Export Factories', in I. Tinker (ed.) *Persistent Inequalities.* Oxford: Oxford University Press.

Lockwood, D. (1958) *The Blackcoated Worker: a Study in Class Consciousness.* London: Unwin.

Loomba, A. (ed.) (1998) *Colonialism/Postcolonialism.* New York: Routledge.

Lovenduski, J. and Norris, P. (eds) (1996) *Women In Politics.* Oxford: Oxford University Press.

Lovering, K. (1997) 'Listening to Girls' "Voice" and Silence: The Problematics of the Menarcheal Body', in E. Marion and V. Grace (eds) *Bodily Boundaries, Sexualised Genders and Medical Discourse.* Palmerston: The Dunmore Press.

Luxton, M. (1980) *More Than a Labour of Love.* Toronto: The Women's Press.

Luxton, M. (1990) 'Two Hands for the Clock: Changing Patterns in the Gendered Division of Labour in the Home', in M. Luxton, H. Rosenberg and S. Arat-Koc (eds) *Through the Kitchen Window: The Politics of Home and Family.* Toronto: Garamond Press.

McClintock, A. (1995) *Imperial Leather: Race, Gender and Sexuality in the Colonial Contest*. London: Routledge.

Mackay, F. (1996) 'The Zero Tolerance Campaign: Setting the Agenda', in J. Lovenduski and P. Norris (eds) *Women In Politics*. Oxford: Oxford University Press.

MacKinnon, C. (1989) *Toward a Feminist Theory of the State*. Cambridge, MA: Harvard University Press.

MacKinnon, C. (1996) 'From Practice to Theory: or What is a White Woman Anyway?', in D. Bell and R. Klein (eds) *Radically Speaking: Feminism Reclaimed*. London: Zed Books.

McNally, F. (1979) *Women for Hire: A Study of the Female Office Worker*. London: Macmillan.

McRobbie, A. (1982) 'The Politics of Feminist Research'. *Feminist Review*, 12: 46–58.

McRobbie, A. (1994) *Postmodernism and Popular Culture*. London: Routledge.

McRobbie, A. (1999) *In the Culture Society: Art, Fashion and Popular Music*. London: Routledge.

Maharaj, Z. (1995) 'A Social Theory of Gender'. *Feminist Review*, 49: 50.

Mahood, L. (1990) *The Magdalenes*. London: Routledge.

Mahood, L. (1995) *Policing Gender, Class and the Family*. London: UCL Press.

Mandel, E. (1973) *An Introduction to Marxist Economic Theory*. New York: Pathfinder Books.

Marchand, M. and Runyan, A.S. (eds) (2000) *Gender and Global Restructuring: Sightings, Sites and Resistance*. London: Routledge.

Martin, E. (1987) *The Woman in the Body*. Boston, MA: Beacon Press.

Matheson, I. (2002) 'The "Lost Girls" of Sudan', BBC News, 7 June, (news.bbc.co.uk/1/hi/world/africa/2031286.stm).

Maynard, M. (1994) 'Methods, Practice and Epistemology: The Debate About Feminism and Research', in M. Maynard and J. Purvis (eds) *Researching Women's Lives From a Feminist Perspective*. London: Taylor and Francis.

Maynard, M. and Purvis, J. (eds) (1994) *Researching Women's Lives From a Feminist Perspective*. London: Taylor and Francis.

Midgley, M. (1992) *Women Against Slavery: The British Campaigns 1780–1870*. London: Routledge.

Mies, M. (1986) *Patriarchy and Accumulation on a World Scale: Women in the International Division of Labour*. London: Zed Books.

Mies, M. (1998) *Patriarchy and Accumulation on a World Scale: Women in the International Division of Labour*. London: Zed Books.

Mies, M., Bennholdt-Thomsen, V. and von Werlhof, C. (eds) (1988) *Women: The Last Colony*. London: Zed Books.

Millett, K. (1970) *Sexual Politics*. London: Roper Hart-Davies.

Mills, C.W. (1959) *The Sociological Imagination*. London: Oxford University Press.

Mills, S. (1998) 'Post-Colonial Feminist Theory', in S. Jackson and J. Jones (eds) *Contemporary Feminist Theories*. Edinburgh: Edinburgh University Press.

Mitchell, J. (1975) *Psychoanalysis and Feminism*. Harmondsworth, Middlesex: Penguin Books.

Mitter, S. (1986) *Common Fate, Common Bond: Women in the Global Economy*. London: Pluto Press.

Modleski, T. (ed.) (1986) *Studies in Entertainment: Critical Approaches to Mass Culture*. Bloomington: Indiana University Press.

Moghadam, V. (1999) 'Gender and the Global Economy', in M. Feree, B. Hess and J. Lorber (eds) *Revisioning Gender*. London: Sage.

Moghadam, V. (n.d.) 'Islamic Feminism and its Discontents: Notes on a Debate', *Iran Bulletin On-Line*, www.iran-bulletin.org/islamic_feminism.htm.

Mohanty, C.T. (1988) 'Under Western Eyes: Feminist Scholarship and Colonial Discourses'. *Feminist Review*. 30.

Mohanty, C.T. (2003) *Feminism Without Borders: Decolonising Theory, Practising Solidarity*. North Carolina: Duke University Press.

Mojab, S. (2001) 'Theorising the Politics of "Islamic Feminism"'. *Feminist Review*, 69 (1): 124–46.

Montag, W. (1988): 'The Debate of Postmodernism?', in E.A. Kaplan (ed.) *Postmodernism and its Discontents*. London: Verso Press.

Morrison, T. (1970) *The Bluest Eye*. New York: Washington Square Press.

Moss, P. (1980) 'Parents at Work', in P. Moss and N. Fonda (eds) *Work and the Family*. London: Temple Smith.

Murray, M. (1995) *The Law of the Father?: Patriarchy in the Transition from Feudalism to Capitalism*. London: Routledge.

Myrdal, A. and Klein, A. (1956) *Women's Two Roles*. London: Routledge and Kegan Paul.

Nash, J. and Safa, H. (eds) (1980) *Sex and Class in Latin America: Women's Perspectives on Politics, Economics and the Family in the Third World*. New York: Bergin Publishers.

New Internationalist (1975) *Women: a World Report*. London: Methuen.

Nicholson, L. (ed.) (1990) *Feminism/Postmodernism*. London: Routledge.

Nochlin, L. (1973) 'Eroticism and Female Imagery in Nineteenth Century Art', in T. Baker and E. Hess (eds) *Art and Sexual Politics: Women's Liberation, Women Artists, and Art History*. London: Collier-Macmillan.

Nochlin, L. (1989) *Women, Art and Power, and Other Essays*. London: Thames and Hudson.

Nyabera, E. (2002) 'Man-eating Lions, Crocodiles, Famine . . .'. *Refugees Magazine*, 126 (April).

Oakley, A. (1972) *Sex, Gender and Society*. London: Maurice Temple Smith.

Oakley, A. (1974) *The Sociology of Housework*. London: Martin Robertson.

Oakley, A. (1979) *Becoming a Mother*. Oxford: Martin Robertson.

Oakley, A. (1980) *Women Confined*. Oxford: Martin Robertson.

Oakley, A. (1981a) *Subject Women*. Oxford: Martin Robertson.

Oakley, A. (1981b) 'Interviewing Women: A Contradiction in Terms', in H. Roberts (ed.) *Doing Feminist Research*. London: Routledge and Kegan Paul.

Oakley, A. (1986) *From Here to Maternity: Becoming a Mother*. Harmondsworth, Middlesex: Penguin Books.

Oakley, A. (2002) *Gender on Planet Earth*. Oxford: Polity Press.

Ollenburger, J.C. and Moore, H.A. (1992) *A Sociology of Women: The Intersection of Patriarchy, Capitalism and Colonization*. Englewood Cliffs, NJ: Prentice Hall.

Omolade, B. (1984) 'Hearts of Darkness', in A. Snitow, C. Stansell and S. Thompson (eds) *Desire: The Politics of Sexuality*. London: Virago.

Pahl, R. (1984) *Divisions of Labour*. Oxford: Basil Blackwell.

Parker, R. and Pollock, G. (eds) (1987) *Framing Feminsim: Art and the Women's Movement 1970–1985*. London: Pandora.

Parsons, T. and Bales, R.W. (1956) *Family Socialization and Interaction Process*. London: Routledge and Kegan Paul.

Paul, J. (2000) 'NGOs and Global Policy Making'. *Global Policy Forum*, June.

Pearson, R. (1992) 'Gender Issues in Industrialisation', in T. Hewitt, H. Johnson and D. Wield (eds) *Industrialisation and Development*. Buckingham: Open University Press.

Pearson, R. (1998) '"Nimble Fingers" Revisited Reflections on Women and the Third World Industrialisation in the Late Twentieth Century', in C. Jackson and R. Pearson (eds) *Feminist Visions of Development*. London: Routledge.

Perutz, K. (1970) *Beyond the Looking Glass*. Harmondsworth, Middlesex: Penguin Books.

Petchesky, R. (1984) *Abortion and Women's Choice: The State, Sexuality and Reproductive Freedom*. New York: Longman.

Peterson, A. (1998) *Unmasking the Masculine*. London: Sage.

Pfeil, F. (1995) *White Guys: Studies in Postmodern Domination and Difference*. London: Verso.

Phillips, A. and Taylor, B. (1980) 'Sex and Skill: Notes Towards a Feminist Economics'. *Feminist Review*, 6: 79–88.

Phizacklea, A. (1990) *Unpacking the Fashion Industry*. London: Routledge.

Phizacklea, A. (1996) 'Women, Migration and the State', in S. Rai and G. Lievesley (eds) *Women and the State: International Perspectives*. London: Taylor and Francis.

Phizacklea, A. and Wolkowitz, C. (1995) *Homeworking Women: Gender, Racism and Class at Work*. London: Sage.

Phoenix, A. (1994) 'Practising Feminist Research: The Intersection of Gender and "Race" in the Research Process', in M. Maynard and J. Purvis (eds) *Researching Women's Lives From a Feminist Perspective*. London: Taylor and Francis.

Pieterse Nederveen, J. (1994) 'Unpacking the West: How European is Europe?', in A. Rattansi and S. Westwood (eds) *Racism, Modernity and Identity*. Cambridge: Polity Press.

Polan, D. (1988) 'Postmodernism and Cultural Analysis Today', in E.A. Kaplan (ed.) *Postmodernism and its Discontents*. London: Verso Press.

Pollert, A. (1981) *Girls, Wives, Factory Lives*. London: Macmillan.

Pollock, G. (1988) *Vision and Difference: Femininity, Feminism and the History of Art*. London: Routledge.

Pope, H., Phillips, K. and Olivardia, R. (2000) *The Adonis Complex: The Secret Crisis of the Male Body*. California: Free Press.

Porter, F. and Verghese, V. (1999) 'Falling Between the Gaps', in M. Porter and E. Judd (eds) *Feminists Doing Development: A Practical Critique*. London: Zed Books.

Price, J. and Sheldrick, M. (eds) (1999) *Feminist Theory and the Body*. Edinburgh: Edinburgh University Press.

Ramazanoglu, C. and Holland, J. (eds) (1993) *Up Against Foucault*. London: Routledge.

Randriamaro, Z. (2002) 'NEPAD, Gender and the Poverty Trap: The NEPAD and the Challenges of Financing for Development in Africa from a Gender Perspective'. Paper presented at the Conference on Africa and the Development Challenges of the New Millennium [Ghana]: (www.aidc.org.za/NEPAD/Gender%20and%20poverty%20trap.htm).

Reif, M. (2000) 'Beyond the Veil: Bigger Issues'. *Christian Science Monitor*.

Riley, D. (1983) *War in the Nursery*. London: Virago.

Roberts, H. (1981) 'Some of the Boys Won't Play Anymore: the Impact of Feminism on Sociology', in D. Spender (ed.) *Men's Studies Modified: The Impact of Feminism on the Academic Disciplines*. Oxford: Pergamon Press.

Roberts, H. (1983) 'Do Her Answers Fit His Questions?', in E. Garmanikov (ed.) *The Public and the Private*. London: Heinemann.

Rodney, W. (1982) *How Europe Underdeveloped Africa*. Washington: Harvard University Press.

Roediger, D. (1992) *The Wages of Whiteness*. London: Verso Press.

Rogers, B. (1980) *The Domestication of Women: Discrimination in Developing Societies*. London: Kogan Page.

Rose, H. and Hanmer, J. (1976) 'Women's Liberation, Reproduction and the Technological Fix', in D. Leonard Barker and S. Allen (eds) *Sexual Divisions and Society: Process and Change*. London: Tavistock.

Rose, K. (1992) *Where Women Are Leaders: The SEWA Movement in India*. London: Zed Books.

Rowbotham, S. (1973) *Woman's Consciousness, Man's World*. Harmondsworth, Middlesex: Penguin Books.

Rowbotham, S. (1982) 'The Trouble with Patriarchy', in M. Evans (ed.) *The Woman Question: Readings on the Subordination of Women*. London: Fontana.

Rowbotham, S. and Linkogle, S. (2001) *Women Resist Globalization: Mobilizing for Livelihoods and Rights*. London: Zed Books.

Rowbotham, S. and Mitter, S. (eds) (1994) *Dignity and Daily Bread: New Forms of Economic Organising Among Poor Women in the Third World and the First*. London: Zed Books.

Rubery, J. and Tarling, R. (1988) 'Women's Employment in Declining Britain', in J. Rubery (ed.) *Women in Recession*. London: Routledge.

Rubin, G. (1975) 'The Traffic in Women: Notes on the "Political Economy of Sex"', in R. Reiter (ed.) *Toward an Anthropology of Women*. London: Monthly Review Press.

Ryle, S. (2001) 'UK Working Mothers Get the Poorest Deal'. *The Guardian*, 21 May.

Saffioti, H. (1978) *Women in Class Society*. New York and London: Monthly Review Press.

Said, E. (1978) *Orientalism*. Harmondsworth, Middlesex: Penguin Books.

Sassen, S. (1991) *The Global City: New York, London, Tokyo*. Princeton: Princeton University Press.

Sayers, J. (1982) *Biological Politics*. London: Tavistock.

Schiebinger, L. (1993) *Nature's Body: Gender in the Making of Modern Science*. Boston, MA: Beacon Press.

Schwartz Cowan, R. (1989) *More Work for Mother*. London: Free Association Books.

Scott, J. and Tilly, L. (1975) 'Women's Work and the Family in Nineteenth Century Europe'. *Comparative Studies in Society and History*, 17(1): 36–64.

Seidman, S. (1998) *Contested Knowledge: Social Theory in the Postmodern Era.* Oxford: Blackwell.

Shabi, R. (2001) 'Muscle Mania'. *The Guardian Weekend,* 21 July.

Sharpston, M. (1976) 'International Subcontracting'. *World Development,* 4 (4).

Sharrat, N. (1983) 'Girls, Jobs and Glamour'. *Feminist Review,* 15: 47–61.

Shiva, V. (1989) *Staying Alive.* London: Zed Books.

Shiva, V. (2001) 'The World on the Edge', in A. Giddens and W. Hutton (eds) *On the Edge: Living With Global Capitalism.* London: Vintage.

Shorter, E. (1983) *A History of Women's Bodies.* Harmondsworth, Middlesex: Penguin Books.

Skeggs, B. (1991) 'Postmodernism: What is All the Fuss About?'. *British Journal of the Sociology of Education,* 12(2): 106–27.

Sklair, L. (2002) *Globalization: Capitalism and its Alternatives.* Oxford: Oxford University Press.

Smith, D. (1974) 'Women's Perspective as a Radical Critique of Sociology'. *Sociological Inquiry,* 44.

Spender, D. (1982) *Women of Ideas (And What Men Have Done to Them).* London: Ark.

Spender, D. (1984) *Time and Tide Wait For No Man.* London: Pandora.

Spindel, C., Levy, E. and Connor, M. (2000) *With an End in Sight: Strategies from the UNIFEM Trust Fund to Eliminate Violence Against Women.* New York: The United Nations Development Fund for Women.

Springer, K. (2002) 'Third Wave Black Feminism?'. *Signs: Journal of Women in Culture and Society,* 27 (4): 1059–83.

Stanley, L. and Wise, S. (1993) *Breaking Out Again.* London: Routledge.

Stanworth, M. (ed.) (1987) *Reproductive Technologies: Gender, Motherhood and Medicine.* Cambridge: Polity Press in association with Blackwell.

Steel, M. (1999) 'Post-eunuch'. *The Guardian,* 10 March.

Stockman, N., Bonney, N. and Xuewen, S. (1992) 'Women's Work in China, Japan and Great Britain'. *Sociology Review,* 2(1): 2–7.

Strachey, R. (1978 [1928]) *The Cause.* London: Virago.

Sydie, R. (1987) *Natural Women, Cultured Men.* Milton Keynes: Open University Press.

Tanesini, A. (1999) *An Introduction to Feminist Epistemologies.* Oxford: Blackwell Publishers.

Taylor, B. (1983) *Eve and the New Jerusalem: Socialism and Feminism in the Nineteenth Century.* London: Virago.

Thomson, D. (1996) 'The Self-contradiction of "postmodernist" feminism', in D. Bell and R. Klein (eds) *Radically Speaking: Feminism Reclaimed.* London: Zed Books.

Tickner, L. (1987) 'The Body Politic: Female Sexuality and Women Artists Since 1970', in R. Parker and G. Pollock (eds) *Framing Feminism: Art and the Women's Movement 1970–1985.* London: Pandora.

Tuchman, G., Daniels, A.K. and Benet, J. (eds) (1978) *Hearth and Home: Images of Women in the Mass Media.* New York: Oxford University Press.

Turshen, M. (1994) 'Women's Health in Sub-Saharan Africa', in N. Aslanbegui, S. Pressman and P. Summerfield (eds) *Women in the Age of Economic Transformation.* London: Routledge.

Udayagiri, M. (1995) 'Challenging Modernisation: Gender and Development, Postmodern Feminism and Activism', in M. Marchand and J. Parpart (eds) *Feminism, Postmodernism, Development.* London: Routledge.

United Nations (1994) 'Declaration on the Elimination of Violence Against Women'. New York: United Nations Resolution No. A/RES/48/104, 23 February.

United Nations Development Programme (UNDP) (2002) *Human Development Report 2001: Making New Technologies Work for Human Development.* New York: UNDP.

Visvanathan, N., Duggan, L., Nisonoff, N. and Wiegersma, F. (eds) (1997) *The Women, Gender and Development Reader.* London: Zed Books.

Walby, S. (1990) *Theorising Patriarchy.* Oxford: Blackwell.

Walby, S. (1997) *Gender Transformations.* London: Routledge.

Waldorf, L. (2001) *Turning the Tide: CEDAW and the Gender Dimensions of the HIV/AIDS Pandemic.* New York: UNIFEM.

Walker, A. (1984) *In Search of Our Mothers' Gardens: Womanist Prose.* London: Women's Press.

Wallerstein, I. (1979) *The Capitalist World-Economy.* Cambridge: Cambridge University Press.

Walter, N. (1998) *The New Feminism.* London: Little Brown.

Walters, M. (1978) *The Male Nude.* Harmondsworth, Middlesex: Penguin Books.

Ware, V. (1992) *Beyond the Pale: White Women, Racism and History.* London: Verso.

Waters, K. (1996) '(Re)turning to the Modern: Radical Feminism and the Post-modern Turn', in D. Bell and R. Klein (eds) *Radically Speaking: Feminism Reclaimed.* London: Zed Books.

Weber, M. (1968) *Economy and Society: Vol. 3.* New York: Bedminster Press.

Wheelock, J. (1990) *Husbands at Home: The Domestic Economy in a Post-industrial Society.* London: Routledge.